Dickens's
ENGLAND

Gad's Hill Place, Higham, Kent, Dickens's home from 1857 until his death in 1870.

Dickens's
ENGLAND

A TRAVELLER'S COMPANION

TONY LYNCH

BATSFORD

First published in the United Kingdom in 2012 by

Batsford
Old West London Magistrates' Court
10 Southcombe Street
London W14 0RA

An imprint of Anova Books Company Ltd

ISBN: 978 1 84994 035 1

A CIP catalogue record for this book is available from the British Library.

18 17 16 15 14 13 12 11
10 9 8 7 6 5 4 3 2 1

Reproduction by Mission, Hong Kong
Printed by 1010 Printing International, China

This book can be ordered direct from the publisher at the website
www.anovabooks.co.uk, or try your local bookshop.

Distributed in the United States and Canada by Sterling Publishing Co.,
387 Park Avenue South, New York, NY 10016, USA

CONTENTS

PREFACE

Charles Dickens was an inveterate traveller who lived through a transport revolution. He knew the last of the great coaching days (celebrated in *The Pickwick Papers*) and he witnessed the birth and the growth of the Railway Age. Dickens was also a phenomenal perambulator who took England in his stride. He thought little of the effort required for a ten-mile (16km) hike in the Kentish countryside, nor for a night-time spent observing life in London's more notorious streets. His enthusiasm for travel echoes in his novels; they abound with journeys.

Charles Dickens's own journey through life began in a small terraced house in Portsmouth on 7 February 1812 and ended 58 years later in a fine country house in Kent. Along the way he became the world's most popular author and one of its best-loved personalities. He wrote 15 major novels (published in weekly or monthly parts), several stage plays, many short stories and innumerable pieces of precise journalism.

Today, the popular legend of Dickens persists as strongly as ever (a typical entry in the visitors' book at the Dickens Birthplace Museum in Portsmouth proclaims the author 'The King', like some latter-day pop idol). His novels remain constantly in print, and hardly a year passes without a dramatic adaptation of one or other of his titles on stage, screen or radio.

Charles Dickens, 1812–1870.

Dickens giving one of his public readings.

Charles Dickens's prime talent lay in the acute observation of his fellow human beings – at their best, their worst and at all stages in between. The England that he knew leaps from the page: at times exciting, at times heavy with the cloying atmosphere we associate with the grimmer aspects of the Victorian era – yet always with the sense of 'being there'.

Dickens's England is a gazetteer of locations associated with his life and novels. It is essentially a tale of *two* countries – the England that he knew in fact, and the 'Dickensland', whose settings were generally borrowed from reality, rebuilt in his imagination and inhabited by all those memorable characters.

CHARLES DICKENS, A CHRONOLOGY

1809 John Dickens, a clerk in the Navy Pay Office, is transferred from London to Portsmouth. He and his wife, Elizabeth, rent 1 Mile End Terrace, Portsea.

1812 7 February: Charles Dickens is born at 1 Mile End Terrace.
4 March: He is christened Charles John Huffam Dickens at St Mary's Church, Kingston, Portsmouth.
24 June: The family moves to 16 Hawk Street, Portsea.

1814 Family is at 39 Wish Street, Southsea, Portsmouth.

1815 1 January: John Dickens is transferred to London. The family takes lodgings in Norfolk Street, off Fitzroy Square.

1817 1 January: John Dickens is transferred to Sheerness, Kent.
March (?): John Dickens is transferred to Chatham, Kent. The family moves into 2 Ordnance Terrace.

1821 Family moves to 18 St Mary's Place, Chatham. Charles begins school in Clover Lane, Chatham.

1822 June: John Dickens is transferred back to London. The family moves into 16 Bayham Street, Camden Town. Charles, however, remains at school in Chatham, probably until the autumn.

1823 26 December: Family moves to 4 Gower Street North, where Elizabeth opens a school for the children of families living in the East Indies. The venture fails.

1824   **January or February:** Charles is employed as a labouring boy at
            Warren's Blacking Warehouse.
            20 February: John Dickens is arrested for debt and imprisoned
            inside the New Marshalsea Debtors' Prison, Southwark.
            March or April: Elizabeth and the younger children also move
            within the walls of the New Marshalsea. Charles is sent to
            lodge first with a Mrs Roylance in Little College Street,
            Camden Town, and later at a house in Lant Street, Southwark.
            28 May: John Dickens is released from the New Marshalsea.
            The family stays with Mrs Roylance in Camden Town.
            John Dickens is retired from the Navy on a superannuation
            of £145 a year.

1825   Family moves to 29 Johnson Street, Somers Town. John Dickens
            leaves the Navy Pay Office.
            Spring: Charles leaves Warren's and becomes a day pupil at the
            Wellington House Academy, Hampstead Road.

1826   John Dickens supplements his Naval pension by working as a
            reporter for the *British Press*. Charles begins to study shorthand.
            December: The *British Press* fails.

1827   **March:** The family is evicted from 29 Johnson Street for non-
            payment of rent. They then lodge at 17 Polygon, Somers
            Town. Charles is removed from Wellington House Academy.
            May: He joins the law firm of Ellis and Blackmore of Gray's Inn,
            as a clerk/messenger at 10 shillings a week.

1828   Charles leaves Ellis and Blackmore and joins the practice of
            Charles Molloy, of Symond's Inn. John Dickens is now
            engaged as a Parliamentary reporter for the *Morning Herald*.

1829   With a distant cousin, Thomas Charlton, Charles rents a reporters'
            box in the Law Courts of Doctors' Commons. Family live at 10
            Norfolk Street, Fitzroy Square.

1830   **February:** Charles obtains a reader's ticket at the British Museum.
He studies, among other subjects, the history of England, and
the works of Shakespeare.
May: He meets, and is infatuated by, Maria Beadnell, the daughter
of a banker. He continues to work at Doctors' Commons.

1832   Charles is invited to join the reporting staff of the *Mirror of
Parliament*. He also begins to contribute general reports to
the *True Sun*.
March: He applies to the Covent Garden Theatre for an
acting audition, but on the appointed day is ill in bed and
unable to attend.
April: He leaves home and takes lodgings in Cecil Street, Strand.
May: He moves to 15 Buckingham Street, Strand.

1833   Family is at 18 Bentinck Street, Marylebone.
May: Maria Beadnell turns cold towards Charles and their
romance ends.
Summer: He begins experimenting with some short fictional pieces.
December: 'A Dinner at Poplar Walk' published in the *Monthly Magazine*.

1834   Several more short pieces appear in the *Monthly Magazine*.
August: Dickens adopts the pseudonym 'Boz'. He also becomes a
Parliamentary reporter for the *Morning Chronicle*.
September: The first of several 'Street Sketches' by 'Boz' appears
in the *Morning Chronicle*.
November: John Dickens is again arrested for debt. Charles
arranges cheap accommodation for his mother and the
younger children at George Street, Adelphi. He also finds
rooms for himself and his younger brother, Fred, at 13
Furnival's Inn, Holborn.

1835   **January:** Dickens is invited to contribute some 'literary sketches' to
the *Evening Chronicle*. He meets Catherine Hogarth.
May: Charles and Catherine become engaged to marry.
September: The first of 12 'Sketches of Scenes and Characters'
appears in *Bell's Life of London*.

1836
7 February: *Sketches by Boz* published.

10 February: Dickens agrees to write a humorous text for Chapman and Hall: this work becomes *The Pickwick Papers*.

17 February: Charles and Fred move to larger chambers at 15 Furnival's Inn.

31 March: First monthly number of *The Pickwick Papers* appears.

2 April: Charles and Catherine are married at St Luke's Church, Chelsea. They live at 15 Furnival's Inn with Fred Dickens. Mary Hogarth, Catherine's 16-year-old sister, often stays at the Furnival's Inn Chambers.

20 April: Robert Seymour, illustrator of *The Pickwick Papers*, commits suicide. Hablot Knight Browne (later known as 'Phiz') is chosen as his successor.

22 August: Dickens agrees to edit *Bentley's Miscellany*.

September: *The Strange Gentleman*, a play adapted by Dickens from a 'Boz' piece, 'The Great Winglebury Duel', is produced at the St James's Theatre, King Street, and runs for 60 performances.

November: Dickens resigns from the *Morning Chronicle*.

December: *The Village Coquettes*, an operetta with libretto by Dickens, is produced at the St James's Theatre.

1837
1 January: *Bentley's Miscellany* first published.

6 January: Dickens's first child, Charles Culliford (Charley), is born.

31 January: First monthly number of *Oliver Twist* appears in *Bentley's Miscellany*.

6 March: Dickens's farce *Is She His Wife?* is produced at the St James's Theatre.

25 March: Charles Dickens takes possession of 48 Doughty Street, Holborn.

7 May: Mary Hogarth dies suddenly at Doughty Street. Dickens is devastated by the loss and is unable to continue with his work. Publication of *The Pickwick Papers* and *Oliver Twist* is suspended for a month.

July: Dickens, Catherine and 'Phiz' visit Flanders.

September: Family is at Broadstairs. Dickens and 'Boz' are publicly revealed to be one and the same man.

31 October: Final instalment of *The Pickwick Papers* appears: its circulation has now reached 40,000 copies per number.

November: Dickens and Catherine stay for one week at The Old Ship Hotel, Brighton. *The Pickwick Papers* appears in volume form: a dinner is held at the Prince of Wales Tavern to celebrate this event. Dickens edits the *Memoirs of Grimaldi* for Richard Bentley.

1838   **January–February:** Dickens and 'Phiz' visit Yorkshire in research for *Nicholas Nickleby*. *The Memoirs of Grimaldi* is published with great success.

6 March: Mary ('Mamie') Dickens is born.

April: First monthly number of *Nicholas Nickleby* appears.

Summer: Family is at Broadstairs.

1839   **March:** Dickens travels to Exeter and finds a suitable cottage in which to retire his parents.

April–August: Family is at Elm Cottage, Petersham, Surrey.

September–October: Family is at Broadstairs. Dickens completes *Nicholas Nickleby*. Kate Macready Dickens is born on 29 October.

December: Family moves to 1 Devonshire Terrace, Regent's Park.

1840   Dickens conceives the idea for *Master Humphrey's Clock*, a monthly miscellany. He travels to Bath with Forster; they visit Walter Savage Landor.

March: Dickens begins writing *The Old Curiosity Shop*.

April: He visits Stratford-upon-Avon, Lichfield and Birmingham.

June: Family is at Broadstairs.

1841   **January:** *Barnaby Rudge* opens in *Master Humphrey's Clock*.

9 February: Walter Landor Dickens is born.

May: Dickens declines an offer to represent the Liberal Party as Parliamentary candidate for Reading.

June: Dickens receives the Freedom of the City of Edinburgh. He and Catherine tour Scotland.

August: Family is at Broadstairs.

November: Dickens undergoes an operation for a fistula, and convalesces

at the White Hart Hotel, Windsor, where he completes
Barnaby Rudge.

1842   **January:** Dickens and Catherine set sail for America aboard the
     steamship *Britannia.* After a rough passage they land first in Halifax,
     Nova Scotia and later in Boston where Dickens gives his
     controversial views on international copyright.

   February: They visit Connecticut and New York. Dickens investigates
     the US prison system.

   March: They visit Philadelphia, Richmond, Washington and Baltimore.
     Dickens criticizes slavery in Virginia.

   April: He investigates solitary confinement, in Pittsburgh.

   May: Charles and Catherine cross the border into Canada: they visit
     Niagara Falls, Montreal, Kingston and Toronto.

   1 July: They return to England. Catherine's younger sister Georgina
     Hogarth joins the household.

   August: Family is at Broadstairs. Dickens writing *American Notes.*

   18 October: *American Notes* is published.

   December: Dickens begins writing *Martin Chuzzlewit.*

1843   **January:** First monthly part of *Martin Chuzzlewit* appears.

   March: Sales of *Martin Chuzzlewit* are disappointing. Dickens rents
     Cobley's Farm, Finchley, in order to concentrate more fully on the
     work. He transports the storyline to America: this turn in the plot
     enrages US readers. Sales in England increase. Dickens quarrels with
     Chapman and Hall over contractual matters.

   October: Dickens presides over the opening of the Athenaeum
     Club, Manchester.

   December: *A Christmas Carol* is published.

1844   **January:** Dickens sues plagiarists of his works.

   15 January: Francis Jeffrey Dickens is born.

   February: Dickens takes the chair at the Mechanics' Institute, Liverpool,
     and the New Polytechnic Institute, Birmingham.

   May: Dickens decides to take the family to Italy. He leases out
     1 Devonshire Terrace and moves temporarily to 9 Osnaburgh
     Terrace, Regent's Park.

June: He signs a new publishing contract with Bradbury and Evans.

July: Final instalment of *Martin Chuzzlewit* appears. Family leaves for Italy. They arrive at Albaro, near Genoa.

October: Dickens rents rooms for the family in the Palazzo Peschiere, Genoa. He begins writing *The Chimes*.

December: Having returned alone to England, through Austria, Germany and France, he reads *The Chimes* to distinguished literary company at John Forster's home, 58 Lincoln's Inn Fields. *The Chimes* is published to great success. Dickens returns to Genoa in time for Christmas.

1845

January–April: Charles and Catherine tour in Italy.

June: The family returns to 1 Devonshire Terrace.

July: Dickens produces amateur theatricals at Fanny Kelly's Theatre in Soho. Family is at Broadstairs.

September: Dickens plays 'Captain Bobadill' in Jonson's play *Every Man in His Humour* at Mrs Kelly's Theatre.

28 October: Alfred D'Orsay Tennyson Dickens is born.

December: *The Cricket on the Hearth* appears. Dickens plans to publish and edit a new independent liberal newspaper, the *Daily News*, with offices in Fleet Street.

1846

21 January: First issue of the *Daily News* appears and includes the first part of *Pictures from Italy*.

9 February: Dickens resigns as editor of the *Daily News*.

May: Family is at Villa Rosement, overlooking Lake Geneva at Lausanne. Dickens studies Swiss prison reform and becomes interested in the work of William Haldimand's Blind Institution.

June: Dickens begins writing *Dombey and Son*.

September: He writes *The Battle of Life*.

October: First monthly part of *Dombey and Son* appears.

November: Family is in Paris.

December: Dickens travels to London to supervise the publication of *The Battle of Life*. He returns to Paris in time for Christmas.

1847   **February:** Family returns to London to be close to young Charley, who has contracted scarlet fever while attending boarding school. They rent 3 Chester Place.

18 April: Sydney Smith Haldimand Dickens is born.

May: Dickens, Catherine and Charley holiday with Georgina Hogarth in Brighton.

June: Family is at Broadstairs.

September: They return to 1 Devonshire Terrace.

December: Dickens takes the chair at the Mechanics' Institute, Leeds. He and Catherine travel to Glasgow where he presides over the opening of the Athenaeum Club. Catherine is unwell, so they remain in Glasgow until the New Year.

1848   **March:** *Dombey and Son* is completed.

May: Dickens plays eight performances at the Theatre Royal Haymarket, as Justice Swallow in *The Merry Wives of Windsor* in aid of the fund for the upkeep of William Shakespeare's birthplace, Stratford-upon-Avon. Dickens subsequently tours with this play, and several others, giving performances in Manchester, Liverpool, Birmingham, Glasgow and Edinburgh.

August: Family is at Broadstairs.

2 September: Dickens's elder sister, Fanny, dies of tuberculosis. She is buried in Highgate cemetery.

November: Dickens writes *The Haunted Man*, while staying at the Bedford Hotel, Brighton.

December: *The Haunted Man* appears. Dickens visits Norwich and Great Yarmouth.

1849   **15 January:** Henry Fielding Dickens is born. Dickens begins work on *David Copperfield*.

May: First instalment of *David Copperfield* appears.

Summer: Family is at Broadstairs, then at Bonchurch, Isle of Wight.

October: Family leaves Bonchurch and returns to Broadstairs. Dickens conceives the idea for a new monthly magazine, *Household Words*.

November: Charles and Catherine stay at Rockingham Castle, Northamptonshire.

1850   **31 March:** The first issue of *Household Words* appears.

April: Dickens visits Knebworth House, Hertfordshire, home of
Edward Bulwer-Lytton. The two men discuss plans to establish a
Guild of Literature and Art. A celebratory dinner is held at the Star
and Garter Hotel, Richmond, in honour of the current success of
David Copperfield.

July: Family is at Broadstairs.

16 August: Dora Annie Dickens is born.

October: *David Copperfield* is completed.

November: Dickens appears in theatrical performances at Knebworth
House in aid of the Guild of Literature and Art.

1851   **January:** Dickens appears in theatrical performances at Rockingham
Castle.

February: Dickens visits Paris.

March: Catherine suffers a nervous collapse. John Dickens dies in
London on 31 March.

14 April: Dora Annie Dickens dies at Devonshire Terrace.

May: Dickens appears before Queen Victoria and Prince Albert,
in a performance of Bulwer-Lytton's play *Not So Bad As We Seem*,
at Devonshire House, Piccadilly. He produces his own play
Nightingale's Diary at the same venue.

July: Family is at Broadstairs.

November: Family leaves 1 Devonshire Terrace and moves to Tavistock
House, Tavistock Square, Bloomsbury. Dickens begins writing *Bleak
House*. Catherine publishes a cookery book, *What Shall We Have For
Dinner?*, under the pseudonym 'Lady Maria Clutterbuck'.

1852   **March:** First monthly part of *Bleak House appears*. Edward Bulwer-
Lytton Dickens is born on 13 March.

July–October: Dickens tours in several performances of *Not So Bad As
We Seem*.

December: A single-volume edition of the *Christmas Books* is published.

1853　**January:** Dickens is honoured in Birmingham for his services to the Mechanics' Institute.

June: Close to a nervous breakdown, Dickens takes time off in Boulogne.

August: *Bleak House* is completed.

September: *A Child's History of England* is completed. Dickens tours Switzerland and Italy with Wilkie Collins and Augustus Egg.

December: Dickens returns to Tavistock House. He gives his first Public Reading from his own works in Birmingham Town Hall.

1854　**January:** Dickens visits Preston, gathering material for *Hard Times*.

April: The first monthly part of *Hard Times* appears in *Household Words*.

Summer: Dickens stays at the Villa Camp de Droit, Boulogne, concentrating on the monthly parts of *Hard Times*.

October: Dickens returns to Tavistock House.

1855　**February:** Dickens and Wilkie Collins spend two weeks in Paris.

May: Dickens meets Maria Beadnell again (now Mrs Winter) and finds her dull and disappointing.

July: Dickens writing *Little Dorrit*, in Folkestone.

November: Family is in Paris.

December: Dickens gives a Public Reading of *A Christmas Carol* in Sheffield.

1856　**March:** Dickens provides the purchase money for Gad's Hill Place, Higham, Kent.

June–August: He is writing *Little Dorrit*, in Boulogne.

1857　**January:** Dickens acts in several performances of Wilkie Collins's *The Frozen Deep* at Tavistock House.

June: He takes possession of Gad's Hill Place. *Little Dorrit is* completed.

July: Marital rift between Charles and Catherine.

August: Dickens meets Ellen Ternan, an actress.

September: Dickens and Wilkie Collins tour the north of England gathering material for *The Lazy Tour of Two Idle Apprentices*.

1858   **February:** Dickens undertakes charitable work for the Hospital for Sick Children, giving a Public Reading in aid of their cause. He later gives sixteen such readings on his own behalf, at St Martin's Hall, London.

May: Charles and Catherine separate.

June: He makes a public statement in *Household Words*, attempting to explain the separation. He quarrels over the matter with Bradbury and Evans.

August: He begins a tour of Public Readings in 44 towns and cities, starting in Clifton, near Bristol, taking in Ireland and Scotland and ending in Brighton on 15 November.

1859   **January:** Dickens conceives the idea for a new monthly magazine, *All the Year Round*.

March: He begins writing *A Tale of Two Cities*.

30 April: First issue of *All the Year Round*, containing first monthly part of *A Tale of Two Cities*.

May: Final issue of *Household Words* appears.

August: Dickens at Broadstairs for one week.

November: Final part of *A Tale of Two Cities* appears.

December: *A Tale of Two Cities* published in volume form.

1860   **January:** *The Uncommercial Traveller* begins in *All the Year Round*.

27 July: Dickens's brother, Alfred Lamert Dickens, dies in Manchester.

September: Dickens gives up Tavistock House and settles permanently at Gad's Hill Place.

November: He begins writing *Great Expectations*. He tours Devon and Cornwall with Wilkie Collins.

December: First part of *Great Expectations* appears in *All the Year Round*.

1861   **March:** Dickens begins a new series of Public Readings at the St James's Hall, Piccadilly.

18 April: Reading Tour ends.

June: Dickens is at Gad's Hill, where he completes *Great Expectations*.

28 October: A new series of Readings begins in Norwich.

1862   **January:** The Reading Tour ends in Chester.

February: Dickens rents 16 Hyde Park Gate.

March: Georgina Hogarth is taken seriously ill. Dickens begins another series of Public Readings at the St James's Hall, Piccadilly: these continue until June.

October: Dickens is in Paris with Georgina Hogarth and his daughter, Mamie. They stay until December.

1863   **January:** Dickens, Georgina and Mamie return to Paris, where he gives a series of charitable Readings at the British Embassy.

March–June: Dickens gives another series of Readings at the Hanover Square Rooms, London.

12 September: His mother, Elizabeth, dies.

November: He begins writing *Our Mutual Friend* at Gad's Hill Place.

31 December: His son Walter dies in India.

1864   Dickens writing *Our Mutual Friend*.

May: First part of *Our Mutual Friend* appears.

1865   **February:** Dickens suffers pains in his left foot; diagnosed as frostbite.

June: He visits Paris with Ellen Ternan.

9 June: Dickens is involved in a serious railway accident at Staplehurst, Kent.

November: Final part of *Our Mutual Friend* appears.

1866   **March:** Dickens suffers heart trouble, but nevertheless accepts an offer to undertake another Reading Tour of 30 venues.

April: Reading Tour begins at St James's Hall. During the tour he complains of exhaustion and pains in his left eye.

October: Dickens's brother, Augustus, dies in Chicago.

1867   **January:** Dickens begins a new Public Reading Tour in Liverpool. He complains again of exhaustion.

14 May: The Reading Tour ends, having taken in 50 venues. Dickens immediately accepts a similar venture to take place in America.

9 November: Dickens sets sail for America, arriving ten days later in Boston where he gives the first of his Readings.

December: He suffers a cold and severe catarrh.

1868   **Winter:** Although in ill-health, Dickens continues his tour of America. He is presented to President Andrew Johnson in Washington.

March: Dickens is close to total exhaustion, but the tour continues.

April: He gives a 'Farewell Reading' in Boston and another in New York, where a celebratory dinner is held for him in Delmonico's restaurant. He sets sail on 22 April.

1 May: He arrives in England and returns to Gad's Hill Place.

October: He begins another Public Reading Tour. His brother, Fred, dies.

November: Reading Tour suspended during the General Election.

1869   **January:** The Reading Tour continues.

April: Dickens is ordered to rest. The Reading Tour is abandoned and future attendance monies returned to the public.

October: Dickens begins writing *The Mystery of Edwin Drood*, at Gad's Hill Place.

1870   **January:** Dickens suffers pains in his left side.

15 March: He gives his final 'Farewell Reading' at St James's Hall.

April: First monthly part of *The Mystery of Edwin Drood* appears.

8 June: Dickens collapses from a cerebral haemorrhage.

9 June: He dies in the evening at Gad's Hill Place.

14 June: Charles Dickens is buried at Poets' Corner in Westminster Abbey.

Dickens's
ENGLAND

DICKENS'S ENGLAND

1 Barnet
2 Chigwell
3 Finchley
4 Hornsey
5 Highgate
6 Holloway
7 Hampstead
8 Camden Town
9 Islington
10 Whitechapel
11 Shadwell
12 Kensington
13 Chelsea
14 Hammersmith
15 Fulham
16 Turnham Green
17 Brentford
18 Putney
19 Richmond
20 Twickenham
21 Petersham
22 Hampton
23 Kingston
24 Brixton
25 Norwood
26 Peckham
27 Dulwich
28 Bow
29 Greenwich
30 Blackheath
31 Gravesend
32 Chalk
33 Cooling

34 Gad's Hill Place
35 Shorne
36 Strood
37 Cobham
38 Rochester
39 Chatham
40 Sheerness
41 West Malling
42 Sandling
43 Maidstone

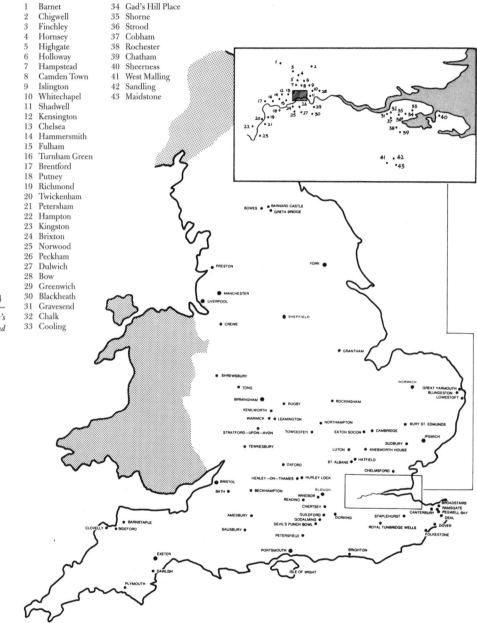

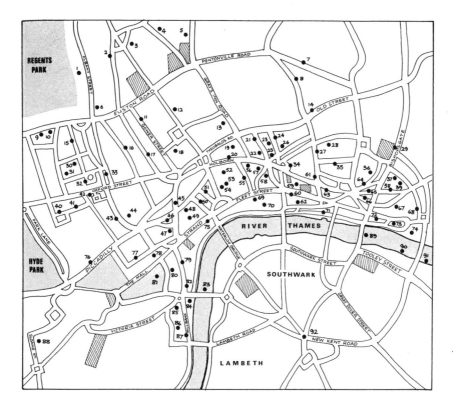

DICKENS'S

LONDON

1	Chester Place
2	Hampstead Road
3	Cranleigh Street
4	Old St Pancras Church
5	King's Cross
6	Osnaburgh Terrace
7	City Road
8	Goswell Road
9	St Marylebone Church
10	Devonshire Terrace (site of)
11	Gower Street
12	Tavistock House (site of)
13	Doughty Street
14	Old Street
15	Harley Street
16	Cleveland Street
17	Tottenham Court Road
18	British Museum
19	Gray's Inn

20	Holborn
21	Hatton Garden
22	Furnival's Inn
23	Saffron Hill
24	Farringdon Street
25	Ely Place
26	Smithfield
27	Aldersgate Street
28	Barbican
29	Bishopsgate
30	Welbeck Street
31	Bentinck Street
32	Cavendish Square
33	Little Portland Street
34	Snow Hill
35	London Wall
36	Austin Friars
37	St Mary Axe
38	Leadenhall Street
39	Aldgate
40	Grosvenor Square
41	Brook Street
42	Tenterden Street
43	Regent Street
44	Golden Square

45	Seven Dials
46	Leicester Square
47	Trafalgar Square
48	Long Acre
49	Covent Garden
50	Bow Street
51	Drury Lane
52	Lincoln's Inn
53	Portsmouth Street
54	Clare Market
55	Chancery Lane
56	Staple Inn
57	Barnard's Inn
58	Thavies Inn
59	Newgate Prison (site of)
60	Ludgate Hill
61	St Martin's-le-Grand
62	Doctors' Commons (site of)
63	Cheapside
64	Threadneedle Street
65	Cornhill
66	Lombard Street
67	St Olave's Church

68	Minories
69	Fleet Street
70	Temple
71	Thames Street
72	Monument
73	Mincing Lane
74	Tower of London
75	Strand
76	Piccadilly
77	Pall Mall
78	Athenaeum Club
79	Whitehall
80	Horse Guards Parade
81	St James's Park
82	Parliament Street
83	Westminster Bridge
84	Houses of Parliament
85	Westminster Abbey
86	Smith Square
87	Millbank
88	Cadogan Place
89	London Bridge
90	Quilp's Wharf (site of)
91	Jacob's Island (site of)
92	Elephant & Castle

A

ALDERSGATE STREET, LONDON — In October 1839 Dickens celebrated the completion of *Nicholas Nickleby* at the Albion Hotel (now demolished), Aldersgate Street. In *Martin Chuzzlewit* the warehouse of 'Chuzzlewit and Son' also stood there. John Jasper, in *The Mystery of Edwin Drood*, stayed in a 'hybrid hotel in a little square behind Aldersgate Street'.

ALDGATE, LONDON — In *The Pickwick Papers* Mr Pickwick and Sam Weller, in pursuit of Alfred Jingle and Job Trotter, leave London aboard Tony Weller's coach from the Bull Inn (site now occupied by Aldgate Avenue), Aldgate. Their fellow Pickwickian, the argumentative Mr Blotton, was 'of Aldgate'.

Aldgate Pump, a famous landmark standing at the junction of Fenchurch Street and Leadenhall Street, features in several novels, most notably *Nicholas Nickleby* and *Dombey and Son*.

The pump is also referred to in the essays 'Shabby-Genteel People' in *Sketches*

The splendid façade of the Athenaeum club, of which Dickens became a member in 1838.

by Boz, and 'Wapping Workhouse' in *The Uncommercial Traveller*.

AMESBURY, WILTSHIRE — The town of Amesbury is one of several locations which provided Dickens with material for 'the little Wiltshire village within an easy journey of the fair old town of Salisbury' in which the story of *Martin Chuzzlewit* begins. The George Hotel is the most likely original of the 'Blue Dragon Inn'. Other Wiltshire towns known to Dickens were Alderbury and Middle Winterslow.

THE ATHENAEUM CLUB, WATERLOO PLACE, LONDON — The Athenaeum Club was founded in 1824 as a gathering place of England's most prominent literary, artistic and scientific figures. In 1830 the club moved to its present premises (a splendid Grecian-style building by Decimus Burton) in Waterloo Place.

Dickens was elected a member of the Athenaeum in June 1838 at the age of twenty-six.

In 1858 the friendship between Dickens and William Makepeace Thackeray became strained when the two men quarrelled over the merits of a controversial article about Thackeray written by Edmund Yates, a young journalist. The feud between the two novelists continued until December 1863 when they met in the elegant hall of the Athenaeum and there – in a celebrated reunion – patched up their differences. Sadly, Thackeray died on Christmas Eve, just a week after this meeting.

AUSTIN FRIARS, LONDON — In *Martin Chuzzlewit* Mr Fips, lawyer to old Martin, has offices in 'a very dark passage on the first floor, oddly situated at the back of a house' in Austin Friars. Dickens had known this street since childhood.

B

BALL'S POND ROAD, LONDON — In *Dombey and Son* Mr Perch, the messenger in Dombey's office, and his ever-pregnant wife live in Ball's Pond Road.

BARBICAN, LONDON — An unspecified inn in this area served Dickens as the meeting place of the 'Prentice Knights in *Barnaby Rudge*. Sim Tappertit makes his way there:

> turning into the narrowest of the narrow streets … It was not a very choice spot for midnight expeditions, being in truth one of more than questionable character, and of an appearance by no means inviting. From the main street he had entered, itself little better than an alley, a low-browed doorway led into a blind court or yard, profoundly dark, unpaved, and reeking with stagnant odours. Into this ill-favoured pit the locksmith's vagrant 'prentice groped his way.

In *Oliver Twist* Bill Sikes and the unwilling young Oliver pass by the Barbican en route to 'crack the crib' at CHERTSEY. The area is also mentioned in *Martin Chuzzlewit* and *Little Dorrit*.

BARNARD CASTLE, CO. DURHAM — Dickens visited Barnard Castle with Hablot Knight Browne in February 1838, during his researches into the 'Yorkshire Schools' system prior to writing *Nicholas Nickleby*. They stayed at the King's Head in Market Place, and used this hotel as a base for their visits to various schools in the North Yorkshire area (see also BOWES, GRANTHAM and YORK).

In *Nicholas Nickleby* Newman Noggs informs Nicholas that 'there is good ale at the King's Head. Say you know me, and I'm sure they will not charge you for it.'

Opposite the King's Head stood a clock-makers' shop under the proprietorship of one Thomas Humphrey. When, in January 1840, Dickens began to consider the publication of a new weekly magazine, he remembered this shop and the owner's name. Thus *Master Humphrey's Clock* was conceived. Dickens transforms the object of the observation into a crippled old fellow who oversees a store of dusty old tales kept inside an ancient grandfather clock: 'I mean to tell how that he has kept odd manuscripts in the old, deep, dark, silent closet where the weights are; and takes from thence to read,' he wrote to John Forster.

BARNARD'S INN, LONDON — In *Great Expectations* Pip and Herbert Pocket share rooms in Barnard's Inn off the south side of HOLBORN. Pip's first impression of the place was one of disappointment:

> ...for, I had supposed that establishment to be an hotel kept by Mr Barnard ... Whereas I now found Barnard to be a disembodied spirit, or a fiction, and his inn the dingiest collection of shabby buildings ever squeezed together in a rank corner for Tom-cats.
>
> We entered this haven through a wicket-gate, and were disgorged by an introductory passage into a melancholy little square that looked to me like a flat burying ground. I thought it had the most dismal trees in it, and the most dismal sparrows, and the most dismal cats, and the most dismal houses (in number half a dozen or so), that I had ever seen.

The two friends later move to an apartment in Garden Court, TEMPLE.

BARNET, HERTFORDSHIRE — Having run away from the workhouse with 'a crust of bread; a coarse shirt; and two pairs of stockings in his bundle', the nine-year-old Oliver Twist finds himself, after a week on the road, wandering along the Great North Road, through the coaching town of Barnet:

> The window shutters were closed; the street was empty; not a soul had awakened to the business of the day...

He had been crouching on the step for some time; wondering at the great number of public-houses (every other house in Barnet was a tavern, large or small), gazing listlessly at the coaches as they passed through, and thinking how strange it seemed that they could do with ease, in a few hours, what it had taken him a whole week of courage and determination beyond his years to accomplish; when he was roused by observing that a boy, who had passed him carelessly some minutes before, had returned, and was now surveying him most earnestly.

This boy, Jack Dawkins, was the sharp-witted 'Artful Dodger' with whom Oliver will share many adventures.

In *Bleak House*, Esther Summerson, Ada Clare and Richard Carstone pass through Barnet on the way to Bleak House in ST ALBANS:

At Barnet there were other horses waiting for us; but as they had only just been fed we had to wait for them too.

While waiting, the trio took 'a long fresh walk over a common and an old battlefield'. This was Hadley Green, scene of the Battle of Barnet in April 1471.

BARNSTAPLE, DEVON — Barnstaple is mentioned in the Christmas story *A Message from the Sea*, which Dickens wrote jointly with Wilkie Collins in 1860 (see also BIDEFORD and CLOVELLY).

BATH, AVON — The youthful Dickens poked mild fun at the very idea of spa towns when he sent the Pickwickians to Bath, following Mr Pickwick's decision to pay 'Not one halfpenny…Not one half-penny' of the costs brought against him, for breach of promise, by Mrs Bardell and her lawyers Dodson and Fogg. (Dickens himself had first visited this beautiful city during his days as a reporter for the *Morning Chronicle*: he had stayed at the Saracen's Head Hotel.)

En route to Bath, the stagecoach causes Sam Weller a certain amount of concern when he sees 'the magic name of PICKWICK' painted upon its door.

He fears that 'the proprietor o' this here coach is a playin' some imperence with us'. Pickwick, however, dismisses the assumption. In fact Dickens was merely giving credit where credit was due, for he had borrowed the surname of his first famous comic creation from one Moses Pickwick, a well-known coach proprietor of Bath. Moses Pickwick also owned the White Hart Hotel (now demolished, site occupied by the Grand Pump Room Hotel).

The Pickwickians eventually arrive at the White Hart:

where the waiters, from their costume, might be mistaken for Westminster boys, only they destroy the illusion by behaving themselves much better.

Next morning Pickwick is welcomed to Bath by Angelo Cyrus Bantam, the Master of Ceremonies, of 12 Queen's Square:

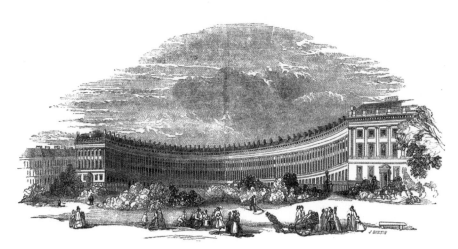

Royal Crescent, Bath, where Mr Winkle has a narrow escape from the wrath of Mr Dowler.

'Welcome to Ba-ath, Sir. This is indeed an acquisition. Most welcome to Ba-ath, Sir. It is long – very long, Mr Pickwick, since you drank the waters. It appears an age, Mr Pickwick. Re-mark-able.'

'It is a very long time since I drank the waters, certainly,' replied Mr Pickwick; 'for to the best of my knowledge I was never here before.'

'Never in Ba-ath, Mr Pickwick!' exclaimed the Grand Master, letting his hand fall in astonishment. 'Never in Ba-ath! He! he! Mr Pickwick, you are a wag. Not bad, not bad. Good, good. He! he! he! Re-markable!'

That evening, before attending the Ball at the Assembly Rooms, Mr Pickwick takes a stroll around the city. He 'arrived at the unanimous conclusion that Park Street was very much like the perpendicular streets a man sees in a dream, which he cannot get up for the life of him.'

Ball Nights in Bath are:

…moments snatched from Paradise; rendered bewitching by music, beauty, elegance, fashion, etiquette, and – and – above all, by the absence of tradespeople, who are quite inconsistent with Paradise, and who have an amalgamation of themselves at the Guildhall every fortnight, which is, to say the least, remarkable.

At the Assembly Rooms Ball:

the hum of many voices, and the sound of many feet, were perfectly bewildering. Dresses rustled, feathers waved, lights shone, and jewels sparkled … In the tea room, and hovering around the card-tables, were a vast number of queer old ladies and decrepit old gentlemen, discussing all the small talk and scandal of the day, with a relish and a gusto which sufficiently bespoke the intensity of the pleasure they derived from the occupation … Lounging near the doors, and in remote corners, were various knots of silly young men, displaying various varieties of puppyism and stupidity … And lastly, seated on some of the back benches, where they had already taken up their positions for the evening, were diverse unmarried ladies past their grand climacteric, who not dancing because there were no partners for them, and not playing cards lest they should be set down as irretrievably single, were in the favourable situation of being able to abuse everybody without reflecting on themselves.

At this function, Mr Pickwick is introduced to 'the elite of Ba-ath' – The Dowager Lady Snuphanuph, young Lord Mutanhead, the Honorable Mr Crushton, Mrs Colonel Wugsby, Miss Bolo and the rest. He also finds himself involved, against his better judgement, in a card game with the ladies: 'Poor Mr Pickwick! he had never played with three thorough-paced female card-players before. They were so desperately sharp, that they quite frightened him.' Contemplating 'a stay of at least two months in Bath', Mr Pickwick next takes lodgings 'in the upper portion of a house in the Royal Crescent'. The Crescent also provides the later scene of Mr Winkle's hilarious nocturnal episode with Mrs Dowler's sedan chair. Pickwick also:

began to drink the waters with the utmost assiduity. He drank a quarter of a pint

before breakfast, and then walked up a hill; and another quarter of a pint after breakfast, and walked down a hill; and after every fresh quarter of a pint, Mr Pickwick declared, in the most solemn and emphatic terms, that he felt a great deal better: whereat his friends were very much delighted, though they had not been previously aware that there was anything the matter with him.

There follows Dickens's magnificent description of the Great Pump Room – a fine piece of journalistic observation, made all the more remarkable considering the fact that he had only previously been in the city for three or four days, and that during the reporting of an election:

The Great Pump Room is a spacious saloon, ornamented with Corinthian pillars, and a music gallery, and a Tompion clock, and a statue of Nash, and a golden inscription, to which all the water drinkers should attend, for it appeals to them in the cause of a deserving charity. There is a large bar with a marble vase, out of which the pumper gets the water; and there are a number of yellow-looking tumblers, out of which the company gets it; and it is a most edifying and satisfactory sight to behold the perseverance and gravity with which they swallow it. There are baths near at hand, in which a part of the company wash themselves; and a band plays afterwards, to congratulate the remainder on their having done so.

There is another pump room, into which infirm ladies and gentlemen are wheeled, in such an astonishing variety of chairs and chaises, that any adventurous individual who goes in with the regular number of toes, is in imminent danger of coming out without them; and there is a third, into which the quiet people go, for it is less noisy than either. There is an immensity of promenading, on crutches and off, with sticks and without, and a great deal of conversation, and liveliness, and pleasantry.

Sam Weller also attends a social gathering – a 'friendly swarry, consisting of a boiled leg of mutton with the usual trimmings', in the select company of the Bath footmen. En route to the 'swarry' with John Smauker, Sam gives his own opinion of the Spa waters: 'I thought they'd a wery strong flavour o' warm flat irons,' he says.

Dickens sets the scene of the footmen's 'swarry' in a parlour behind a greengrocer's shop, the identity of which has never been firmly proven. It is known, however, that the footmen of the city held occasional soirees at the Beaufort Arms in Princes Street.

Dickens revisited Bath in 1840, staying with Catherine and John Forster at the York House Hotel (now the Royal York Hotel). They also visited the home of Dickens's good friend Walter Savage Landor, at 35 St James's Square, where Dickens first conceived the idea for Little Nell, the central character of *The Old Curiosity Shop* and one of his most enduring creations.

According to Forster, Landor 'had meant to purchase [the house], and then and there to have burnt it to the ground, to the end that no meaner association should ever desecrate the birthplace of Little Nell'.

Landor himself provided Dickens with the inspiration for 'the most impetuous man', Laurence Boythorn in *Bleak House*. In the same novel Miss Volumnia Dedlock is 'retired to Bath; where she lives slenderly on an annual present from Sir Leicester…'.

BEAK STREET, LONDON — In *Nicholas Nickleby*, Newman Noggs's letter to Nicholas recommends the Crown Inn (now gone), Silver Street (now Beak Street): 'It is at the corner of Silver Street and James Street, with a bar door both ways.'

BECKHAMPTON, WILTSHIRE — The Waggon and Horses Inn at Beckhampton is generally regarded as Dickens's original for the inn in *The Pickwick Papers* wherein Tom Smart had his adventure with:

> a strange grim-looking high-backed chair, carved in the most fantastic manner, with a flowered damask cushion, and the round knobs at the bottom of the legs carefully tied up in red cloth, as if it had got the gout in its toes.

BENTINCK STREET, LONDON — 18 Bentinck Street, Manchester Square, Marylebone, was Dickens's parents' home during 1833–34. The house has since been rebuilt.

BEVIS MARKS, LONDON — In *The Old Curiosity Shop* Sampson Brass, the 'attorney of no very good repute', has offices in Bevis Marks. In the same novel the inn so favoured by Dick Swiveller is most probably the Red Lion, which once stood in that street.

BIDEFORD, DEVON — Dickens and Wilkie Collins visited Bideford in November 1860 during their researches for *A Message from the Sea* (see also BARNSTAPLE and CLOVELLY). After a twelve-hour train journey Dickens wrote to Georgina Hogarth:

> I write (with the most impracticable pen on earth) to report our safe arrival here in a beastly hotel…We had a stinking fish for dinner, and have been able to drink nothing, though we have ordered wine, beer, and brandy and water…The landlady is playing cribbage with the landlord in the next room (behind a thin partition), and they seem quite comfortable.

BILLINGSGATE, LONDON — The famous fish market features in *Little Dorrit* as one of several places where Tip Dorrit enjoys a brief spell of employment. In *Great Expectations* 'old Billingsgate market' is viewed by Pip and Herbert Pocket as they row along the Thames on their way to assist in the departure of Abel Magwitch. In *The Uncommercial Traveller* the 'Uncommercial' reports on the fish market at night in the essay 'Night Walks'.

BIRMINGHAM, WEST MIDLANDS — Mr Pickwick and his friends travel to Birmingham by stagecoach, in order to visit Mr Winkle senior. Dickens vividly describes their entry into the great industrial centre:

> It was quite dark when Mr Pickwick roused himself sufficiently to look out of the window. The straggling cottages by the road-side, the dingy hue of every object visible, the murky atmosphere, the palls of cinders and brick-dust, the deep red glow of furnace fires in the distance, the volumes of dense smoke issuing heavily forth from high toppling chimneys, blackening and obscuring everything around; the glare of distant lights, the ponderous waggons which toiled along the road, laden with flashing rods of iron, or piled with heavy goods – all betoken their rapid approach to the great working town of Birmingham.

Having settled in at the Old Royal Hotel in Temple Row, Pickwick, Ben Allen and Bob Sawyer walk to the home of Winkle senior:

> About a quarter of a mile off, in a quiet, substantial-looking street, stood an old red-brick house with three steps before the door, and a brass plate upon it, bearing in fat Roman capitals, the words 'Mr Winkle'. The steps were very white, and the bricks were very red and the house was very clean.

Dickens's model for this house, afterwards known as 'Mr Winkle's House', stood at the corner of Easy Row (now gone) and Edmund Street: it was demolished in the late 1800s.

Birmingham also features briefly in *Oliver Twist*, *Nicholas Nickleby*, *Master Humphrey's Clock*, *Barnaby Rudge* and *Dombey and Son*.

Dickens often visited England's second city, initially as a reporter for the *Morning Chronicle*, then as an amateur actor, and in later life as a public performer of his own works.

In February 1844 he presided over a meeting held in support of the New Polytechnic Institute. In June 1848 he acted at the Theatre Royal (now gone: site later occupied by a department store), New Street, in a fundraising effort for the upkeep of William Shakespeare's birthplace at STRATFORD-UPON-AVON. He acted again, at the Town Hall, in 1852 in aid of the Guild of Literature and Art, the brainchild of his good friend Lord Lytton (see also KNEBWORTH HOUSE). In January 1853 Dickens was presented with a silver salver and a diamond ring at a 'Banquet in Honour of Literature and Art' held at Dee's Hotel (now gone).

And it was in Birmingham in December 1853 that Charles Dickens began what may be called his second career, when he fulfilled a promise to the Birmingham and Midland Institute by giving a charitable reading of *A Christmas Carol* and *A Cricket on the Hearth* in the Town Hall.

The event was a resounding success, raising more than £400 on behalf of the Institute. Within a week Dickens was seriously considering the possibility of becoming a Public Reader. Indeed, by the time of his next visit to Birmingham, in October 1858, he was a professional, giving a reading at the Music Hall in Broad Street (later to become the Prince of Wales Theatre – now gone). There were further readings in Birmingham in 1859, 1861 and 1866.

During the last of these performances at the Town Hall, an incident occurred which further serves to illustrate precisely how popular Dickens had by then become as a Public Reader of his own works. He wrote of the event to Georgina Hogarth:

> We had a tremendous hall at Birmingham last night, £230 odd, 2100 people; and I made a most ridiculous mistake. Had Nickleby on my list to finish with, instead of Trial. Read Nickleby with great go, and the people remained. Went back again at 10 o'clock, and explained the accident; but said if they liked I would give the Trial. They did like it, and I had another half hour of it in that enormous place.

Dickens returned to Birmingham to give more Public Readings in February 1867 and April 1869, by which time his health was failing him.

BISHOPSGATE, LONDON — In *Dombey and Son* 'one Brogley, sworn broker and appraiser' had a shop in Bishopsgate, not far from Sol Gills's establishment (see also LEADENHALL STREET), in which:

every description of second-hand furniture was exhibited in the most uncomfortable aspect, and under circumstances and in combinations the most completely foreign to its purposes.

BLACKHEATH, LONDON — Salem House, the place of David Copperfield's first formal education, is situated 'down by Blackheath':

Salem House was a square brick building with wings, of a bare and unfinished appearance ... I gazed upon the schoolroom ... as the most forlorn and desolate place I had ever seen. I see it now. A long room, with three long rows of desks, and six of forms, and bristling all round with pegs for hats and slates. Scraps of old copybooks and exercises litter the dirty floor. Some silkworms' houses, made of the same materials, are scattered over the desks. Two miserable little white mice, left behind by their owner, are running up and down in a fusty castle made of pasteboard and wire, looking in all the corners with their red eyes for anything to eat. A bird, in a cage a very little bigger than himself, makes a mournful rattle now and then in hopping on his perch, two inches high, or dropping from it, but neither sings nor chirps. There is a strange unwholesome smell upon the room, like mildewed corduroys, sweet apples wanting air, and rotten books. There could not well be more ink splashed about it, if it had been

roofless from its first construction, and the skies had rained, snowed, hailed, and blown ink through the varying seasons of the year.

How closely this description is based upon Dickens's own school, the Wellington House Classical and Commercial Academy, it is impossible to say (see also HAMPSTEAD ROAD). It is more than probable, however, that he drew upon memories of his own schooldays when conjuring up young Copperfield's schoolfriends and masters; Steerforth, Traddles, Sharp, Mell et al.

Later, on his lonesome trek towards DOVER to find his aunt, young Copperfield spends a night under a haystack close to Salem House.

The action of *A Tale of Two Cities* begins as the Dover mail coach lumbers up Shooter's Hill 'on a Friday night late in November' 1775. In *Our Mutual Friend* the newlyweds John and Bella Rokesmith set up home in Blackheath: 'A modest little cottage but a bright and a fresh.'

BLUNDESTON, SUFFOLK — 'I was born at Blunderstone, in Suffolk, or "thereby" as they say in Scotland,' so states the hero of Dickens's eighth novel *David Copperfield* (1849–1850). Dickens based his 'Blunderstone' on the charming village of Blundeston, which he had visited in 1848.

Blundeston Rectory was his original for 'The Rookery', birthplace of young Copperfield and scene of the first triumphant entry of his Aunt Betsey Trotwood:

'In the name of Heaven, why Rookery?'
'Do you mean the house, ma'am?' asked my mother.
'Why Rookery?' said Miss Betsey.
'Cookery would have been more to the purpose, if you had any practical ideas of life, either of you.'

'The name was Mr Copperfield's choice,' returned my mother. 'When we bought the house, he liked to think that there were rooks about it.'...

'Where are the birds?' asked Miss Betsey.

'The —?' My mother had been thinking of something else.

'The rooks – what has become of them?' asked Miss Betsey.

'There have not been any since we have lived here,' said my mother. 'We thought – Mr Copperfield thought – it was quite a large rookery; but the nests were very old ones, and the birds have deserted them a long while.'

'David Copperfield all over!' cried Miss Betsey. 'David Copperfield from

The Rookery, Blundeston ('Blunderstone' in the book), birthplace of David Copperfield.

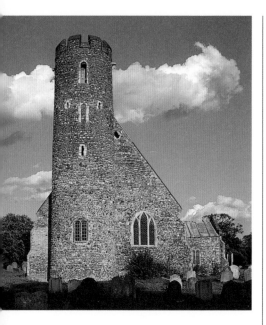

There is nothing half so green that I know anywhere, as the grass of that churchyard; nothing half so shady as its trees; nothing half so quiet as its tombstones. The sheep are feeding there, when I kneel up, early in the morning, in my little bed in a closet within my mother's room, to look out at it; and I see the red light shining on the sun-dial, and think within myself, 'Is the sun-dial glad, I wonder, that it can tell the time again?'

Blundeston churchyard, where David Copperfield Senior lies buried beneath a 'white gravestone'.

A sundial still remains above the porch of the church and any one of several now dulled tombstones may have provided Dickens with his model for the 'white gravestone' of David Copperfield senior.

'Our village alehouse', departure point of Mr Barkis's cart to Great Yarmouth, is based upon the Plough Inn, Blundeston.

David Copperfield is the most 'autobiographical' of Dickens's novels. Indeed, he had made several 'autobiographical notes' which were eventually absorbed into the book, and many events and characters in the narrative are clearly based upon the realities of his own life – Wilkins Micawber is an affectionate portrait of John Dickens; Murdstone and Grinby's establishment derives from Warren's Warehouse (see also STRAND and COVENT GARDEN), and Salem House School is probably based on the Wellington House Academy (see also HAMPSTEAD ROAD and BLACKHEATH). The novel became a favourite with the public, and Dickens called *David Copperfield* 'my favourite child'.

head to foot! Calls a house a rookery when there's not a rook near it, and takes the birds on trust, because he sees the nests!'

This fine house still stands in the village of Blundeston, although it no longer serves as a rectory (the church relinquished the deeds and sold off the property in 1976) and its name has been changed to 'The Rookery'!

The church of St Mary the Virgin, Blundeston, is the church visible to young David from his mother's room (although Dickens describes it as having a spire when, in fact, the church boasts a round tower):

BOW, LONDON — In *Nicholas Nickleby* the kindly Cheeryble brothers, Charles and Edwin, having engaged Nicholas as a clerk at their office in the city (exact location unknown), next provide a home for the impoverished Nickleby family at:

> …that little cottage in Bow which is empty, at something under the usual rent. …'

For Nicholas, the daily return to this house in the then rural district of Bow was full of surprises:

> One day it was a grape vine, and another day it was a boiler, and another day it was the key of the front parlour closet at the bottom of the water-butt, and so on through a hundred items. Then this room was embellished with a muslin curtain, and that room was rendered quite elegant by a window-blind, and such improvements were made as no one would have supposed possible…

In short the poor Nicklebys were social and happy, while the rich Nickleby was alone and miserable.

BOWES, NORTH YORKSHIRE — By the winter of 1838 Dickens had decided that his next novel would deal with the notorious 'Yorkshire Schools' system, in which certain northern 'educational establishments' openly advertised to take in children for as little as twenty guineas a year. These terms often included such added inducements as 'no extra charges' and 'no vacations'. Thus, any number of illegitimate or otherwise unwanted offspring could be banished from sight for as long as their parents or guardians so desired.

A late 19th-century illustration of Dotheboys Hall, based by Dickens on Bowes Academy.

Bowes Academy as it appeared in the 20th century. It has now been divided into flats.

Many prospective parents were completely taken in by the flowery language and high promises of the advertisements – 'Youths are carefully instructed in the English, Latin and Greek languages, Writing, Common and Decimal Arithmetic, Bookkeeping, Mensuration, Surveying, Geometry, Geography and Navigation, with the most useful branches of Mathematics, and are provided with Board, Clothes and every necessary at twenty guineas per annum each.'

Thus, under the misapprehension that they were providing their children with a rounded education and a good start in life, and all at a reasonable cost, they would unwittingly pack them off, all too often to a life of misery.

Many pupils of the 'Yorkshire Schools' were subjected to ill-treatment. In certain cases they never returned home again, and several actually died from the effects of their 'education'.

Dickens had first become aware of the 'Yorkshire Schools' during his childhood days at Chatham: 'I know my first impressions of them were picked up at that time,' he wrote, 'that they were somehow or other connected with a suppurated abscess that some boy had come home with, in consequence of his Yorkshire Guide, Philosopher, and friend having ripped it open with an inky penknife'.

Now, having made arrangements with Chapman and Hall for the publication of the work – to be entitled *Nicholas Nickleby* – Dickens decided to travel to Yorkshire to investigate the situation at first hand.

On 30 January 1838 he set off, in the company of Hablot Knight Browne (Phiz), by stagecoach from the Saracen's Head, SNOW HILL. For two days they travelled through a bleak winter landscape, stopping only at GRANTHAM in Lincolnshire, and arriving shortly before midnight of the second day at the George and New Inn,

GRETA BRIDGE. Next day they travelled on to BARNARD CASTLE, from where they set out to visit several schools in the area.

One such establishment stood in the village of Bowes, and was run by a one-eyed headmaster named William Shaw. (In 1823 Shaw had been found guilty of cruelty towards certain of his pupils – ten of whom had gone blind while in his care. Yet, fifteen years later, his business still thrived.)

Using an assumed name, and posing as a prospective customer seeking a suitable school on behalf of a recently widowed friend in London, Dickens visited Bowes Academy and met with William Shaw. Understandably, the headmaster was wary of all visitors and refused to show this prospective client around the establishment. In Bowes churchyard Dickens and Browne came upon the graves of several unfortunate pupils of Shaw's school. One tombstone in particular moved the author to tears. It reads:

Here lie
the remains of
George Ashton Taylor
of Trowbridge Wilts
who died suddenly at
Mr William Shaw's Academy
of this place April 13th 1822
aged 19 years
Young reader thou must die
But after this the judgement

Bowes

Bowes Churchyard. Here lie buried William Shaw, headmaster of Bowes Academy, and several of his pupils.

Dickens later wrote 'I think his ghost put Smike into my mind, upon the spot.'

That evening, back in Barnard Castle, the two travellers were joined by the solicitor who had arranged their introductions to several of the schoolmasters in the area. Throughout the evening he refused to be drawn on the subject of the schools. However, as he was preparing to leave, he confessed to Dickens that he could not 'gang to bed and not tell 'ee, for weedur's sak', to keep the lattle boy . . . while that's a harse to hoold in Lunnon'.

With his suspicions thus obliquely confirmed and his own impressions firmly stamped in his mind Dickens – and Browne – returned, via YORK, to London. On 7 February 1838, his 26th birthday, he began work on *Nicholas Nickleby*.

William Shaw became the model for Wackford Squeers, while Bowes Academy was Dickens's prototype for Dotheboys Hall:

…a long, cold-looking house one story high, with a few straggling outbuildings behind and a barn and stable adjoining…

Mr Squeers having bolted the door to keep it shut, ushered him into a small parlour scantily furnished with a few chairs, a yellow map hung against the wall, and a couple of tables – one of which bore some preparations for supper, while on the other a tutor's assistant, a Murray's grammar, half-a-dozen cards of terms, and a worn letter to Wackford Squeers, Esquire, were arranged in picturesque confusion…

This was the Squeers's parlour, a luxurious apartment compared to the school itself:

It was such a crowded scene, and there were so many objects to attract attention, that, at first, Nicholas stared about him, really without seeing anything at all. By degrees, however, the place resolved itself into a bare and dirty room, with a couple of windows, where of a tenth part might be of glass, the remainder being stopped up with old copy-books and paper. There were a couple of long old rickety desks, cut and notched, and inked, and damaged, in every possible way, two or three forms, a detached desk for Squeers, and another for his assistant. The ceiling was supported, like that of a barn, by cross beams and rafters, and the walls were so stained and discoloured that it was impossible to tell whether they had ever been touched with paint or whitewash…

Pale and haggard faces, lank and bony figures, children with the countenances of old men, deformities with irons upon their limbs, boys of stunted growth, and others whose long meagre legs would hardly bear their stooping bodies, all crowded on the view together; there were the bleared eye, the hair-lip, the crooked foot … There were little faces which should have been handsome, darkened with the scowl of sullen dogged suffering; there was childhood with the light of its eyes quenched, its beauty gone, and its helplessness alone remaining; there were the vicious-faced boys, brooding, with leaden eyes, like malefactors in a jail; and there were young creatures on whom the sins of their frail parents descended … what an incipient Hell was breeding here!

Nicholas Nickleby was an immediate success, with the opening number selling upwards of 50,000 copies on its first day of sale. The third and fourth numbers, detailing the horrors inside Dotheboys Hall, were immensely successful in turning the tide of public opinion against the 'Yorkshire Schools' system. In his preface to the novel's first cheap edition in 1848, Dickens was able to report 'There were, then, a good many Yorkshire schools in existence. There are few now.'

BOW STREET, LONDON — In *Oliver Twist*, the Artful Dodger is taken to the Bow Street Police Court, having been caught returning a stolen handkerchief (it was, he had discovered, a second-hand one) to its owner's pocket. In *Barnaby Rudge*, Barnaby is also questioned in the Police Court. In *Nicholas Nickleby* the actor Snevellici is 'to be found in Broad Court, when I'm in town'. Broad Court is a turning off Bow Street. Bow Street is also mentioned in the essay 'Prisoners' Van' in *Sketches by Boz*.

BRENTFORD, MIDDLESEX — In *Oliver Twist* Brentford is passed through by Bill Sikes and his unwilling accomplice Oliver on their way to 'crack the crib' at CHERTSEY. In *Great Expectations*, Compeyson's house was, according to Abel Magwitch, 'over nigh Brentford'. And in *Our Mutual Friend*, 'the abode of Mrs Betty Higden was not easy to find, lying in such complicated back settlements of muddy Brentford'.

BRIGHTON, SUSSEX — Brighton was a favourite seaside resort for Dickens (see also BROADSTAIRS and ISLE OF WIGHT). He considered the town 'a gay place for a week or so'. He first stayed there, with Catherine, at the Old Ship Hotel, King's Road, in November 1837. On this occasion the weather was bad. 'On Wednesday night,' he wrote to John Forster:

> it blew a perfect hurricane, breaking windows, knocking down shutters, carrying people off their legs, blowing the fires out, and causing universal consternation. The air was for some hours darkened with a shower of black hats (second hand) which are supposed to have blown off the heads of unwary passengers in remote parts of the town, and have been industriously picked up by the fishermen.

Despite this blustery experience Dickens stayed again in Brighton in 1841.

In 1847 he wrote part of *Dombey and Son* while staying at 148 King's Road. The original of Dr Blimber's school in that novel was Chichester House, Chichester Terrace, and although Mrs Pipchin's 'castle' has never been satisfactorily identified, Brighton does possess several narrow streets which answer to Dickens's description of 'a steep by-street ... where the soil was more than usually chalky, flinty, and sterile, and the houses were more than usually brittle and thin'. In the same novel Miss Pankey's aunt lived at nearby Rottingdean.

In November 1848 Dickens stayed at the Bedford Hotel (site now occupied by the Holiday Inn) while writing *The Haunted Man*. He stayed there again in 1849. This hotel would also serve as his Brighton base during the later reading tours.

The original Phiz illustration of Dr Blimber's school from *Dombey and Son*.

BRISTOL, AVON — Bristol features in *The Pickwick Papers*, following Mr Winkle's escape from Mr Dowler in BATH. Winkle puts up at the Bush Inn (now gone) and then explores the streets of the city:

which struck him as being a shade more dirty than any place he had ever seen. Having inspected the docks and

shipping, and viewed the cathedral, he inquired the way to Clifton, and being directed thither, took the route which was pointed out to him. But, as the pavements of Bristol are not the widest or cleanest upon earth, so its streets are not altogether the straightest or least intricate; and Mr Winkle being greatly puzzled by their manifold windings and twistings, looked about him for a decent shop in which he could apply afresh for counsel and instruction. His eye fell upon a newly-painted tenement which had recently been converted into something between a shop and a private-house, and which a red lamp, projecting over the fanlight of the street-door, would have sufficiently announced as the residence of a medical practitioner, even if the word 'Surgery' had not been inscribed in golden characters on a wainscot ground, above the window of what, in times bygone, had been the front parlour.

This turns out to be the surgery of Bob Sawyer (see also SOUTHWARK) 'late Nockemorf', and is based, it is believed, on a chemist's shop which once stood at the foot of a hill in Park Street, although this establishment is more likely a product of Dickens's imagination.

Sam Weller, despatched on behalf of Mr Winkle to ascertain the whereabouts of Arabella Allen in the picturesque suburb of Clifton, meets his valentine, Mary the housemaid (see also IPSWICH), near a 'stable door at the bottom of a long back lane without a thoroughfare'. Through Mary, he learns that Arabella is living at the 'very next house', but 'only walks in the garden in the evening'. Armed with this intelligence Weller is able to arrange an interview between Mr Winkle and Miss Allen; the couple later marry in secret.

Bristol also features in *Barnaby Rudge* when, a month after the NEWGATE executions:

> Mr Haredale … stood alone in the mail office … his appearance was greatly altered. He looked much older, and more care-worn … He was now a solitary man, and the heart within him was dreary and lonesome … he was about to revisit London for the last time, and look once more upon the walls of their old home, before turning his back on it, for ever.

Charles Dickens had first visited Bristol in 1835, as a reporter for the *Morning Chronicle*. In 1851 he acted at the Victoria Rooms, Queens Road, in aid of the Guild for Literature and Art. He gave Public Readings in Bristol in 1858, 1866 and 1869; on this last occasion, he gave a particularly inspired reading of the murder of Nancy from *Oliver Twist*. Afterwards he wrote to Georgina Hogarth:

> At Clifton on Monday night we had a contagion of faintings; and yet the place was not hot. I should think we had from a dozen to twenty ladies taken out rigid at various times! It became quite ridiculous.

'Quite ridiculous', perhaps, but further testament to Dickens's powers as a public performer of his own works.

THE BRITISH MUSEUM, LONDON — The ambitious young Dickens resolved to continue his self-education. On 7 February 1830 – his eighteenth birthday – he obtained to this end, a reader's ticket at the British Museum in Great Russell Street, Bloomsbury. There, amid the dusty tomes of the Old Reading Room, he studied among other subjects the history of England and the works of William Shakespeare. In later years he would count his study of this self-imposed curriculum amongst the wisest decisions of his life.

BRIXTON, LONDON — A genteel suburb in the 1800s where, in *The Pickwick Papers*, Mr Pickwick undertakes some of his 'unwearied researches'. Brixton is also mentioned in *Martin Chuzzlewit* and *The Uncommercial Traveller*.

BROADSTAIRS, KENT — Dickens first stayed at Broadstairs, with Catherine and

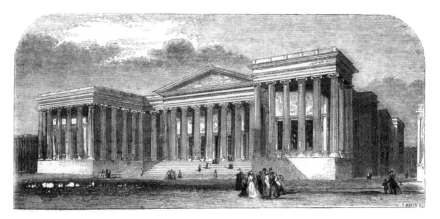

The British Museum, where Dickens studied in the Reading Room in his early career.

the eight-month-old Charley, in September 1837, during the writing of *The Pickwick Papers*. They stayed at 12 High Street (now 31 High Street) where Dickens continued with his work between bouts of taking the bracing sea air. He wrote to John Forster of the nude bathing:

> I have seen ladies and gentlemen walking upon the earth in slippers of buff, and pickling themselves in the sea in complete suits of the same.

He also notes:

> I have found that our next neighbour has a wife and something else under the same roof with the rest of his furniture – the wife deaf and blind, and the something else given to drinking.

Dickens was so taken with the resort of Broadstairs that he returned there each summer, except for two, until 1851.

40 Albion Street was his residence in autumn 1839, a house later incorporated into the Albion Hotel (Dickens stayed at the hotel in 1845 and 1849). In 1840, during the writing of *The Old Curiosity Shop* and *Barnaby Rudge* the family stayed at Lawn House (now Archway House), Albion Street. In 1842 following his American sojourn (see also LIVERPOOL) he wrote his *American Notes* in Broadstairs. In 1847 and 1848 he stayed at Chandos Place, but was dissatisfied there because of the noise from the street. Again he wrote to John Forster:

> Vagrant music is getting to that height here, and is so impossible to be escaped from, that I fear Broadstairs and I must part company in time to come. Unless it pours of rain I cannot write half-an-hour without the most excruciating organs, fiddles, bells or glee-singers. There is a

Broadstairs, Dickens's favourite resort, with Fort House (now known as Bleak House) on the cliff.

violin of the most torturing kind under the window now (time, ten in the morning) and an Italian box of music on the steps – both in full blast.

Indeed, Dickens and Broadstairs did part company in the summer of 1849 when he took a house in Bonchurch (see also BRIGHTON and ISLE OF WIGHT). However, this experiment did not work out and he was back on the Kentish coast by October.

In 1850 he took the house most closely associated with him in Broadstairs, Fort House (now called 'Bleak House'), a tall and imposing building overlooking the town on its northernmost promontory. Here, in his study overlooking the North Sea, Dickens completed *David Copperfield*. A house in Nuckell's Place (now Victoria Parade) suggested Betsey Trotwood's house

in that novel (although Dickens removed it in his imagination to DOVER). Aunt Betsey was in fact partly modelled upon the owner of this house, one Mary Pearson Strong, who, like her fictional counterpart, had a strong aversion to donkeys.

The connection between Broadstairs and Betsey Trotwood's house was confirmed by Charles ('Charley') Dickens junior in his 'Notes on Some Dickens Places and People' which appeared in an edition of the *Pall Mall* magazine in 1894:

The Trotwood donkey fights did not take place at Dover at all, but at Broadstairs; where a certain Miss Strong – a charming old lady who was always most kind to me as a small boy, and to whose cakes and tea I still look back with fond and unsatisfied regret – lived in a little double-fronted cottage in the middle of Nuckell's Place, on the seafront, firmly convinced of her right to stop the passage of donkeys along the road in front of her door. Never shall I forget being carried by a wilful donkey, who evidently enjoyed the fun, across this sacred ground, and seeing my old friend making vigorously hostile demonstrations at me with the hearth-broom. It was a long time before she could be brought to understand that I really had been an unwilling and perfectly innocent trespasser.

Miss Strong's house, now known as Dickens House, displays many interesting items including a writing-box presented to Dickens by John Forster, the calendar used in the offices of *All the Year Round*, and several letters written by Dickens. The small garden fronting the house (now fenced off) is Nuckell's Place, the same spot of greenery upon which Miss Strong/Aunt Betsey suffered the attack of donkeys.

In his essay 'Our English Watering-place', published in *Household Words* and later in *Reprinted Pieces*, Dickens affectionately describes Broadstairs:

Sky, sea, beach and village lie as still before as if they were sitting for a picture. It is dead low water. A ripple plays upon the ripening corn upon the cliff, as if it were faintly trying from recollection to

The Dickens House Museum, Broadstairs, the model for Betsey Trotwood's home in David Copperfield.

imitate the sea ... But the ocean lies winking in the sunlight like a drowsy lion – its glassy waters scarcely curve upon the shore – the fishing boats in the tiny harbour are all stranded in the mud – our two colliers (our watering place has a maritime trade employing that amount of shipping) have not an inch of water within a quarter of a mile of them, and turn, exhausted, on their sides ... We have a pier – a queer old wooden pier, fortunately without the slightest pretensions to architecture, and very picturesque in consequence. Boats are hauled up upon it, ropes are coiled over it; lobster pots, nets, masts, oars, spare sails, ballast and rickety capstans make a perfect labyrinth of it.

We have an excellent hotel – capital baths, warm, cold and shower – first rate bathing machines – and as good butchers, bakers and grocers, as heart could desire ... You would hardly guess which is the main street of our watering-place, but you may know it by its being always stopped up with donkey-chaises. Whenever you come here, and see harnessed donkeys eating clover out of barrows drawn completely across a narrow thoroughfare, you may be quite sure you are in our High Street.

Dickens made one more visit to Broadstairs in 1859 when, feeling unwell, he believed that 'nothing but sea-air and sea water will set me right'.

BROOK STREET, LONDON — In *Dombey and Son*, Mrs Skewton:

> had borrowed a house in Brook Street, Grosvenor Square, from a stately relative (one of the Feenix brood), who was out of town, and who did not object to lending it, in the handsomest manner, for nuptial purposes, as the loan implied his final release and acquittance from all further loans and gifts to Mrs Skewton and her daughter.

The 'nuptial purposes' in question were the wedding celebrations of Mr Dombey and Edith Granger.

In *Little Dorrit*, William Dorrit lives for a while at an hotel in Brook Street.

BURY ST EDMUNDS, SUFFOLK — In *The Pickwick Papers* Mr Pickwick and Sam Weller, in pursuit of Alfred Jingle, are perched on the outside of a stagecoach bound for 'the good old town of Bury St Edmunds'.

The coach eventually stops at 'a large inn situated in a wide, open street, nearly facing the old Abbey'. This is the Angel Hotel, where Sam Weller secretly books Pickwick into a private room before passing the evening 'in his own way' inside the tap-room. Next morning we meet him again in the courtyard 'dispelling the feverish remains of the previous evening's conviviality', by rewarding a young man with a halfpenny to 'pump over his head and face until he is perfectly restored'.

Glancing up from under the pump, Weller spots a 'young man in Mulberry-coloured livery' who turns out to be none other than Job Trotter, manservant to Alfred Jingle.

Trotter confides to Weller that Jingle is about to elope in the dead of night with a pupil from Westgate House, a nearby boarding school for girls. Later, Pickwick attempts to prevent the elopement by scaling the school wall, with Weller's assistance; he destroys three gooseberry bushes and a rose tree in the process. Then, Sam's footsteps depart, 'leaving Mr Pickwick alone in the garden' to await the appointed hour when he was to knock on the door which would, as pre-arranged, be opened from the inside by Job Trotter:

Lights occasionally appeared in the different windows of the house, or glanced from the staircases, as if the inmates were retiring to rest. Not caring to go too near the door until the appointed time, Mr Pickwick crouched into an angle of the wall, and awaited its arrival.

…Mr Pickwick had meditated himself into a doze, when he was roused by the chimes of the neighbouring church ringing out the hour – half-past eleven.

'That is the time,' thought Mr Pickwick, getting cautiously on his feet. He looked up at the house. The lights had disappeared, and the shutters were closed – all in bed, no doubt. He walked on tip-toe to the door, and gave a gentle tap…

At length the sound of feet was audible upon the stairs, and then the light of a candle shone through the key-hole of the door. There was a good deal of unchaining and unbolting, and the door was slowly opened…

Unfortunately for Pickwick, it is a maidservant who opens the door and not Trotter as expected. He hides beneath a tree just as a thunderstorm erupts. In fact, the whole episode has been a ruse arranged by Jingle and Trotter, and Pickwick succeeds only in wakening the entire population of the school, 'consisting of the spinster lady of the establishment, three teachers, five female servants, and thirty boarders, all half dressed and in a forest of curl papers'. These good ladies, thinking Pickwick no better than a common burglar, lock him inside a closet until Sam Weller arrives on the scene to explain his master's true identity and purpose.

Bury St Edmunds does boast a 'large old, red brick house' called Southgate House which might well have provided the original of the Westgate House School. However, it is more likely that Dickens based the school on Eastgate House, in ROCHESTER, a building known to him since his childhood.

C

CADOGAN PLACE, LONDON — In *Nicholas Nickleby* the home of Mr and Mrs Wititterly – where Kate lodges for a while – stands in Cadogan Place which 'looks down upon Sloane Street, and thinks Brompton low'.

CAMBRIDGE, CAMBRIDGESHIRE — The famous university city is featured in *A Tale of Two Cities*. Charles Darnay was treated among the undergraduates as 'a sort of tolerated smuggler who drove a contraband trader in European languages'. In *Great Expectations* Herbert Pocket had 'distinguished himself at Cambridge'.

The City is also mentioned in *Mrs Lirriper's Lodgings* and *George Silverman's Explanation*. Dickens gave Public Readings in the Guildhall in October 1859, March 1867 and March 1869.

CAMDEN TOWN, LONDON — Following John Dickens's naval transfer from Chatham to London in June 1822, he settled his family into 16 Bayham Street, Camden Town. This was a terraced house which was later described by John Forster as 'a mean small tenement, with a wretched little back garden abutting on a squalid court'. The annual rental of the property was £22.

In the pre-railway days of the 1820s Camden Town was a pleasant, if impoverished, suburb of the City (on a clear day, the dome of St Paul's Cathedral could be glimpsed beyond the distant fields). The populace of the area was a mixture of artists, artisans and labourers; among the Dickens's closest neighbours were a Bow Street Runner and a washerwoman.

For the sensitive 10-year-old Charles, however, the misery of the recent move from Chatham was merely compounded as he grew more and more familiar with the district. He took distinct objection to the fact that the inhabitants of the area were

16 Bayham Street, Camden Town (now gone).

prone to tossing their rubbish out into the streets, making the place untidy 'on account of the cabbage leaves'.

During the early part of John Dickens's imprisonment for debt (see also SOUTHWARK) Charles was sent to lodge with a Mrs Roylance in Little College Street, Camden Town; he was later removed to Lant Street, Southwark. Upon John's release from prison in May 1824 the family lodged briefly with Mrs Roylance.

Charles Dickens was never able to give Camden Town a happy place in his memory – and the Bayham Street house would later inspire the pathetic abodes of the Cratchit family in *A Christmas Carol*, and of the Micawbers in *David Copperfield* (albeit removed to Windsor Terrace, CITY ROAD). The house was demolished in 1910.

The 'euphonius locality' known as Stagg's Garden in *Dombey and Son* was also set in Camden Town:

> a little row of houses, with little squalid patches of ground before them, fenced off with old doors, barrel staves, scraps of tarpaulin, and dead bushes with bottomless tin kettles and exhausted iron fenders thrust into the gaps. Here the Stagg's Gardeners trained scarlet beans, kept fowls and rabbits, erected rotten summer houses (one was an old boat), dried clothes and smoked pipes.

According to Dickens, Stagg's Garden 'vanished from the earth', with the coming of the railway.

CANTERBURY, KENT — Dickens sets several scenes in the ancient cathedral city of Canterbury. In *David Copperfield* the young David pauses there en route to DOVER:

> The sunny streets of Canterbury, dozing as it were in the hot light; and with the sight of its old houses and gateways, and the stately gray Cathedral, with the rooks sailing round the towers.

When Aunt Betsey decides to send David to school, it is to Dr Strong's establishment in Canterbury. She drives him there by pony and chaise:

> We came to Canterbury where, as it was market day, my aunt had a great opportunity of insinuating the gray pony among carts, baskets, vegetables, and hucksters' goods. The hair-breadth turns and twists we made, drew down upon a variety of speeches from people standing about, which were not always complimentary, but my aunt drove on with perfect indifference.

They arrive at Mr Wickfield's house (believed to have stood at 71 St Dunstan's Street) to be greeted there by Uriah Heep: 'a very old house bulging out over the road … so that I fancied the whole house was leaning forward, trying to see who was passing on the narrow pavement below'.

The actual location of Dr Strong's school is uncertain. Indeed, Dickens told

Canterbury Cathedral, the 'stately grey Cathedral' of *David Copperfield*.

his tour manager George Dolby that 'there were several [buildings] that would do'. It is generally thought that the author based the school on the famous King's School standing in Green Court in the shadow of the Cathedral, although this is far too grand a building for Strong's more humble establishment. The ''umble dwelling' (now demolished) of the obnoxious Uriah Heep stood, according to tradition, in North Lane. Mr Dick stays on alternate Wednesdays at the County Inn, based on the Fountain Hotel (now gone). The Sun Inn, Sun Street, where 'Mr Micawber put up and occupied a little room', is now The Sun Hotel and Tea Rooms. It is here that David, Mr Dick, Tommy Traddles and Aunt Betsey all stay during their unmasking of Uriah Heep on behalf of Mr Micawber. A plaque now commemorates the building's association with the novel. Canterbury is also mentioned in *Little Dorrit* and *The Uncommercial Traveller*.

CAVENDISH SQUARE, LONDON — In *Nicholas Nickleby* the showrooms of Madame Mantalini, milliner and dressmaker, are situated 'near Cavendish Square'. Kate Nickleby finds employment there.

> There was a shop to the house, but it was let off to an importer of otto of roses. Madame Mantalini's showrooms were on

the first floor: a fact which was notified to the nobility and gentry by the casual exhibition, near the handsomely curtained windows, of two or three elegant bonnets of the newest fashion, and some costly garments in the most approved taste.

Silas Wegg, the ballad-monger, keeps a fruit stall in the vicinity of Cavendish Square in *Our Mutual Friend*.

CHALK, KENT — In April 1836 the newlyweds, Charles and Catherine Dickens, spent a week's honeymoon in the delightful Kentish village of Chalk (one week being all the time Dickens's busy writing schedule would allow). Three cottages in the village have since staked claims to being the 'Honeymoon Cottage' of the famous author.

In later years, when living at GAD'S HILL PLACE, Dickens would often walk to Chalk's eleventh-century church to admire a stone effigy set above the porch which represented 'a comical old monk who, for some incomprehensible reason, sits carved in stone, cross-legged, with a jovial pot'. In more recent years this lewd, yet comical figure apparently upset the sensibilities of a prominent lady parishioner and was consequently removed from public view.

The village of Pip's youth in *Great Expectations* is an amalgam of Chalk and

The weatherboarded cottage in Chalk, Kent, where Charles and Catherine Dickens spent their honeymoon.

Chalk

A scene from *Great Expectations* showing
Joe Gargery's forge.

childhood were replaced by the stocky resilience that would fuel his future energies. He clothed himself as fashionably as his pocket would allow in a rather flashy blue jacket and a military-style cap which he tilted at a jaunty angle: he must have been quite a provocative sight as he crossed Chancery Lane one morning, for as he later reported: 'a big blackguard fellow knocked my cap off … He said "Halloa, sojer," which I could not stand, so I struck him and he hit me in the eye'. The eye was black and swollen for several days afterwards.

Dickens found working for Molloy to be as dull as ever. Yet his time as a legal messenger-boy was far from wasted. While ferrying about the writs and deeds and wills and other bits and pieces of legal paraphernalia, he was also observing the odd and queer characters associated with the profession of the silk: observations subconsciously stored in his mind for future use.

Chancery Lane and its immediate vicinity appear chiefly in *Bleak House*, Dickens's immense study of the evil effects engendered by the interminable Chancery Court case of Jarndyce and Jarndyce. Tom Jarndyce 'in despair blew his brains out at a coffee-house in Chancery Lane', while:

> On the eastern borders of Chancery Lane, that is to say, more particularly in Cook's Court, Cursitor Street, Mr Snagsby, Law-Stationer, pursues his lawful calling. In the shade of Cook's Court, at most times a shady place, Mr

COOLING. A forge on the old Dover Road was the original of Joe Gargery's home where Pip was 'brought up by hand', the 'hand' in question being that of Georgina Gargery. This house still stands.

CHANCERY LANE, LONDON — In November 1828 Charles Dickens left the employ of Ellis and Blackmore (see also GRAY'S INN) and entered the office of another solicitor, Charles Molloy, at 6 Symond's Inn (now gone), Chancery Lane. By this time he had grown into a rather elegant young man; and the sickly ailments that had often plagued him in

Snagsby has dealt in all sorts of blank forms of legal process; in skins and rolls of parchment, in paper – foolscap, brief, draft, brown, white, whitey-brown, and blotting; in stamps; in office quills, pens, ink, India-rubber, pounce, pins, pencils, sealing-wax, and wafers; in red tape and green ferret; in pocket-books, in almanacks, diaries, and law lists; in string boxes, rulers, inkstands – glass and leaden, pen-knives, scissors, bodkins, and other small office-cutlery; in short, in articles too numerous to mention.

Cook's Court was in fact based on Took's Court, off Cursitor Street, which is indeed 'a shady place'. A house on the eastern side now bears the name of 'Dickens House', although there is no substantial evidence to suggest that this is the house of Snagsby's lawful calling.

The office of Vholes, solicitor to Richard Carstone (John Jarndyce's ward), is situated in Symond's Inn.

John Rokesmith, in *Our Mutual Friend*, spots Mr Boffin – 'The Golden Dustman' – walking ahead of him in Chancery Lane: 'I took the liberty of following you, trying to make up my mind to speak to you,' he explains, before offering services as Boffin's secretary (see also FLEET STREET).

CHATHAM, KENT — In 1817 John Dickens was transferred from London, first and briefly to SHEERNESS, and then to the Pay Office at Chatham, a major naval town on the estuary of the river Medway in Kent.

He settled the family – there were three children by now – into 2 (now 11) Ordnance Terrace, Chatham. This pleasant, three-storey Georgian house, which commanded a splendid view of the river, was to remain as the family homestead for the next four years.

Elizabeth Dickens's recently widowed sister, Mary – known to the family as Aunt Fanny – also joined the household at Ordnance Terrace. In addition, there were two live-in servants: one, Mary Weller (whose surname would later be immortalized in The Pickwick Papers), told young Charles many tales of terror – of ghosts and murderers – which often kept him awake at night, long after their telling, for fear that they might come true if he dared to close his eyes.

Elizabeth Dickens taught her son to read and to write in Chatham. He also discovered in the attic a hoard of books belonging to his father, a collection of romantic and adventurous fiction. He read them all avidly and their plots and characters whirled around in his mind for days afterwards. 'I have been Tom Jones ... for a week together,' he later wrote. 'I have sustained my own idea of Roderick Random for a month at a stretch.' Mary Weller would later describe him as 'a terrible boy to read'.

Although a small and somewhat sickly child who seldom joined in the games of the neighbourhood children, Charles Dickens was never shy or retiring in any way. In fact he was quite the opposite, and developed a talent for mimicry and for singing comic songs. His proud father would sometimes stand him on the dining-room table to entertain visitors to the house.

Occasionally he accompanied his father on naval business, sometimes sailing up and down the river Medway on board the Navy Pay Yacht *Chatham*. The sights and sounds on the river further stirred his already lively imagination: he saw ships putting out to sea, tiny fishing smacks bobbing on the water, and the dismally dark convict hulks laying offshore, each awaiting its sad cargo like some 'wicked Noah's Ark'.

On shore his father often took him on long, rambling walks through Chatham and neighbouring ROCHESTER and into the countryside and villages beyond.

Standing on the main Gravesend-to-Rochester road was an impressive country house called GAD'S HILL PLACE. Whenever they passed it, father would turn to son and advise him always to work hard so that one day he might own a house just like it. Such a fanciful prospect must have seemed an absolute impossibility to so sensible a child – and yet his father's words were indeed prophetic, as later years would prove.

In 1821 the quick-witted, eager boy began school at William Giles's establishment in Clover Lane (now Clover Street), Chatham. Giles, the son of a Baptist minister, was a good teacher and was quick to recognize young Dickens's academic potential. He therefore concentrated rather more than was usual on the boy's educational development. In turn, Charles responded well and began to enjoy the learning process. It was during this period that he put pen to paper creatively for the first time, composing a naive tragedy entitled *Misnar, Sultan of India* (now lost).

The happy times at Chatham might have continued, but by 1821 and despite the fact that John Dickens was then earning in excess of £300 per annum, he found himself sinking into a new well of debt. That spring he was forced to move the family to cheaper accommodation; lower in the town this time, at 18 St Mary's Place, a wooden building (now demolished), situated off a street called The Brook.

In June 1822 John Dickens was transferred back to London. The family moved on to the capital while young Charles was allowed to remain in Chatham to complete a final term with William Giles. On the last day of term he was packed along with his few belongings (including a bound volume of Oliver Goldsmith's *The Bee*, presented by Giles) into a stagecoach romantically named 'The Blue-Eyed Maid'. He was the only passenger and it rained all the way. As he sat amongst the damp straw, eating his soggy sandwiches, he thought life 'sloppier than I had expected to find it'.

John Forster called Chatham 'the birthplace of his [Dickens's] fancy', and undoubtedly, the bustling port provided the ideal stimulus to the lively imagination of the future novelist. Indeed Dickens returns to Chatham several times in his works.

In *The Pickwick Papers* Mr Pickwick, newly arrived in the town, described it thus:

The principal production ... appears to be soldiers, sailors, Jews, chalk, shrimps, officers and dockyard men. The commodities chiefly exposed for sale in the public streets are marine stores, hardbake, apples, flat fish and oysters. The streets present a lively and animated appearance, occasioned chiefly by the conviviality of the military. It is truly delightful to the philanthropic mind, to see these men staggering along under the influence of an overflow, both of animal and ardent spirits; more especially when we remember that the following them about, and the jesting with them, affords a cheap and innocent amusement for the boy population...

In the same novel the duel between Mr Winkle and Doctor Slammer – Surgeon to the 97th Regiment – is scheduled to take place at Fort Pitt, a disused fortification (now a recreation ground) which overlooks a bend in the river. 'It was a dull and heavy evening when they sallied forth on their awkward errand.' They arrive 'in excellent time', just as the sun is setting. 'Mr Winkle looked at the declining orb, and painfully thought of the probability of his "going down" himself, before long.' Thankfully, the whole episode is discovered to be no more than a case of mistaken identity. The duel is called off in the nick of time and Mr Winkle lives on to delight us in future episodes.

Being 'an enthusiastic admirer of the army', Mr Pickwick next accompanies his fellow Pickwickians to a Military Review on the Great Lines – then a large military training area lying between Chatham and Gillingham (now the site of the War Memorial). Such reviews were common occurrences in military towns in the early 1800s. They provided a fine form of free entertainment for the locals – who would turn out in their thousands.

The spectacle is to comprise the taking of a 'Citadel' and the springing of a mine: it promises to be an excellent subject for the observation of character and manners, to which cause the noble Pickwickians are entirely dedicated. However, thanks to some pushing and shoving among the enthusiastic crowd, Mr Pickwick does not manage to complete his passive observation of the scene before him. Instead, he is actively engaged in the spectacle when 'jerked forward for several yards, with a degree of elasticity highly inconsistent with the general gravity of his demeanour', and is soon 'fully occupied in falling about, and disentangling himself, miraculously, from between the legs of horses'.

The Pickwickians manage to extricate themselves from this difficulty, only to find themselves on the make-believe battlefield and staring wide-eyed into the barrels of the regimental muskets – thankfully these are loaded with nothing more sinister than blanks. This unnerving experience is followed almost immediately by a charge of the opposing lines with our noble observers of human nature caught somewhat nervously between them.

The situation is rescued by a 'fine gentle wind' which blows Mr Pickwick's hat from his head to 'gambol playfully away in perspective' until it stops against the wheels of an open carriage belonging to Mr Wardle of Dingley Dell (see also SANDLING) who immediately welcomes him aboard, thereby transporting us into the next delightful episode of *The Pickwick Papers*.

David Copperfield passes through Chatham on his long, foot-slogging trek to find his Aunt Betsey in DOVER:

> ... toiling into Chatham, – which, in that night's aspect, is a mere dream of chalk, and drawbridges, and mastless ships in a muddy river, roofed like Noah's arks, – I crept, at last, upon a sort of grass-grown battery overhanging a lane ... Here I lay down, near a cannon; and happy in the society of the sentry's footsteps ... slept soundly until morning.

The following day sees young Copperfield negotiating the sale of his jacket, for fourpence, to a second-hand clothes dealer before continuing his journey to Dover.

The Mitre Inn, Chatham High Street (now demolished and replaced by a department store), features in 'The Holly Tree' and becomes 'The Crozier' in *Edwin Drood*. Dick Datchery announced himself at 'The Crozier':

> (orthodox hotel, where he put up with a portmanteau) as an idle dog who lived on his means; and he further announced that

he had a mind to take lodgings in the picturesque old city for a month or two, with a view of settling down there altogether. Both announcements were made in the coffee room of the Crozier, to all whom it might, or might not, concern.

Chatham also provides the model for 'Mudfog' in *The Mudfog Papers*, etc. (an edition of collected pieces published in 1880) and, with ROCHESTER, becomes 'Dullborough' in *The Uncommercial Traveller* – in which Dickens describes a return visit to the town of his childhood:

> As I left Dullborough in the days when there were no railroads in the land, I left in a stage-coach ... with this tender remembrance upon me, I was cavalierly shunted back into Dullborough the other day by train ... When I had sent my disfigured property to the hotel, I began to look around me; and the first discovery I made, was, that the station had swallowed up the playing field.
>
> It was gone. The two beautiful hawthorn-trees, the hedge, the turf, and all those buttercups and daisies, had given place to the stoniest of jolting roads: while, beyond the station, an ugly dark monster of a tunnel kept its jaws open, as if it had swallowed them and were ravenous for more destruction.

An old school friend fails to recognize the Uncommercial Traveller when he calls on him. And when he spies a greengrocer of old acquaintance he accosts him and reminds him that he had left the town as a child:

> 'Had I?... And did I find it had got on tolerably well without me?' Such is the difference ... between going away from a place and remaining in it. I had no right, I reflected, to be angry with the greengrocer for his want of interest. I was nothing to him, whereas he was the town, the cathedral, the bridge, the river, my childhood, and a large slice of my life, to me.'

Chatham is now home to the Dickens World attraction, which opened in 2007.

CHEAPSIDE, LONDON — Cheapside appears as a place for random encounters in several of the novels. In *The Pickwick Papers* Mr Pickwick meets Sam Weller's father, Tony, at an inn in the vicinity. Pickwick partakes of brandy and warm water here, following his unnerving encounter with the lawyers Dodson and Fogg. In *Nicholas Nickleby* Tim Linkinwater is spotted walking along Cheapside in the company of an 'uncommonly handsome spinster'.

In *Martin Chuzzlewit* Mr Mould, the undertaker, had his establishment 'Deep in the city and within the ward of Cheap ... abutting on a churchyard'. Mr Carker 'went gleaming up Cheapside' on horseback in *Dombey and Son*; and Arthur Clennam passed that way whilst walking to his mother's house, in *Little Dorrit*. In *Great Expectations* Mr Jaggers meets Pip in Cheapside and invites the young man to dinner.

It was at the Cross Keys Inn (now gone) in Cheapside that the 10 year-old Dickens was met by his father following his trip from Chatham in the autumn of 1822. John Dickens then took Charles to the new family home at Bayham Street, CAMDEN TOWN. This famous coaching inn features in *Little Dorrit* as the spot where John Baptist Cavalletto is involved in an accident with a stagecoach. Arthur Clennam asks a bystander what has happened:

> 'An accident going to the hospital?' he asked of an old man beside him, who stood shaking his head, inviting conversation.
> 'Yes,' said the man, 'along of them Mails. They ought to be prosecuted and fined, them Mails. They come a-racing out of Lad Lane and Wood Street at twelve or fourteen miles an hour, them Mails do. The only wonder is, that people ain't killed oftener by them Mails.'

In *Great Expectations* Pip arrives from ROCHESTER at the Cross Keys, and later meets Estella there.

CHELMSFORD, ESSEX — While working as a Parliamentary reporter for the *Morning Chronicle* (1834–1835) Dickens wrote to his friend Henry Austin that he had been:

> ordered on a journey, the length of which is at present uncertain ... Don't laugh.

I am going alone in a gig ... I am going into Essex and Suffolk. It strikes me I shall be spilt before I pay a turnpike. I have a presentiment I shall run over an only child before I reach Chelmsford, my first stage.

Thankfully the rather grim prediction did not prove true.

In *The Pickwick Papers* Tony Weller informs Mr Pickwick that Alfred Jingle and Job Trotter had boarded the Ipswich coach 'at the Black Boy at Chelmsford . . . and I took 'em up, right through to Ipswich'. The Black Boy Inn was demolished in 1857.

CHELSEA, LONDON — The wedding of Charles Dickens and Catherine Hogarth took place on 2 April 1836 in the then recent church of St Luke's, Sydney Street, Chelsea. The ceremony was attended by the Hogarth family and the John Dickens household. Tom Beard, a fellow Parliamentary Reporter of Dickens, and John Macrone, publisher of *Sketches by Boz*, were the only non-family members present.

After the ceremony a simple wedding breakfast was held at Catherine's home, 18 York Place, and in the afternoon the newlyweds left for a week's honeymoon in the village of CHALK near GRAVESEND in Kent.

In *The Pickwick Papers* Sam Weller informs the tearful Job Trotter that 'Chelsea Water-works is nothin' to you', while Nicholas Nickleby informs us that 'Crummles is NOT a Prussian, having been born in Chelsea'. Miss Sophie Wackles in *The Old Curiosity Shop* lived in Chelsea. She:

resided with her widowed mother and two sisters, in conjunction with whom she maintained a very small day-school for young ladies of proportionate dimensions – a circumstance which was made known to the neighbourhood by an oval board over the front first-floor window, whereon appeared, in circumnambient flourishes, the words, 'Ladies' Seminary,' and which was further published and proclaimed at intervals between the hours of half-past nine and ten in the morning, by a straggling and solitary young lady of tender years standing on the scraper on the tips of her toes and making futile attempts to reach the knocker with a spelling-book.

In *Barnaby Rudge* 'few would venture to repair at a late hour ... to Chelsea [among other places], unarmed and unattended'.

CHERTSEY, SURREY — In *Oliver Twist* Bill Sikes takes young Oliver along with him to 'crack the crib' at Chertsey. Going, 'slap through the town ... They hurried through the main street':

which at that late hour was wholly deserted. A dim light shone at intervals from some bedroom window, and the hoarse barking of dogs occasionally broke the silence of the night. But there was nobody abroad, and they had cleared the town as the church-bell struck two.

A little further on, they scale the wall of a

house, where the unwilling Oliver is forced through 'a little latticed window, about five and a half feet above the ground', with orders to open the door and let his accomplices in (the couple have been joined by Toby Crackit). The attempted burglary fails, however, and Oliver is shot by one of 'two terrified half-dressed men at the top of the stairs'. As the boy loses consciousness, Sikes drags him back through the window. Oliver is left lying in a ditch, where:

> The grass was wet, the pathways and low places were all mire and water, and the damp breath of an unwholesome wind went languidly by with a hollow moaning.

The exhausted boy eventually retraces the route back to the house where he explains himself to Rose and Mrs Maylie, who with the aid of Dr Losberne, tend him through his illness and even shield him from the law.

The original of Mrs Maylie's house is either a house in Gogmore Lane, or Pyrcroft House (now a school), Pyrcroft Street. A pantry window from Pyrcroft House – known as 'Oliver's Window' – is preserved in the Morning Room at the Dickens House Museum in DOUGHTY STREET, London.

CHESTER PLACE, LONDON — In February 1847 Dickens and Catherine rented 3 Chester Place, Regent's Park. They had had to return suddenly from France, in order to be close to their eldest son, Charley, who had contracted scarlet fever whilst attending boarding school. (Their home at 1 DEVONSHIRE TERRACE had been leased out for the family's trip to Switzerland and France.)

CHIGWELL, ESSEX — 'Chigwell, my dear fellow, is the greatest place in the world': so wrote Charles Dickens to John Forster on 25 March 1841:

> Name your day for going. Such a delicious old Inn opposite the Churchyard – such a lovely ride – such beautiful scenery – such an out of the way rural place – such a sexton! I say again, name your day.

Ye Olde King's Head, Chigwell, now a restaurant.

The day was duly named, and the visit duly made. 'Dickens's promise,' wrote Forster:

> was exceeded by our enjoyment; and his delight in the double recognition of himself and of Barnaby, by the landlord of the nice old inn, far exceeded any pride he would have taken in what the world thinks the highest sort of honour.

The 'delicious old Inn' in question was the King's Head, which probably served as Dickens's original for the Maypole Inn of *Barnaby Rudge* (though he took the name from a real Maypole Inn at Chigwell Row).

The plot of *Barnaby Rudge* revolves around the Maypole – under the proprietorship of John Willet – from Solomon Daisy's telling of the murder of Ruben Haredale, through the Gordon 'No Popery' riots, to Barnaby's eventual happy life with Grip the raven spent on the Maypole Farm. The inn was:

> An old house, a very old house, perhaps as old as it claimed to be, and perhaps older ... upon the borders of Epping Forest ... [with] more gable ends than a lazy man would care to count on a sunny day; huge zig-zag chimneys, out of which it seemed as though even smoke could not choose but come in more than naturally fantastic shapes, imparted to it in its tortuous progress ... Its windows were old diamond pane lattices ... Its floors were sunken and uneven, its ceilings blackened by the hand of time

and heavy with massive beams. Over the doorway was an ancient porch, quaintly and grotesquely carved; and here on summer evenings the more favoured customers smoked and drank – ay, and sang many a good song too, sometimes – reposing on two grim-looking high-backed settles, which, like the twin dragons of some fairy tale, guarded the entrance to the mansion.

And the King's Head still remembers the author; a 'Charles Dickens Lodge' was established there in 1899, and a theatre used by Bransby Williams, the actor who specialized in the portrayal of Dickensian characters, was added later. A portrait of Dickens hangs in the bar, so that he may always look down on his 'delicious old Inn'.

The Warren, home of Geoffrey Haredale, and a 'dreary, silent building, with echoing courtyards, desolated turret-chambers, and whole suites of rooms shut up and mouldering to ruin' has never been satisfactorily identified, although Peter Warren M.P. lived in Chigwell in 1770 and gave his name to the house which may have served as Dickens's original.

Despite its obvious power, *Barnaby Rudge* was unable to compete in the public's affections with its predecessor *The Old Curiosity Shop* and the touching travails of Little Nell and her grandfather. Consequently sales of *Master Humphrey's Clock* (in which both stories were serialized) fell dramatically. With a circulation down to around 30,000 copies a week, Dickens decided to close the

Tom-all-alones, based on Clare Market. Original Phiz illustration from *Bleak House*, 1853.

magazine with the conclusion of *Barnaby Rudge* in November 1841.

CITY ROAD, LONDON — Location of the 'Charitable Grinders' school in *Dombey and Son*, the place where 'little Biler' was taught. In *David Copperfield* Mr Micawber gives his address as 'Windsor Terrace, City Road': 'I – in short,' said Mr Micawber, with the same genteel air, and in another burst of confidence – 'I live there.' This house was probably based upon Dickens's childhood home in Bayham Street, CAMDEN TOWN.

CLARE MARKET, LONDON — Most Dickensians agree that the author based 'Tom-all-alones', the notorious slum district in *Bleak House*, upon the area around Clare Market (largely rebuilt in the early 1900s during the development of Kingsway). Here lives Jo, the Crossing Sweeper:

> Jo lives – that is to say, Jo has not yet died – in a ruinous place, known to the like of him by the name of Tom-all-alones. It is a black, dilapidated street, avoided by all decent people; where the crazy houses were seized upon, when their decay was

Jo the Crossing Sweeper, from *Bleak House*.

far advanced, by some bold vagrants, who, after establishing their own possession, took to letting them out in lodgings. Now, these tumbling tenements contain, by night a swarm of misery…

Twice, lately, there has been a crash and a cloud of dust, like the springing of a mine, in Tom-all-alone's; and each time a house has fallen.

In *Sketches by Boz* Dickens describes certain gin shops in the vicinity of Clare Market.

CLERKENWELL, LONDON — It is at a bookstall near Clerkenwell Green in *Oliver Twist*, that the Artful Dodger, Charley Bates and Oliver Twist spot an old gentleman (Mr Brownlow) as he browses through the wares on display. ' "He'll do," said the Dodger. "A prime plant," observed Master Charley Bates.' This pair then relieve the old gentleman's pocket of its handkerchief. In that instant, the reasons behind Fagin's 'training' become horribly apparent to young Oliver. In the confusion that follows, our hero is captured for the crime.

Later in Oliver Twist, Mr Bumble proceeds to

The Artful Dodger and
Oliver Twist.

the Clerkenwell Session House, having advised Mrs Mann that:

' …A legal action is coming on, about a settlement; and the board has appointed me – me, Mrs Mann – to depose the matter before the quarter-session at Clerkinwell. And I very much question,' added Mr Bumble, drawing himself up, 'Whether the Clerkinwell Sessions will not find themselves in the wrong box before they have done with me.'

'Oh! you mustn't be too hard upon them, Sir,' said Mrs Mann, coaxingly.

'The Clerkinwell Sessions have brought it upon themselves, Ma'am,' replied Mr Bumble; 'and if the Clerkinwell Sessions find that they come off worse than they expected, the Clerkinwell Sessions have only themselves to thank.'

In *Barnaby Rudge*, the locksmith Gabriel Varden lives:

In the venerable suburb – it was a suburb once – of Clerkenwell, towards that part of its confines which is nearest to the Charter House, and in one of those cool, shady streets, of which a few, widely scattered and dispersed, yet remain in such old parts of the metropolis, – each tenement quietly vegetating like an ancient citizen who long ago retired from business…

Varden lived in:

a modest building, not very straight, not large, not tall; not bold faced, with great staring windows, but a shy, blinking house, with a conical roof going up to a peak over its garret window of four small panes of glass, like a cocked-hat on the head of an elderly gentleman with one eye.

In *A Tale of Two Cities* Jarvis Lorry 'walked along the sunny streets of Clerkenwell, where he lived, on his way to dine with the Doctor.' (See also SOHO.) In *Our Mutual Friend*, Mr Venus, the preserver of animals and birds, was found residing 'in a narrow and dirty street', in Clerkenwell.

CLEVELAND STREET, LONDON — Charles Dickens first came to London as a two-year-old, when his father was transferred back there from Portsmouth in January 1815. The family took lodgings in Norfolk Street (now Cleveland Street), off Fitzroy Square, and close to the Middlesex Hospital. They stayed until 1817 when John Dickens was relocated yet again by the Navy (see also CHATHAM and SHEERNESS). There is little documented evidence of their stay here, only that many years later Dickens told his good friend, John Forster, that he had a vague memory of leaving Portsmouth and arriving in London in the depths of winter. The house in question was swallowed up in the later development of the Middlesex Hospital.

In 1829–30 the family again lived in Norfolk Street at Number 10; above a greengrocer's shop (now 22 Cleveland Street), this being the address given by Dickens when applying for a reader's ticket at the BRITISH MUSEUM in February 1830.

CLOVELLY, DEVON — Clovelly was the original of 'Steepways', in the 1860 Christmas Story *A Message from the Sea* which Dickens wrote jointly with Wilkie Collins. ' "And a mighty singular and pretty place it is, as ever I saw in all the days of my life," says Captain Jorgen, looking up at it … Captain Jorgen had to look high to look

The steep, winding main street of Clovelly, Devon.

at it, for the village was built sheer up the face of a steep and lofty cliff.'

The Captain and Tom Pettifer:

> climbed high up the village – which had the most arbitrary turns and twists in it, so that the cobbler's house came dead across the ladder, and to have held a reasonable course, you might have gone through his house and through him too, as he sat at his work between two little windows, with one eye microscopically on the geological formation of that part of Devonshire, and the other telescopically on the open sea.

COBHAM, KENT — 'Really for a misanthrope's choice, this is one of the prettiest and most desirable places of residence I ever met with': so exclaims Mr Pickwick to his fellow clubmen as they enter the delightful Kentish village of Cobham in search of their downhearted friend, Tracy Tupman (Tupman has been duped out of a new-found happiness with Rachel Wardle, and ten pounds sterling, by the unscrupulous Alfred Jingle).

The Pickwickians approached the village via Cobham Park, passing by the grandeur of Cobham Hall, well known to Dickens since his childhood days:

> an ancient hall, displaying the quaint and picturesque architecture of Elizabeth's time. Long vistas of stately oaks and elm trees appeared on every side; large herds of deer were cropping the fresh grass; and occasionally a startled hare scoured along the ground, with the speed of the

Clovelly

The Leather Bottle, Cobham, scene of the Pickwickians' reunion with Tracy Tupman.

shadows thrown by the light clouds which sweep across a sunny landscape like a passing breath of summer.

The three friends find Tupman in the 'clean and commodious ale-house', The Leather Bottle. His recent tribulations have not, it seems, dulled his appetite, for he is seated at a table 'well covered with a roast fowl, bacon, ale and et ceteras'.

Following this meal Mr Pickwick walks Mr Tupman up and down in the graveyard of the church of St Mary Magdelene, which stands opposite the inn: 'for half an hour their forms might be seen pacing to and fro'. During the pacing, Pickwick manages to persuade Tupman to rejoin the warmth and companionship of the Pickwick Club.

Returning with Tupman to The Leather Bottle, Pickwick makes his famous 'immortal discovery' when his eye falls 'upon a small broken stone, practically buried in the ground in front of a cottage door'. A closer inspection reveals some sort of inscription, which is enough to excite Pickwick into purchasing the object from the owner of the cottage.

Upon cleaning the stone in The Leather Bottle the inscription became clear, although its meaning remains a mystery – it reads:

+

BILST

UM

PSHI

S.M

ARK

'Mr Pickwick's eyes sparkled with delight as he sat and gloated over the treasure he had discovered.' In fact he considers the find so important that he has the stone transported, by river, to London for further examination.

The discovery makes Pickwick the 'envy of every antiquarian in this or any other country'. He writes a 96-page pamphlet, detailing the find and offering 27 possible interpretations of the mysterious inscription. As a result he is 'elected an honarary member of seventeen native and foreign societies'.

No expert is able to decipher the meaning of the stone, although a certain Mr Blotton takes a trip to Cobham and speaks with the cottage owner from whom Pickwick purchased the stone. Blotton is, however, ridiculed by Pickwick's followers for his supposition that the man's name, being William Stumps, was in fact:

crudely carved by himself in an idle mood, and to display the letters being neither more nor less than the simple construction of – 'Bill Stumps, His MARK': and that Mr Stumps, being little in the habit of original composition, and more accustomed to be guided by the sound of words, than by the strict rules of orthography, had omitted the concluding 'L' of his christian name.

The argument dragged on through seventeen nations and was referred to ever afterwards as 'The Pickwick Controversy'. 'And to this day the stone remains, an illegible monument of Mr Pickwick's greatness, and a lasting trophy of the littleness of his enemies.' In fact, a keen Dickensian later took the trouble to carve a stone precisely to the description given by Dickens in *The Pickwick Papers*. This now stands in the car park, against the wall of The Leather Bottle, for all to see.

The inn became a favourite watering-hole for Dickens in his later life, while living at nearby GAD'S HILL PLACE. The Leather Bottle successfully retains even today a certain 'Pickwickian' atmosphere. One room of the restaurant is designated 'The Dickens Room' and has been described as a 'living museum'. Indeed the walls are covered with Dickensian prints and among several relics is the leather case in which the author carried the privately printed reading version of the works featured in his later Public Reading Tours. A chair, reputed to be the one used by Dickens whenever he dined at the inn, is still in use and is often the cause of great surprise to unsuspecting diners when its former occupant is mentioned to them. It was through Cobham Wood that Charles Dickens took his last walk, on the eve of his death in 1870.

COOLING, KENT — Amid a bleak landscape on 'the marsh country, down by the river, within, as the river wound, twenty miles of the sea', lies the Kentish village of Cooling, whose churchyard was once a favourite destination of Dickens's on country walks from GAD'S HILL PLACE. Here, in *Great Expectations*, 'on a

'Pip's Graves', St James's Churchyard, Cooling, Kent.

memorable raw afternoon towards evening', Philip Pirrip ('Pip') gazes down at the grave of his parents and at the:

five little stone lozenges, each about a foot and a half long, which were arranged in a neat row beside their grave, and were sacred to the memory of five little brothers of mine – who gave up trying to get a living, exceedingly early in that universal struggle.

As he reflects on his place in life, Pip is suddenly attacked by the escaped convict, Magwitch, who will later prove to be the source of the boy's 'Great Expectations'. There are, in fact, thirteen lozenge-shaped body stones in a plot located to the south of St James's Churchyard. The children interned here in the late 1700s number three from the Barker family, and ten from the Comport family, none of whom survived more than seventeen months of life.

The Horseshoe and Castle inn at Cooling provided the author with his model for the Three Jolly Bargemen, where Joe Gargery 'had been ... from a quarter after eight o'clock to a quarter before ten'.

CORAM'S FIELDS, LONDON — Now a children's playground, Coram's Fields, to the north of Guilford Street in Bloomsbury, occupies the former site of the Foundling Hospital (founded in 1739 by Thomas Coram, for the care of destitute children). Between 1837 and 1839 Dickens lived just a few streets away, at 48 DOUGHTY STREET, and was a frequent visitor to the children in the hospital. He often attended divine service in the Foundation Chapel, and corresponded with the chaplain there, one Mr Brownlow, whose name found its way into the pages of *Oliver Twist*.

In *Little Dorrit* the Meagles's decided to adopt 'Tattycorum' (Harriet Beadle) after hearing the children of the Foundling Hospital singing on a Sunday morning in church.

CORNHILL, LONDON — The offices of the lawyers Dodson and Fogg – acting on behalf of Mrs Bardell against Mr Pickwick, in the matter of a breach of promise to marry – were situated in Freeman's Court, off Cornhill, of which Dickens's original was Newman's Court (now rebuilt). The office was:

> a dark, mouldy, earth-smelling room with a high wainscotted partition to screen the clerks from the vulgar gaze: a couple of old wooden chairs, a very loud ticking clock, an almanack, an umbrella-stand, a row of hat pegs, and a few shelves, on which were deposited several bundles of dirty papers, some old deal boxes with paper labels, and sundry decayed stone ink bottles of various shapes and sizes.

Pickwick and Weller are eventually brought before the partners, who proceed to reiterate Mrs Bardell's claim for damages of £1500. Pickwick's anger at being asked so huge a sum for so small a charge incenses him enough to hurl insults at the two lawyers. They, in turn, simply egg him on, while ensuring, of course, that there are enough witnesses present to hear him do so. Once again Sam Weller steps in to rescue his master: 'You just come avay,' he advises. 'Battledore and Shuttlecock's a very good game, when you ain't the shuttlecock.'

In Change Alley, another turning off Cornhill, stood the famous coffee house of Garraway's (demolished in 1874) from which Mr Pickwick wrote one of his letters to Mrs Bardell. This was read aloud by Sergeant Buzfuz in evidence in the court case at the GUILDHALL:

' "Garraway's, twelve o'clock. Dear Mrs B – Chops and tomato sauce. Yours, PICKWICK." Gentlemen, what does this mean? Chops and tomato sauce. Yours, Pickwick! Chops! Gracious heavens! and Tomato sauce! Gentlemen, is the happiness of a sensitive and confiding female to be trifled away, by such shallow artifices as these?'

In *Martin Chuzzlewit* Mr Nadgett, the private detective of the Anglo Bengalee Insurance Company, is observed sitting in Garraway's and was 'occasionally seen drying a very damp pocket handkerchief before the fire'. Jeremiah Flintwitch of *Little Dorrit* was also a regular patron of the coffee house. Dickens also describes Garraway's on a Sunday in *The Uncommercial Traveller*. 'And here is Garraway's, bolted and shuttered hard and fast! It is possible to imagine the man who cuts the sandwiches, on his back in a hayfield.'

The opening sentence of *Barnaby Rudge* refers to 'the standard in Cornhill', and later in the same novel, Cornhill is one of several points at which 'iron chains were drawn across the street' during the Gordon riots. In *A Christmas Carol* Bob Cratchit celebrated the festive season, he: 'went down a slide on Cornhill, at the end of a lane of boys, twenty times in honour of its being Christmas-eve.'

In the churchyard of St Peter's Cornhill, Bradley Headstone, passionately in love with Lizzie Hexam, implores her to marry him – in *Our Mutual Friend*:

The court brought them to a churchyard; a paved court, with a raised bank of earth about breast high, in the middle, enclosed by iron rails.

Lizzie refuses Headstone in favour of Eugene Wrayburn.

COVENT GARDEN, LONDON — Young Charles Dickens had expected that his father's release from the New Marshalsea Prison (see also SOUTHWARK), in May 1824, would automatically secure his own release from the purgatory of Warren's Warehouse (see also STRAND). But when the blacking business was moved to new premises in Chandos Street, Covent Garden (site now occupied by a department store) he moved with it.

He sat with his fellow worker Bob Fagin at a window overlooking the street, and a small crowd would often gather to watch the deft-fingered boys at work. One day in the spring of 1825 John Dickens, in the company of another man, witnessed this humiliating spectacle for himself and was shocked to see his own son on public display, as it were. He quarrelled with Lamert over the matter, with the result that Charles was sent home for good. Elizabeth Dickens, ever conscious of the family's precarious financial position, was appalled by this turn in events and wanted John to return next morning to patch things up with Lamert. 'I shall never forget, I can never forget,' Charles Dickens later wrote 'that my mother was warm for my being sent back.'

However, his father was adamant, stating that the bright young boy ought to be in school (see also HAMPSTEAD ROAD).

Doubtless Dickens's experience inside Warren's Warehouse contributed towards the creation of such waifs and strays as Oliver Twist, Smike and Little Jo the crossing sweeper; and, of course, the warehouse itself provided the model for Murdstone and Grinby's establishment in *David Copperfield*. But, whatever creative processes were later actioned by his memories, Dickens managed to keep his time at Warren's a secret from his wife and children throughout his lifetime. They did not learn of it until the publication of John Forster's *The Life of Charles Dickens* in 1872, two years after Dickens's death. Forster himself had stumbled upon the information by accident. In 1847 he innocently asked Dickens if he had ever made the acquaintance of a certain Mr Dilke, a former friend of John Dickens. It transpired that Dilke had been the man accompanying Dickens senior on the day in 1824 when he had discovered young Charles at work in Warren's window.

'He was very silent for a moment,' wrote Forster. 'I felt that I had unintentionally touched a painful place in his memory.' Dickens then went on to relate the story of his time in the warehouse, concluding that: 'For many years, when I came near to Robert Warren's in the Strand, I crossed over to the opposite side of the way, to avoid a certain smell of the cement they put upon the blacking-corks, which reminded me of what I once was. It was a long time before I liked to go up Chandos Street. My old way home by the Borough made me cry after my eldest child could speak.'

Covent Garden was an area known to Dickens since 1822, when he had first read a vivid description of the market place in George Colman's *Broad Grins*, loaned to him by Mrs Manson, a bookshop owner and friend of the family (see also SOHO). The passage had conjured up 'the flavour of faded cabbage leaves as if it were the very breath of comic fiction'. Upon finishing the piece young Dickens went directly to the famous market to compare its reality with Colman's description.

Dickens's own impressions of Covent Garden appear in several of his books; the first of these, 'The Streets – Morning' (*Sketches by Boz*), tells us that:

> Covent Garden market, and the avenues leading to it, are thronged with carts of all sorts, sizes, and descriptions, from the heavy lumbering waggon, with its four stout horses, to the jingling costermonger's cart, with its consumptive donkey. The pavement is already strewn with decayed cabbage-leaves, broken haybands, and all the indescribable litter of a vegetable market; men are shouting,

carts backing, horses neighing, boys fighting, basket-women talking, piemen expatiating on the excellence of their pastry, and donkeys braying. These and a hundred other sounds form a compound discordant enough to a Londoner's ears, and remarkably disagreeable to those of country gentlemen who are sleeping at the Hummums for the first time.

'The Hummums' was an hotel that once occupied the corner of Russell Street, and which also features in *Great Expectations* as Pip's destination, following Wemmick's warning 'Don't go home'.

Job Trotter, having delivered his important news of Mr Pickwick to Perker the Lawyer in *The Pickwick Papers*, went directly 'to Covent Garden Market to spend the night in a vegetable basket'.

In *Oliver Twist*, Bill Sikes wonders 'fiercely' of Fagin:

'... wot makes you take so much pains about one chalk-faced kid, when you know there are fifty boys snoozing about Common (sic) Garden every night and you might pick and choose from?'

'Because they're of no use to me, my dear,' replied the Jew, with some confusion, 'not worth the taking. Their looks convict 'em when they get into trouble, and I lose 'em all.'

Master Humphrey, the narrator at the beginning of *The Old Curiosity Shop*, describes the market:

at sunrise, too, in the spring or summer, when the fragrance of sweet flowers is in the air, overpowering even the unwholesome steams of last night's debauchery, and driving the dusky thrush, whose cage has hung outside a garret window all night long, half mad with joy.

In *Martin Chuzzlewit*, Ruth and Tom Pinch stroll through the market. And the hungry young David Copperfield 'strolled ... as far as Covent Garden Market, and stared at the pineapples' – an experience shared many years earlier by the hungry young Dickens.

Also in *David Copperfield* Steerforth refuses David's offer of breakfast because 'I am going to breakfast with one of these fellows who is at the Piazza Hotel, in Covent Garden.' (The Piazza stood at the corner of James Street. Dickens stayed there as a guest in 1844 upon his brief return from Italy, during which he first read *The Chimes* to distinguished literary company gathered at John Forster's house in LINCOLN'S INN

The blue plaque marking the former *All The Year Round* offices, Covent Garden.

FIELDS.) Later in the novel, David buys a bouquet for Dora in the Market, and later still, he takes 'a temporary lodging in Covent Garden' with his Aunt Betsey.

The offices of Dickens's magazine *All the Year Round* stood at 26 Wellington Street, an address which doubled as the starting point for the journeys of *The Uncommercial Traveller* and which also served briefly as a base during Dickens's later Public Readings in London.

The area also features in *Our Mutual Friend* when Mr Cleaver, the drunken father of Jenny Wren:

staggered into Covent Garden Market and there bivouacked to have an attack of the trembles succeeded by an attack of the horrors…

In March 1832 whilst nurturing theatrical ambitions, Dickens applied to George Bartley, stage manager at the Covent Garden Theatre, asking for an acting audition with the company there. Bartley replied, inviting the would-be actor to attend the theatre and perform anything he pleased in audition. However, when the appointed day arrived, Dickens was ill in bed with a heavy cold and inflammation of the face and was unable to attend – a cruel blow for the stage-struck youth perhaps, but a fortunate one for the world of literature. (Dickens was granted a second audition some months later, but he did not attend on this occasion because of his then growing success as a journalist.)

CRANLEIGH STREET, LONDON — In the winter of 1825 (the year after John Dickens's brief period of imprisonment; see also SOUTHWARK) the Dickens family moved into a terraced house at 29 Johnson Street (now Cranleigh Street), Somers Town, a move which coincided with John Dickens's retirement from the Navy Pay Office.

The family appears to have enjoyed a period of modest prosperity at this time, as John started to supplement his naval pension by working as a reporter for the *British Press*, while young Charles became a pupil at the Wellington House Academy in HAMPSTEAD ROAD, an experience which he greatly enjoyed, following the seeming purgatory of Warren's Warehouse (see also COVENT GARDEN and STRAND).

Unfortunately, in December 1826 the *British Press* failed, thereby dealing a severe blow to John Dickens's pocket. The situation had worsened considerably by March of the following year and the family were evicted from 29 Johnson Street for non-payment of rent. The house fell victim to German bombs during World War II.

CREWE, CHESHIRE — Charles Dickens's grandparents William and Elizabeth Dickens were employed as steward and housekeeper at Crewe Hall (now owned by a commercial concern) in the late 1700s.

Crewe Hall was then owned by John Crewe (later Lord Crewe), MP for Chester. It is believed that through his influence John Dickens later gained his first position in the Navy Pay Office.

D

Dawlish, Devon — In *Nicholas Nickleby*, Godfrey Nickleby, father of Ralph and Nicholas senior:

> purchased a small farm near Dawlish in Devonshire, whither he retired with his wife and two children, to live upon the best interest he could get for the rest of his money, and the little produce he could raise from his land.

Deal, Kent — This seaside town was well known to Dickens during his holidays at nearby BROADSTAIRS.

Richard Carstone is stationed in Deal in *Bleak House*. Esther Summerson relates her journey there from London to find him:

> At last we came into the narrow streets of Deal: and very gloomy they were, upon a raw misty morning. The long flat beach, with its little irregular houses, wooden and brick, and its litter of capstans, and great boats, and sheds, and bare upright poles with tackle and blocks, and loose gravelly waste places, overgrown with grass and weeds, were as dull in appearance as any place I ever saw. The sea was heaving under a thick white fog; and nothing else was moving but a few early rope makers, who, with the yarn twisted round their bodies, looked as if, tired of their present state of existence, they were spinning themselves into cordage.
>
> But when we got into a warm room in an excellent hotel, and sat down, comfortably washed and dressed, to an early breakfast (for it was too late to think of going to bed), Deal began to look more cheerful ... Then the fog began to rise like a curtain; and a number of ships, that we had no idea were near, appeared. I don't know how many sail the waiter told us were there lying in the Downs. Some of those vessels were of grand size: one was a large Indiaman, just come home: and when the sun shone through the clouds, making silvery pools in the dark sea, the way in which these ships brightened, and shadowed, and changed, amid the bustle of boats putting off from the shore to them and from them to the shore, and a general life and motion in themselves and everything around them, was most beautiful.

Deal is most probably the 'Out of Season' town to which Dickens walked from Folkestone in *Reprinted Pieces*:

> A walk of ten miles brought me to a seaside town without a cliff, which, like the town we had come from, was out of season too. Half the houses were shut up; half of the other half were to let; the town might have done as much business as it was doing then, if it had been at the bottom of the sea.

DEVIL'S PUNCH BOWL, SURREY — In *Nicholas Nickleby*, the third day of their walk towards Portsmouth proves, for Nicholas and Smike, 'a harder day's journey than yesterday, for there were long and weary hills to climb; and in journeys, as in life, it is a great deal easier to go down hill than up'. Eventually they:

> walked upon the rim of the Devil's Punch Bowl, and Smike listened with greedy interest as Nicholas read the inscription upon the stone which, reared upon that wild spot, tells of a murder committed there by night. The grass on which they stood had once been dyed with gore; and the blood of the murdered man had run down, drop by drop, into the hollow which

gives the place its name. 'The Devil's Bowl,' thought Nicholas, as he looked into the void, 'never held fitter liquor than that!'

DEVONSHIRE TERRACE, MARYLEBONE ROAD, LONDON — In December 1839, with his fame growing daily and his children now numbering three (Charley, Mamie and Kate), Dickens left his DOUGHTY STREET home and moved into 1 Devonshire Terrace, near Regent's Park. And, although he called it a 'frightful first-class Family Mansion, involving awful responsibilities', this house became Dickens's own favourite amongst all his homes. He would remain here for the next twelve years, during which time and among all his other activities, he would complete

No. 1 Devonshire Terrace, Dickens's home from 1839 to 1851. It was demolished in 1959.

five novels and establish himself as the most popular novelist of all time.

Dickens's study at Devonshire Terrace was described by his daughter Mamie as 'a pretty room, with steps leading directly into the garden from it, and with an extra baize door to keep out all sounds and noise'.

Since Dickens – like many Victorian heads of family – was in the habit of spending much time away from home – chiefly at BROADSTAIRS, or on the Continent – the house was occasionally let, with the consequence that on their return the family would sometimes have to find temporary accommodation until their own home was free again (see also OSNABURGH TERRACE and CHESTER PLACE).

Devonshire Terrace was demolished in 1959 in order to make way for an office block. A frieze in bas-relief depicting the author and the chief characters from the novels written at Devonshire Terrace reminds us that Dickens once lived there.

DOCTORS' COMMONS, LONDON — Doctors' Commons no longer exists. In its day the main ancient, chapel-like building – which lay in the City between St Paul's Cathedral and the river Thames – housed the chief Ecclesiastical, Probate and Admiralty Courts.

In 1829 Dickens quit his job with Molloy (see also CHANCERY LANE) and took the ambitious step of renting a reporters' box (with Thomas Charlton, a distant cousin) at 5 Bell Yard, within Doctors' Commons.

A Doctors' Commons reporter simply sat and waited until a proctor engaged him to record a particular case. And, while waiting, Dickens was able to continue his scrutiny of the legal eagles – the clerks, the secretaries, the proctors, the red-robed, grey-wigged doctors and all. The work itself was as tedious as it was exhausting. However, for the past three years Dickens had been studying the craft of shorthand and was able to take things in his stride. He quickly earned himself a reputation for speed and accuracy, and was therefore in constant demand.

He features Doctors' Commons in several stories, describing it in *Sketches by Boz* as:

> the place where they grant marriage-licences to love-sick couples, and divorces to unfaithful ones; register the wills of people who have any property to leave, and punish hasty gentlemen who call ladies by unpleasant names.

In *The Pickwick Papers* Sam Weller gives directions there to Alfred Jingle. 'Paul's churchyard, sir; low archway on the carriage-side, booksellers at one corner, hotel on the other, and two parties in the middle as touts for licences.' Weller then relates his own father's matrimonial experience on a visit to Doctors' Commons after which, being in possession of a brand-new licence, he felt compelled to procure a second wife for himself. Later Mr Pickwick sends out to the Horn Coffee house in nearby Knightrider Street for 'a bottle or six' with which to celebrate Mr Winkle's visit to the Fleet Prison (see also FARRINGDON STREET). The coffee house at 29 Knightrider Street later became the Horn Tavern (now rebuilt).

David Copperfield is articled to Mr Spenlow in Doctors' Commons; and Mr Boffin in *Our Mutual Friend* describes proceedings inside 'Doctor Scommons'.

The main building was demolished in 1867, ten years after the dissolution of the office. All remaining buildings associated with the courts were destroyed during World War II bombing raids, the exception being the Deanery of St Paul's, which now serves as an office suite.

A plaque on the wall of the Faraday Building in Queen Victoria Street now commemorates the former site of Doctors' Commons.

DORKING, SURREY — The Marquis of Granby inn of *The Pickwick Papers* stood in Dorking. This house, kept by Tony Weller and his second wife, Susan, 'was quite a model of a road-side public house of the better class – just large enough to be convenient, and small enough to be snug.'

In fact the 'Markis Gran' was entirely a product of Dickens's imagination for he was never particularly familiar with the town of Dorking. However, several inns in the area made later claims as to being the author's original, notably the King's Arms, The White Horse and the King's Head (site later occupied by the Post Office).

DOUGHTY STREET, LONDON — The beginning of 1837 saw Charles Dickens's rise from hard-working journalist to highly successful, though equally hard-working, author. By then *The Pickwick Papers* was well on the way to popular success, while *Oliver Twist* had begun its own journey into literary history. Dickens had also known some theatrical success and had accepted the editorship of a new monthly magazine, *Bentley's Miscellany* (in which *Oliver Twist* was appearing in instalments). He began to look around for a new home: somewhere more fitting to his rapidly improving social position as a man of letters. In March he decided upon a twelve-roomed house at 48 Doughty Street, Holborn, which he leased for three years at an annual rental of £80.

The Charles Dickens Museum, Doughty Street.

Doughty Street was a pleasant residential thoroughfare with a lodge-gate at each end, both of which were policed by porters who would lock the gates at night.

The family – Charles, Catherine and Fred Dickens with Mary Hogarth as a constant guest – left FURNIVAL'S INN and moved in to Number 48 on 25 March 1837. And here Dickens worked, in an upstairs study which overlooked the walled-in garden. Many visitors came to the house. Harry Burnett (the fiancée of Charles's elder sister Fanny) remembered one such visit:

> [We] were sitting round the fire cosily enjoying a chat, when Dickens, for some purpose, came suddenly into the room. 'What, you here!' he exclaimed; 'I'll bring down my work.' It was his monthly portion of 'Oliver Twist' for Bentley's. In a few minutes he returned, manuscript in hand, and while he was pleasantly discoursing he employed himself in carrying to a corner of the room a little table, at which he seated himself and recommenced his writing. We, at his bidding, went on talking about our 'little nothings', he – every now and then (the feather of his pen moving rapidly from side to side), put in a cheerful interlude. It was interesting to watch, upon the sly, the mind and the muscles working (or, if you please playing), in company, as new thoughts were being dropped upon the paper. And to note the working brow, the set of mouth, with the tongue pressed against the closed lips, as was his habit.

Those early days at Doughty Street also had their moment of tragedy. On 7 May 1837, following a family outing to the St James's Theatre to see Dickens's farce *Is She His Wife?*, Mary Hogarth collapsed suddenly and later died in her room.

Dickens had grown extremely fond of his young sister-in-law during her brief stay in his household. He was utterly devastated by the loss and was quite unable to continue with his work. Consequently publication of the imminent parts of both *The Pickwick Papers* and *Oliver Twist* was suspended for a month during which Dickens, Catherine and baby Charley spent a period of mourning at Wylde's Farm in HAMPSTEAD.

Mary Hogarth was buried in Kensal Green Cemetery, Harrow Road. Dickens composed the lines inscribed on her tombstone:

> Young Beautiful and Good,
> God in his Mercy
> Numbered her with his Angels
> At the Early Age of
> Seventeen

Memories of Mary Hogarth and of the pure and innocent qualities she had represented to him remained with Dickens for many years to come and she became the inspiration for several of the 'child angels' who would appear in future novels.

Besides completing *The Pickwick Papers* and *Oliver Twist* at Doughty Street, Dickens also wrote most of *Nicholas Nickleby* and

A corner of the carefully restored drawing room at 48 Doughty Street.

the beginning of *Barnaby Rudge* there. Two daughters were born in the house, Mary (known always as 'Mamie') on 6 March 1838, and Kate on 29 October 1839.

As 1839 drew to a close Dickens – by then a household name – began to look for a larger house, and in December the family moved to 1 DEVONSHIRE TERRACE near Regent's Park.

Although Dickens spent less than three years at 48 Doughty Street, the house did not forget him. In the summer of 1922 the building was rescued, by the Dickens Fellowship, from the threat of the demolisher's hammers. By appeal, the Fellowship raised enough money to purchase the freehold of the property. A further sum, enough to endow the house as a museum, was raised by public subscription. The house became the headquarters of the Dickens Fellowship, founded in 1902 by B. W. Matz as 'a common bond of friendship [of] lovers of that great master of humour and pathos, Charles Dickens'.

In 1925 Number 48 was opened to the public, under the direction of an independent trust, as The Dickens House Museum (now the Charles Dickens Museum), and has remained a popular literary shrine ever since. Each year the house welcomes many thousands of visitors from all over the world. Indeed a visit to the Doughty Street museum is essential for all keen Dickensians: the house is a treasure trove of relics from his life and times. Included among them are a Spanish mahogany sideboard purchased by the author in 1839; a grandfather clock, once the property of Moses Pickwick, coachman of BATH, whose surname was borrowed and immortalized by Dickens in *The Pickwick Papers*, a bust of Dickens (1842) by Henry Dexter of Boston; the family Bible, showing Dickens's own record of the family history; the hall clock from GAD'S HILL PLACE; the original 'Little Midshipman' figure-head of *Dombey and Son* (see also LEADENHALL STREET) and the gold-beater's sign of *A Tale of Two Cities* (see also SOHO).

Dickens's writing desk and chair from GAD'S HILL PLACE are preserved at Doughty Street. On the eve of his death he wrote his

The handsome front door of Dickens's former home at Doughty Street, now the Charles Dickens Museum.

last two letters at this desk. The table from his Swiss Chalet (see also GAD'S HILL PLACE and ROCHESTER) at which he wrote the final pages of the unfinished *Edwin Drood* is also on display.

The Dickens Reference Library, containing the collections of B. W. Matz and F. G. Kitton, is also on view at Doughty Street, as is the Suzannet collection of Dickensiana (the Comte Alain de Suzannet, 1882–1950, a former vice-president of the

Dickens Fellowship, devoted much of his time to the assembly of this fascinating array of books, letters, portraits, prints etc).

The room once occupied by Mary Hogarth contains one of the two remaining letters written in her own hand, as well as a pendant presented to her by Dickens in 1835 and worn by him on his watch-chain after her death in 1837. Between 1980 and 1983 the museum's curator, Dr David Parker, undertook the daunting task of restoring Charles Dickens's Doughty Street drawing-room to its apparent condition of 1837–1839. This project involved detailed detective work, gently scraping away at layers of paint on the walls; finding carpets, curtains and other furnishings matching those shown in sketches made by Dickens's good friend George Cruickshank; and painstakingly tracking down pieces of furniture once owned by Dickens. The results of this remarkable enterprise are now on public view. Further refurbishments were made ahead of the Dickens Bicentennial celebrations of 2012.

David Copperfield with Betsey Trotwood.

DOVER, KENT — In *David Copperfield* young David treks from London to Dover in order to be with his Aunt, Betsey Trotwood. Unsure of the whereabouts of her cottage he sits 'on the step of an empty shop at a street corner, near the market place'. Eventually a friendly fly driver acquaints the boy with Miss Trotwood's maid who in turn leads him to 'a very neat little cottage with cheerful bow windows: in front of it, a small square gravelled court or garden, full of flowers carefully tended, and

smelling deliciously'. This is Betsey Trotwood's cottage, which Dickens's literary imagination had transferred several miles along the Kentish coastline from BROADSTAIRS.

In *A Tale of Two Cities* Jarvis Lorry always stays at the Royal George Hotel (now gone). Dover is also mentioned in *The Pickwick Papers*, *Little Dorrit* and *The Uncommercial Traveller*. In 1852, during the writing of *Bleak House*, Dickens stayed for three months at 10 Camden Crescent. He considered Dover 'infinitely too genteel … But the sea is very fine and the walks are quite remarkable'.

Dickens gave one of his Public Readings in Dover on 5 November 1861 and thought the audience there had 'the greatest sense of humour'.

DRURY LANE, LONDON — In his days as a labouring boy at Warren's Blacking Warehouse (see also COVENT GARDEN and STRAND), Dickens worked alongside a boy named 'Poll' Green, whose father was a fireman at the famous Drury Lane Theatre.

Dickens's original for Jo's churchyard, in *Bleak House*, where Captain Hawdon (lover to Lady Dedlock and father of Esther Summerson) is buried, was based upon a cemetery in Drury Lane:

> a hemmed-in churchyard, pestiferous and obscene, whence malignant diseases are communicated to the bodies of our dear brothers and sisters who have not departed; while our dear brothers and sisters who hang about official backstairs – would to heaven they had departed! – are very complacent and agreeable.

Later poor Jo brings Lady Dedlock here to view the grave:

> 'He was put there,' says Jo, holding to the bars and looking in.
>
> 'Where? Oh, what a scene of horror.'
>
> 'There,' says Jo, pointing. 'Over yinder. Among them piles of bones, and close to that there kitchen winder! They put him wery nigh the top. They was obliged to stamp on it to git it in. I could unkiver it for you, with my broom, if the gate was open. That's why they locks it, I s'pose,' giving it a shake. 'It's always locked. Look at the rat!' cries Jo, excited. 'Hi! Look! There he goes! Ho! Into the ground!'

Lady Dedlock later dies near the spot. Today the site of this graveyard is occupied by a children's playground known as Drury Lane Gardens.

In *Nicholas Nickleby* Miss Petowker, a member of Vincent Crummles's travelling theatrical troupe, is 'of the Theatre Royal, Drury Lane.' In *The Old Curiosity Shop* the lodging place of Dick Swiveller 'had the advantage of being over a tobacconists shop', in Drury Lane.

Dickens, like his 'favourite child' David Copperfield, had once, while working as a labouring boy at Warren's Blacking Warehouse in Covent Garden, ordered a plate of beef in Johnson's Alamode Beef House in Clare Court, Drury Lane. (This street has long since gone; its site now occupied by Kean Street.)

DULWICH, LONDON — The end of *The Pickwick Papers* sees Mr Pickwick retiring to 'a house which exactly suited my fancy', where he is to live out the rest of his days tended to by Sam Weller and his wife Mary.

> 'The house I have taken,' said Mr Pickwick, 'is at Dulwich; it has a large garden, and is situated in one of the most pleasant spots near London. It has been fitted up with every attention to substantial comfort; perhaps to a little elegance besides…'

And, in the final paragraph of the book we learn that Mr Pickwick is:

> somewhat infirm now, but he retains all his former juvenility of spirit, and may still be frequently seen contemplating the pictures in the Dulwich Gallery, or enjoying a walk about the pleasant neighbourhood on a fine day. He is known by all the poor people about, who

never fail to take their hats off as he passes with great respect; the children idolise him, and so indeed does the whole neighbourhood.

E

EATON SOCON, CAMBRIDGESHIRE — The stagecoach carrying Nicholas Nickleby, Wackford Squeers, and a party of new pupils to Yorkshire, in *Nicholas Nickleby*, halts for a while at an unnamed inn at 'Eton Slocomb' for which Dickens's original was Eaton Socon, near St Neots. The adult passengers enjoyed 'a good coach dinner' here, whilst 'the five little boys were put to thaw by the fire, and regaled with sandwiches'.

ELEPHANT AND CASTLE, LONDON — In *Bleak House* Mrs Bagnet is found by Mr George 'washing greens', in 'a street of shops' in the vicinity of 'the far-famed Elephant who has lost his Castle'.

ELY PLACE, LONDON — In *David Copperfield* Mr Waterbrook, agent to the lawyer Wickfield, lived with his wife 'in Ely Place, Holborn'. Here, David visits Agnes Wickfield and apologizes to her for his earlier boorish behaviour (Agnes later becomes the second Mrs Copperfield).

EXETER, DEVON — At the end of April 1835 Dickens was sent by the *Morning Chronicle* to Exeter, to record and report upon a speech made by the prospective parliamentary candidate for South Devon, Lord John Russell. Dickens's transcription of this speech – delivered in pouring rain in Castle Yard – was followed by a breakneck race back to London against the man from the *Times*. Dickens not only won the race but presented the better story to his readers. The *Times* retaliated by calling the *Morning Chronicle* 'that squirt of filthy water'. In turn the *Chronicle* bounced back with 'the poor old *Times* in its imbecilic ravings'. No doubt encounters such as this later inspired the journalistic battles between the rival editors Pott and Slurk in *The Pickwick Papers*.

In February 1839 Charles Dickens learned that his father was once again indulging in his old, spendthrift ways. It transpired that for the previous two years, John Dickens had been borrowing odd sums of money from, among others, the

Exeter Castle, where Dickens reported on Lord John Russell's parliamentary speech in 1835.

publishers Chapman and Hall. By the time the son learned of the father's latest financial lapse the amount in question had reached embarrassing proportions.

Charles took it upon himself to resolve the situation once and for all. He quickly settled all his father's debts and then, in March, travelled to Exeter to find a suitable cottage in which to retire his parents.

Using the New London Inn as a base, he began his search. On the Plymouth High Road he spotted a 'For Rent' sign outside Mile End Cottage, Alphington. He quickly agreed with the owner to a rental of £50 per annum.

On 5 March he wrote to John Forster:

> I took a little house for them this morning, and if they are not pleased with it I shall be grievously disappointed. Exactly a mile beyond the city on the Plymouth High Road there are two white cottages: one is theirs and the other belongs to the landlady … The paint and paper throughout are new and fresh and cheerful-looking, the place is clean beyond all description, and the neighbourhood I suppose the most beautiful in this most beautiful of English counties.

He brought in various bits and pieces of furniture and then summoned his parents to Exeter via the earliest available stagecoach. A few days later John and Elizabeth Dickens dutifully moved in to Mile End Cottage.

Initially they enjoyed the rural life, but the novelty soon began to wear thin. Both parents found themselves missing the hustle and bustle of London, and both wrote reproachful letters to Charles, chiding him for his seemingly too prompt action in exiling them so far from the capital. Gradually, however, they came to accept the situation and remained at Mile End Cottage for the next three years.

In *Nicholas Nickleby* Godfrey and Ralph Nickleby 'had been brought up together at a school near Exeter'. Dickens gave two of his Public Readings in Exeter, one in 1858 and the other in 1862.

F

FARRINGDON STREET, LONDON — In *The Pickwick Papers*, Mr Pickwick finds himself incarcerated in the notorious Fleet Prison in Farringdon Street following his refusal to pay the costs laid against him by Mrs Bardell.

> 'The tipstaff, just looking over his shoulder to see that his charge was following close at his heels, preceded Mr Pickwick into the prison.

Here Mr Pickwick is studied by turnkeys and warders so that they might take his 'likeness': 'We're capital hands at likenesses

here. Take 'em in no time, and always exact.'
This ceremony enables the prison staff to
distinguish inmates from visitors.

Pickwick is next led into the prison
proper, by Mr Roker:

'This here is the hall flight'.

'Oh,' replied Mr Pickwick, looking
down a dark and filthy staircase, which
appeared to lead to a range of damp and
gloomy stone vaults beneath the ground,
'and those, I suppose, are the little cellars
where the prisoners keep their small
quantities of coal. Ah! unpleasant places
to have to go down to; but very
convenient, I dare say.'

'Yes, I shouldn't wonder if they was
convenient,' replied the gentleman, 'seeing
that a few people live there pretty snug.
That's the Fair, that is.'

'My friend,' said Mr Pickwick, 'you
don't really mean to say that human beings
live down in those wretched dungeons?'

'Don't I?' replied Mr Roker, with
indignant astonishment; 'why shouldn't
I?'

'Live! – Live down there!' exclaimed Mr
Pickwick.

'Live down there! Yes, and die down
there, too, wery often!'

The remainder of Pickwick's tour of the Fleet
is equally depressing to him, nothing more
so than when shown his own future quarters:

It was getting dark; that is to say, a few gas
jets were kindled in this place, which was
never light, by way of compliment to the
evening, which had set outside. As it was
rather warm, some of the tenants of the
numerous little rooms which opened into
the gallery on either hand had set their
doors ajar … there, four or five great
hulking fellows, just visible through a
cloud of tobacco smoke, were engaged in
noisy and riotous conversation over half-
emptied pots of beer, or playing at all-
fours with a very greasy pack of cards. In
the adjoining room, some solitary tenant
might be seen, poring, by the light of a
feeble tallow candle, over a bundle of
soiled and tattered papers, yellow with
dust and dropping to pieces from age,
writing, for the hundredth time, some
lengthened statement of his grievances,
for the perusal of some great man, whose
eyes it would never reach, or whose heart
it would never touch…

Mr Pickwick remains for three months in
the Fleet, during which time he is surprised
to find that Alfred Jingle and Job Trotter
become his fellow inmates. Generously, he
arranges their release together with a
passage to Demerara. Later, Mrs Bardell is
also imprisoned in the Fleet, on behalf of
Dodson and Fogg for failure to pay their
costs. Once more Pickwick's generosity
relieves the situation and Mrs Bardell goes
free, on condition that she drops all charges
against him.

The Fleet Prison was demolished in
1846 (site later occupied by the New
Congregational Memorial Hall).

The northern continuation of Farringdon Street is Farringdon Road; here at its northernmost end stood the notorious Coldbath Fields Prison (now gone, site occupied by the Mount Pleasant Post Office). Dickens wrote of this prison in the essay 'Prisoner's Van' in *Sketches by Boz*.

FINCHLEY, LONDON — In the winter of 1843 Dickens's public was slow to respond to his new novel *Martin Chuzzlewit*, just as they had been to its predecessor *Barnaby Rudge*. With the opening numbers of *Chuzzlewit* selling a mere 20,000 copies, both publishers and author realized that the story was not going to be the resounding success they had so eagerly anticipated.

In March, while brooding over the possibility that his public had deserted him, Dickens ensconced himself at Cobley's Farm, an out-of-the-way retreat in Finchley, in order to concentrate solely on the improved development of his storyline. Here, a possible solution suggested itself. He decided to draw upon his recent trip to America (see also LIVERPOOL) and to transport young Martin and his servant Mark Tapley across the Atlantic.

The couple travel, aboard 'that noble and fast sailing line-of-packet ship "The Screw" ', to New York and then by land to the 'thriving city' of Eden – probably based on Cairo, Illinois – where Chuzzlewit intends to set himself up as an architect and surveyor. Unfortunately the reality of Eden disappoints him. First impressions show:

a flat morass, bestrewn with fallen timber; a marsh on which the good growth of the earth seemed to have been wrecked and cast away, that from its decomposing ashes vile and ugly things might rise; where the very trees turn to the aspect of huge weeds, begotten of the slime from which they sprung, by the hot sun that burnt them up; where fatal maladies, seeking whom they might infect, came forth at night in misty shapes, and creeping out upon the water, hunted them like spectres until days where even the blessed sun, shining down on festering elements of corruption and disease, became a horror; this was the realm of Hope through which they moved.

Young Martin falls victim to swamp fever and is nursed back to health by Tapley, who in turn is also claimed by the same malady. After much further misadventure both men return, disillusioned, to England.

While this turn in the tale did help to increase the circulation of *Martin Chuzzlewit* in Britain – albeit by a mere 3,000 copies – it also enraged American readers, just as Dickens's *American Notes* had done a few months earlier.

The increased sales were not enough, however, to prevent Chapman and Hall from invoking a clause in their contract with Dickens which entitled them to deduct £50 from his monthly fee in the event that *Chuzzlewit*'s profits did not cover advances already paid to him. A bitter quarrel ensued which sowed the seeds of Dickens's eventual break with his first publishers. The incident also soured his appetite for the writing of *Martin Chuzzlewit*. But he soon knuckled down and was later able to report to John Forster: 'I think Chuzzlewit is a hundred points immeasurably the best of my stories.'

The best thing to come out of Dickens's Finchley sojourn was the creation of Sairey Gamp – the midwife with a liking for liquor. The site of Cobley's Farm is now occupied by 70 Queens Avenue, where Dickens's brief stay is commemorated by a plaque.

In *The Old Curiosity Shop* the Garland family lived in Finchley at 'Abel Cottage':

> To be sure it was a beautiful little cottage, with a thatched roof and little spires at the gable-ends, and pieces of stained glass in some of the windows almost as large as pocketbooks.

Abel Cottage has never been positively identified.

In *Barnaby Rudge* Rudge senior and Rudge junior spend a night in a shed in a field in Finchley following their escape from NEWGATE PRISON. In *Dombey and Son* Mr Toots gives his reason for being late: 'I went up as far as Finchley first, to get some uncommonly fine chickweed that grows there, for Miss Dombey's bird.'

FLEET STREET, LONDON — In the summer of 1833 Charles Dickens, by then very well aware of his own acute powers of observation, began to experiment with some short fictional pieces based upon scenes from London life. By October he was confident enough to drop the first of these literary efforts 'with fear and trembling into a dark letterbox, in a dark office, up a dark court in Fleet Street'. The letterbox was that of a new publication, the *Monthly Magazine*, in Johnson's Court off the north side of Fleet Street.

Shrewdly, Dickens had reasoned that this journal would not yet be inundated with prospective and hopeful contributions to its pages, and that his piece would rise quickly to the top of the editor's pile. The piece in question was an essay entitled 'A Sunday Out of Town' and tells of the thwarted efforts of the obnoxious Octavius Budden to extract funds from a wealthy but unwilling relative, Augustus Minns.

Two months later an anxious Dickens entered a bookshop in the STRAND and asked the small fellow behind the counter for a copy of the latest *Monthly Magazine*. He made the purchase and stepped out into the street again. With nervous, trembling fingers he opened the magazine's pages and there 'in all the glory of print' he found his story under the title 'A Dinner at Poplar Walk'.

Needing to be alone to savour this exquisite moment, he walked in a euphoric daze to his regular reporting haunt, Westminster Hall (see also HOUSES OF PARLIAMENT), and 'turned into it for half an hour because my eyes were so dimmed with joy and pride that they could not bear the street, and were not fit to be seen there'.

Captain Holland, proprietor and editor of the *Monthly Magazine*, could not afford to pay his contributors, but was ever willing to encourage promising writing talent. He was greatly impressed with 'A Dinner at Poplar Walk' and asked Dickens for more 'sketches' along the same lines. Consequently several other short pieces, penned by Dickens, appeared at regular intervals in the *Monthly Magazine*. At first they appeared uncredited, then in August 1834 the second part of 'The Boarding House' bore the signature 'Boz'. (Dickens had borrowed this pseudonym from the nickname of his youngest brother Augustus, whose nasal pronunciation of the word 'Moses' had flattened the word to 'Boses' and eventually to 'Boz'. The name had stuck and had been in family usage for several years. Now it was a name destined for a far wider fame.)

The letterbox of the *Monthly Magazine* remained in Johnson's Court for several years – a reminder of the part that it had played in the history of English Literature – until the original building was demolished to make way for Hulton House.

Dickens had been familiar with Fleet Street since his days at Warren's Blacking Warehouse (see also COVENT GARDEN and STRAND). He knew it, too, as a newspaper reporter; and in 1845, when he decided to publish his own liberal newspaper, the *Daily News*, he took editorial offices in Whitefriars, to the south of Fleet Street.

His favourite tavern, The Olde Cock Inn, was situated on the northern side of Fleet Street (the same business is now to be found in newer premises on the south side).

Ye Olde Cheshire Cheese, frequented by Dickens.

Fleet Street features in several of the novels: David Copperfield shares Charles Dickens's hungry childhood experience of gazing longingly into a food-shop window there. Later he takes Peggotty to see Mrs Saloman's 'perspiring waxworks' at 17 Fleet Street; and with his Aunt Betsey he 'made a pause at a toy-shop in Fleet Street to see the giants of St Dunstan's strike upon the bells'. This church, rebuilt in 1831, inspired the Christmas Story *The Chimes*.

In *A Tale of Two Cities*, Sydney Carton leads Charles Darnay down LUDGATE HILL to Fleet Street, and so up a covered way into a tavern, where they enjoy a 'good plain dinner and good wine'. The most likely original for this setting is Ye Olde Cheshire Cheese, in Wine Office Court, off the north side of Fleet Street. Dickens often visited this beautiful old inn (rebuilt in 1667), as did many other literary figures of the past, including Dr Johnson, James Boswell and Oliver Goldsmith.

Tellson's Bank in *A Tale of Two Cities* is based upon Child's Bank at 1 Fleet Street (demolished in 1879, now rebuilt), which Dickens described as:

> an old fashioned place ... very small, very dark, very ugly, very incommodious ... After bursting open a door of idiotic obstinacy with a weak rattle in its throat, you fell into Tellson's down two steps, and came to your senses in a miserable little shop with two little counters, where the oldest of men made your cheque shake as if the wind rustled it, while they examined the signature by the dingiest of windows.

Beside the bank stood Temple Bar, a 'leaden old obstruction' which marked the entrance to the City of London, and was later removed, stone by stone, to Theobald's Park in Hertfordshire. It has since been replaced at the City boundary by a single 'Griffin'. A painstaking reconstruction of Temple Bar in Paternoster Square near St Paul's Cathedral was completed in 2004.

Beside the Bar in *A Tale of Two Cities* squatted the odd-job-man Jerry Cruncher, 'as well known to Fleet Street and the Temple as the Bar itself'. Cruncher and his wife live in an apartment in Hanging Sword Alley, Whitefriars – Mrs Cruncher always 'flopping' down in prayer. (Temple Bar also features briefly in *Barnaby Rudge*, *Martin Chuzzlewit*, *Little Dorrit*, *David Copperfield* and *Bleak House*.)

Clifford's Inn, the oldest inn of Chancery, which once stood off Fetter Lane, to the north of Fleet Street, provides office accommodation for Melchisedech, solicitors to Joshua Smallweed in *Bleak House*. In *Little Dorrit* Tip Dorrit was employed at twelve shillings a week by a solicitor of Clifford's Inn. In *Our Mutual Friend*, John Rokesmith offers his secretarial services to Mr Boffin, at Clifford's Inn, having followed him along CHANCERY LANE.

Temple Bar, reconstructed in the City in 2004.

A house (now gone) in Fetter Lane laid claim to being the original of Dickens's 'Old Curiosity Shop'.

FOLKESTONE, KENT — In the summer of 1855 Dickens took a holiday in Folkestone, staying with his family at 3 Albion Villas, where he wrote part of *Little Dorrit*. On 16 September he gave a Public Reading of extracts from his works, the proceeds of which went to deserving local charities.

Folkestone appears in the stories 'The Flight', and 'Out of Season' in which it becomes the original of Pavilionstone: 'Within a quarter of a century, it was a little fishing town, and they do say, that the time was, when it was a little smuggling town.'

FULHAM, LONDON — The MP Sir Barnet Skettles and his wife Lady Skettles reside in a villa at Fulham in *Dombey and Son*. Florence Dombey stays with them for a while.

FURNIVAL'S INN, LONDON — In 1834 John Dickens lost his job with the *Mirror of Parliament* and, despite finding occasional employment with the *Morning Herald*, he was once again indulging in his old extravagant ways and living far beyond his means. This situation worsened, and by November he found himself up to his neck in debt and languishing inside a sponging house. Charles – by then a successful reporter with the *Morning Chronicle* – decided to take control of the situation.

The house at Furnival's Inn where Dickens rented rooms in the 1830s.

During the next three months the dutiful son exhausted his own financial resources and mortgaged those of his immediate future in order to extricate his family from its latest difficulties. He quickly arranged cheaper accommodation for his mother and the younger children at 21 George Street, Adelphi (see also STRAND), and also found rooms for himself and his fourteen-year-old brother, Frederick, at 13 Furnival's Inn, High Holborn, where the advance rental of £35 left him broke. Indeed, there were no funds available at the end of the day for homely comforts such as knives and forks or curtains or carpets.

While living here Dickens increased the literary reputation of 'Boz' by leaps and bounds. His 'sketches' for the *Monthly Magazine* had ceased in February 1834, but he had since contributed several more pieces to the *Morning Chronicle*, the *Evening Chronicle* and *Bell's Life of London*. Through the novelist Harrison Ainsworth he had also been introduced into the best literary salons. Among his new acquaintances was an up-and-coming young publisher named John Macrone who suggested that the 'Boz sketches' might be collected together and published in a two-volume edition; all that was needed, he added, were a few more items. Naturally Dickens was elated and excited by the proposition. He leapt at the opportunity and quickly set to work on the extra pieces.

The morning of 7 February 1836 – Dickens's 24th birthday – saw the publication of *Sketches by Boz*. Three days later he answered a knock at the door of his Furnival's Inn chambers: a small man stood on the doorstep and introduced himself as William Hall, junior partner in the publishing firm of Chapman and Hall: he asked if he might discuss a matter of business.

Dickens recognized Hall immediately as the small fellow who, two years and two months earlier, had sold him a copy of the *Monthly Magazine* containing his first literary effort 'A Dinner at Poplar Walk' (see

also FLEET STREET and STRAND). Reasoning that such a coincidence could only be a good omen, he invited Hall to step inside 'and so fell to business'.

William Hall suggested that Charles Dickens should write a humorous text linking together certain illustrations which featured a fictional 'Nimrod Club' – a sporting organization whose members' collective lack of skill and dexterity would embroil them in all kinds of comical situations. The drawings were the work of Robert Seymour, a popular cartoonist, and had been submitted for consideration by Chapman and Hall for quite some time. Now Seymour was quite understandably growing anxious as to the future of his project: to him it was simply a matter of finding a journeyman writer capable of supplying the necessary text. The current success of 'Boz' had obviously brought Dickens into consideration for the commission.

The work, explained Hall, would be published in twenty monthly numbers, each 12,000 words in length. The fee offered to Dickens was 14 guineas per number. Considering his then current financial plight, this offer was more than tempting to him. And yet, he had the good sense to pause to consider the immensity of the task, and to foresee the difficulties that might arise from so narrow a concept. He explained to Hall that he was not a sporting man, and he argued that Seymour's idea was not an original one. In short, he agreed to undertake the project, provided that his text would form the core of the work and that Seymour's illustrations would then arise directly from the storyline as dictated by its author.

This was not the reaction William Hall had expected. However, so impressed was he by the young author's obvious strength of will that he returned to his senior partner, Edward Chapman, and put Dickens's proposal to him.

Chapman considered the matter at length, perhaps weighing the growing popularity of 'Boz' against that of Seymour. Two days later he agreed to the new scheme and his decision was conveyed back to Furnival's Inn. Dickens was delighted and he put his mind to the new story at once. 'My views being deferred to,' he later wrote, 'I thought of Mr Pickwick.' Within a week the first number of *The Pickwick Papers* was begun in earnest.

The opening numbers of the story met with a lukewarm critical reception, however, with many copies returned unsold to Chapman and Hall; and the second number was halted by tragedy when Robert Seymour committed suicide.

Publication of *The Pickwick Papers* was suspended for a month while the search for a replacement artist was made. The most obvious choice was George Cruickshank – he had illustrated *Sketches by Boz* – but he was heavily committed to other projects. A number of other possibilities came forward, but after a faltering restart with the inexperienced Robert Buss, publishers and author finally settled on Hablot Knight Brown ('Phiz'), who would later illustrate several of Dickens's works.

In the fourth monthly number of *The Pickwick Papers* Dickens introduced the irrepressible cockney 'boots' Sam Weller who, with his quick wit, worldly-wise ways and apposite epigrams, provides the perfect foil to the essentially naive and innocent Mr Pickwick. Subsequent sales rose from around 4,000 per number to upwards of 40,000.

The Pickwick Papers became a publishing sensation. The story was enjoyed by rich and poor alike; indeed, many groups of poor people would club their funds together to buy, or even to rent the monthly numbers; while many of the illiterate would contrive to have the episodes read aloud to them.

An entire 'Pickwickian Industry' was built up around the phenomenal popularity of the work. Besides pirated copies and unashamed plagiarisms, there were several stage adaptations and numerous 'Pickwickian dances'. And any amount of merchandise was available, including song books, hats, coats, cigars, ornamental figurines *et al.*, each item bringing in a handsome profit for the sharp-witted entrepreneurs who had so swiftly leapt aboard the bandwagon. Pickwick also found fame abroad: editions in English were read as far afield as Australia and America, while numerous translations found their ways about the world. Dickens rarely profited from the additional ventures so closely associated with his own work, and he would henceforth champion the fight for authors' rights.

The circumstances of Charles Dickens's life altered radically during the writing of *The Pickwick Papers*. An increase in his monthly income meant that he and Fred Dickens could move to larger chambers at 15 Furnival's Inn. These comprised three rooms on the third floor together with the use of a kitchen in the basement. Here they brought in more furniture and made themselves more comfortable.

Charles Dickens had first met Catherine Hogarth when her father, George Hogarth, editor of the *Evening Chronicle*, invited him to dine at his home 18 York Place, Fulham Road, in January 1835. Catherine was then a dark-haired and good-looking girl of twenty. During the course of several subsequent visits the young couple fell in love and by May were engaged: they were married on 2 April 1836 (see also CHALK and CHELSEA). After a brief honeymoon the couple settled at 15 Furnival's Inn with Fred Dickens and Catherine's 16-year-old sister Mary Hogarth as a constant guest.

Their first son, Charley, was born here on 6 January 1837, and they stayed at Furnival's Inn until moving to 48 DOUGHTY STREET in March of the same year. Dickens later wrote: 'I shall never be so happy again, as I was in those chambers ... never if I roll in wealth and fame.'

Like Dickens, John Westlock in *Martin Chuzzlewit* also occupied chambers in Furnival's Inn:

a shady, quiet place, echoing the footsteps of the stragglers who have business there; and rather monotonous and gloomy on summer evenings.

In *The Mystery of Edwin Drood*, Mr Grewgious took meals at Wood's Hotel, which stood within the Inn. In the same book Rosa Bud stayed at this hotel.

Furnival's Inn was demolished in 1889. The site was later occupied by the rather grandiose offices of The Prudential Assurance Company. A plaque, and a bust of Dickens set beneath the elegant portico commemorates the fact that he once lived there. The building is now known as Holborn Bars.

G

GAD'S HILL PLACE, KENT — As a child living in Chatham between 1817 and 1822, Charles Dickens was often taken on long walks into the surrounding countryside by his father, John Dickens. Amongst the places they visited was the village of Higham, some five miles from Chatham along the main Rochester to Gravesend road.

There, at the top of a hill and standing a little way back from the main road, was a large country house of red brick, known as

Gad's Hill Place. Whenever they passed it they would pause there: father would turn to son and advise him to work hard so that one day he might own a house just like it.

By the summer of 1855 Charles Dickens was a world-famous author and editor who, apart from relatively short periods spent in America, Italy, Switzerland and France, had lived most of his life in London. It was then that he decided to leave TAVISTOCK HOUSE and buy a home in the country.

By coincidence William Wills, Dickens's chief sub-editor on *Household Words*, had at the time an appointment with Mrs Lynn Linton, a regular contributor to the magazine. Over dinner she told Wills, in passing, that she knew Gad's Hill Place very well. She had, in fact, spent her childhood in the house, because her father had been rector of Higham. The rector had recently died, leaving the house to his daughter.

Knowing of Dickens's feelings for the house, Wills returned to the *Household Words* office next morning and proclaimed to the author, 'It is written that you are to have that house at Gad's Hill ... So, you must buy it. Now or Never!'

Negotiations began at once. Dickens initially offered £1,500 for the house, but meeting with a certain resistance from Mrs Linton, he finally paid £1,790 on Friday 14 March 1856: 'Now isn't it an extraordinary thing', he said to Wills. 'Look at the day – Friday. I have been drawing it [the purchase money] half a dozen times

when the lawyers have not been ready, and here it comes round as a matter of course'. (The 'matter of course' referred to was the fact that the most important events of Dickens's life – birth and marriage – had each occurred on a Friday.) Purchase eventually included a small shrubbery, known as the wilderness, on the opposite side of the main road, and a twenty-seven year's lease of the meadow-land behind the house, some eleven acres in all.

Rear view of Gad's Hill Place.

Gad's Hill Place, Higham. Dickens's childhood ideal, and his last home.

Although he spent much time and money on improving the property, Dickens did not in fact move into Gad's Hill Place on a more permanent basis until 1860 (by which time he and Catherine had separated, and his household was being managed by his sister-in-law Georgina Hogarth), preferring to travel intermittently between London and Kent.

In the summer of 1858 he wrote to his Swiss friend William de Cerjat of a stay at Gad's Hill:

At the present moment I am on my little Kentish freehold looking on as pretty a view out of my study window as you will find in a long day's English ride. My little house is a grave red brick house (time of George the First, I suppose) which I have added to and stuck bits upon in all manner of ways, so that it is pleasantly irregular, and as violently opposed to all architectural ideas, as the most hopeful man could possibly desire.

Dickens was incorrect as to the period of construction of Gad's Hill Place. It was, in fact, built in the late 1770s – during the reign of King George III – for a certain Mr Stevens, an illiterate man who rose in life to become a successful brewer, and Mayor of Rochester.

During his fourteen-year ownership of Gad's Hill Place Dickens made many 'pleasantly irregular' alterations, including the conversion of a bedroom into a library, the enlargement of the drawing-room, and the construction of the conservatory at the eastern end of the house. In his study he had dummy books painted on the door and part of the walls, for which he invented several amusing titles, including *Lady Godiva and her Horse*, *Evidences of Christianity* by King Henry VIII, *Cats' Lives* in nine volumes, *Five Minutes in China*, *Swallows, on Emigration* and *History of a Short Chancery Suit* in nineteen volumes.

Perhaps the most interesting addition to the property came in the form of a gift from

The Swiss Chalet presented to Dickens by Charles Fechter in 1864, which now stands in Rochester.

a friend – the Swiss actor Charles Fechter. It arrived in December 1864: 98 pieces packed in 58 boxes, which when constructed formed a splendid two-storey Swiss Chalet. 'It really will be a pretty thing,' wrote Dickens, 'and in the summer (supposing it is not blown away in the spring), the upper room will make a charming study.' He had the chalet erected in the shrubbery (in 1859, a tunnel had been driven beneath the road, joining the main garden to the shrubbery).

Dickens often worked in the chalet and eventually installed five mirrors inside it:

and they reflect and refract, in all kinds of ways, the leaves that are quivering at the windows, and the great fields of waving corn, and the sail-dotted river. My room is up among the branches of the trees; and the birds and the butterflies fly in and out, and the green branches shoot in at the open windows, and the lights and shadows come and go with the rest of the company.

In the flower garden to the rear of the house is a replica of the grave of one of Dickens's pets, a canary. The epitaph on the slim wooden marker reads:

This is the Grave of
DICK
THE BEST OF BIRDS
Born at Broadstairs, Midsummer, 1851
Died at Gad's Hill Place,
October 14, 1866

Dickens grew to love Gad's Hill Place and the surrounding district. He often entertained the local villagers in the grounds, occasionally arranging running races or cricket matches for them. He also kept several horses there. He frequented the Sir John Falstaff Inn, which still stands across the road from Gad's Hill Place. And he often set out from Higham on long walks through the countryside perhaps to SHORNE, or COBHAM through Cobham Wood, or even further to COOLING on the marshlands of the Isle of Grain.

Dickens wrote *A Tale of Two Cities*, *The Uncommercial Traveller*, *Great Expectations*, *Our Mutual Friend* and the unfinished *Edwin Drood* while living at Gad's Hill. In the essay 'Travelling Abroad' in *The Uncommercial Traveller* the 'Uncommercial' comes across a 'queer small boy' on the road between Gravesend and Rochester:

'Where do you live?'

'At Chatham,' says he.

'What do you do there?' says I.

'I go to school,' says he.

I took him up in a moment, and we went on. Presently the very queer small boy says, 'This is Gadshill we are coming to, where Falstaff went out to rob those travellers, and ran away.'

'You know something about Falstaff, eh?' said I.

'All about him,' said the very queer small boy. 'I am old (I am nine), and I read all sorts of books. But do let us stop at the top of the hill, and look at the house there, if you please!'

'You admire that house?' said I.

'Bless you, sir,' said the very queer small boy, 'when I was not more than half as old as nine, it used to be a treat for me to be brought to look at it. And ever since I can recollect, my father, seeing me so fond of it, has often said to me, 'If you were to be very persevering and were to work hard, you might some day come to live in it! Though that's impossible!' said the queer small boy, drawing a low breath, and now staring at the house out of window with all his might.

I was rather amazed to be told this by the very queer small boy; for that house happens to be my house, and I have reason to believe that what he said was true.

On Sunday 5 June 1870 Dickens sat with his daughter Kate in the conservatory at Gad's Hill Place. As they sat long into the night, their conversation turned to *The Mystery of Edwin Drood*, which Dickens hoped would be a great success 'If, please God, I live to finish it'.

On Wednesday 8 June he worked all day in the chalet on the manuscript of *Edwin Drood*, stopping only for lunch. That afternoon he left the chalet later than usual and returned to the house to write some letters. Later, during dinner, he suddenly exclaimed that he must go to London at once. He then rose from his chair and collapsed from a cerebral haemorrhage. Shortly before 6 o'clock in the evening of the following day, he died.

Although he had expressed a wish to be buried without fuss in either his beloved ROCHESTER or alternatively in COBHAM or SHORNE, the monumental event of his death brought great pressure to bear on his family, and they were persuaded that he should be buried amongst the finest English writers at Poets' Corner in Westminster abbey.

After Dickens's death Gad's Hill Place was taken over by his son Charley, who in 1897 sold it to one Major Budden for £7,000.

Today Gad's Hill Place continues its life as a school. Dickens's chalet stands in the grounds of Eastgate House in ROCHESTER.

GODALMING, SURREY — In *Nicholas Nickleby*, Nicholas and Smike, en route to Portsmouth, spend a night in Godalming:

To Godalming they came at last, and here they bargained for two humble beds, and slept soundly. In the morning they were astir, though not quite so early as the sun, and again afoot, if not with all the freshness of yesterday, still with enough hope and spirit to bear them cheerily on.

GOLDEN SQUARE, LONDON — An elegant square situated to the west of Soho, where Ralph Nickleby lived, in:

a spacious house ... which, in addition to a brass plate upon the street-door, had another brass plate two sizes and a half smaller upon the left hand doorpost surmounting a brass model of an infant's fist grasping a fragment of a skewer, and displaying the word 'Office', it was clear that Mr Ralph Nickleby did, or pretended to do, business of some kind ...

7 Golden Square (now rebuilt) is the most likely original of this house as Dickens reputedly knew its owner, one William a' Beckett. 35 Golden Square has also been suggested as Dickens's original for Nickleby's house.

> ...Although a few members of the graver professions live about Golden Square, it is not exactly in anybody's way to or from anywhere ... It is a great resort for foreigners. The dark-complexioned men who wear large rings, and heavy watch-guards, and bushy whiskers, and who congregate under the Opera colonnade, and about the box-office in the season, between four and five in the afternoon, when they give away the orders, – all live in Golden Square, or within a street of it...
>
> This would not seem a spot very well adapted to the transaction of business, but Mr Ralph Nickleby had lived there notwithstanding for many years, and uttered no complaint on that score.

Newman Noggs, Ralph Nickleby's clerk, and confidant of Nicholas, also lodged nearby.

In *David Copperfield*, David and Martha Endell find Little Em'ly at a house near Golden Square:

> The house swarmed with inmates. As we went up, doors of rooms were opened and people's heads put out; and we passed other people on the stairs, who were coming down ... rot, damp and age had weakened the flooring, which in many cases was unsound and even unsafe. Some attempts had been made, I noticed, to infuse new blood into this dwindling frame, by repairing the costly old woodwork here and there with common deal; but it was like the marriage of a reduced old noble to a plebeian pauper, and each party to the ill-assorted union shrank away from each other.

GOSWELL ROAD, LONDON — In *The Pickwick Papers* Dickens is precise as to the location of Mr Pickwick's chambers inside Mrs Bardell's house: 'sitting room on the first floor front, bedroom on the second floor front', which stood in Goswell Street:

> Goswell Street extended on his right hand – as far as the eye could reach, Goswell Street extended on his left hand; and the opposite side of Goswell Street was over the way.

Goswell Street now forms part of Goswell Road. Thankfully Mr Pickwick is not content to simply gaze upon such a 'narrow view ... without one effort to penetrate the hidden countries which on every side surround it' and is soon off on his delightful adventures.

Later in the story, before departing for 'Eatanswill' (see also SUDBURY) Mr

Pickwick attempts to explain to Mrs Bardell his need for a manservant. Unfortunately the landlady misunderstands the explanation and believes that he is in fact proposing marriage to her. She faints away in his arms just as his fellow Pickwickians arrive. They witness this dramatic scene in an embarrassed silence.

Mrs Bardell, encouraged by the lawyers Dodson and Fogg, later brings a case of Breach of Promise against Mr Pickwick (see also CORNHILL, FARRINGDON STREET and GUILDHALL).

GOWER STREET, LONDON — In 1823, and in a fit of misguided inspiration, Elizabeth Dickens decided that an improvement in the family's fortunes would come only at her initiative. She planned to open a school for the children of families who were living in the East Indies – even though tuition of this kind was something of which she had little knowledge and even less experience.

John Dickens agreed with the scheme and the couple hurriedly found a six-roomed house at 4 Gower Street North (now demolished) where the rental was a staggering £50 per annum. They moved in during December and attached a brass plate to the door, announcing 'Mrs Dickens's Establishment'.

'Nobody ever came to the school,' Charles Dickens later wrote. 'Nor do I recollect that anybody ever proposed to come, or that the least preparation was ever made to receive anybody.' The scheme proved an utter failure and merely worsened the Dickens's financial plight. In *David Copperfield* Mrs Micawber opens a similar educational establishment with equally disastrous results.

Local tradesmen began to press for payment for services already rendered and cash to meet their bills came from the pawning and sale of various family belongings. Among the first of these items to be sold off for a few shillings was Charles's much-prized collection of books, which had been brought up from CHATHAM.

GRANTHAM, LINCOLNSHIRE — On his way north with Hablot Knight Browne to investigate the Yorkshire Schools for *Nicholas Nickleby* in 1838, Dickens stayed overnight at the George Inn in Grantham, and described it as 'the very best inn I have ever put up at'.

Here, by coincidence, he met with 'a very queer old lady' who turned out to be the mistress of a Yorkshire School returning northwards after a holiday in London. 'She was very communicative, drank a great deal of brandy and water and towards evening became insensible, in which state we left her.' (See also BARNARD CASTLE, BOWES and YORK.)

GRAVESEND, KENT — Gravesend was known to Dickens since his childhood days in nearby CHATHAM.

In the essay 'The Tuggses at Ramsgate' in *Sketches by Boz*, the Tuggs family, discussing a suitable holiday venue, consider that 'Gravesend is low'. In *Barnaby Rudge* the newly enlisted soldier Joe Willet is transported by river from London to Gravesend, from where he is marched onwards to Chatham.

In *David Copperfield*, David and his Aunt Betsey travel to Gravesend in order to say farewell to the Micawbers, who are setting sail for a new life in Australia. In *Great Expectations* Pip's attempt to escort Abel Magwitch out of the country ends on the river at Gravesend. In *Bleak House* Prince Turveydrop and Caddy Jellyby spend their honeymoon in the town.

GRAY'S INN, LONDON — In December 1826 John Dickens lost his job as a reporter with the *British Press*. Consequently the family was evicted from 16 Johnson Street (see also CRANLEIGH STREET) for non-payment of rent.

Elizabeth Dickens again set her mind to finding a fresh source of income. She visited Edward Blackmore, a solicitor and a partner in the firm of Ellis and Blackmore of 5 Holborn Court (now 1 South Square), Gray's Inn. Blackmore agreed to her proposal that his firm should take on her bright young son as a clerk/messenger at 10s a week, beginning in May 1827.

Had he stayed long enough in the Law to complete its wearisome apprenticeship, then Charles Dickens might well have become a solicitor; this would have been one way of securing the prosperous future he now so desired. However, he found the

work to be made of very dull stuff indeed, and never attempted to climb above the bottom rung on the legal ladder.

Shortly after he joined Ellis and Blackmore the firm moved to larger premises at 1 Raymond Buildings, Gray's Inn. The more he worked here, the more he hated the area. This feeling remained with him well into later life, for 32 years later he vilified Gray's Inn in the essay 'Chambers' in *The Uncommercial Traveller*: 'Can anything be more dreary than its arid square, Saharah Desert of the Law?' he asks. And, in the same piece, his 'imagination gloats' over the day when Gray's Inn would crumble to dust.

The area also features in several of the novels. In *The Pickwick Papers* the chambers of the lawyers Mr Perker and Mr Phunky are both situated in Gray's Inn. In *David Copperfield* Tommy Traddles occupies chambers on the top storey of 2 Holborn Court, while his friend Copperfield stays in the Gray's Inn Coffee House (at Gray's Inn Gateway) during his search for Traddles. In the same novel Mr Micawber – posing as Mr Mortimer – lives in Gray's Inn Lane.

In *Little Dorrit* Christopher Casby, the unscrupulous landlord of Bleeding Heart Yard:

> lived in a street in the Gray's Inn Road,
> which had set off from that thoroughfare
> with the intention of running at one heat
> down into the valley, and up again at the
> top of Pentonville Hill; but which had

run itself out of breath in twenty yards and had stood still ever since.

GREAT YARMOUTH, NORFOLK — In *David Copperfield*, the kindly Peggotty takes young David for two weeks' holiday in Great Yarmouth (he returns to find that his mother has married the unyielding Mr Murdstone). They travel there aboard the cart of one Mr Barkis. En route they take 'so many deviations up and down lanes and were such a long time in delivering a bedstand at a public house'; this was most probably the Village Maid Inn at Lound. Eventually the cart rattles into sight of Great Yarmouth:

> I was quite tired and very glad when we saw Yarmouth. It looked rather spongy and soppy, I thought, as I carried my eye over the great dull waste that lay across the river; and I could not help wondering, if the world were really as round as my geography-book said, how any part of it came to be so flat. But I reflected that Yarmouth might be situated at one of the poles; which would account for it.
>
> As we drew a little nearer, and saw the whole adjacent prospect lying a straight low line under the sky, I hinted to Peggotty that a mound or so might have improved it; and also that if the land had been a little more separated from the sea, and the town and the tide had not been quite so mixed up, like toast and water, it would have been nicer. But Peggotty said, with greater emphasis than usual, that we must take things as we find them, and

that, for her part, she was proud to call herself a Yarmouth Bloater.

> When we got into the street (which was strange enough to me), and smelt the fish, and pitch, and oakum, and tar, and saw the sailors walking about, and the carts jingling up and down over the stones, I felt that I had done so busy a place an injustice; and said as much to Peggotty, who heard my expressions of delight with great complacency, and told me it was well known (I suppose to those who had the good fortune to be born Bloaters) that Yarmouth was, upon the whole, the finest place in the universe.

At an inn (unidentified) Peggotty meets her nephew, Ham, who leads them towards Dan'l Peggotty's house:

> We turned down lanes bestrewn with bits of chips and little hillocks of sand, and went past gas-works, rope-walks, boat-builders' yards, ship-wrights' yards, ship-breakers' yards, rigger's lofts, smiths' forges, and a great litter of such places, until we came out upon the dull waste I had already seen at a distance.

Ham next leads them towards:

> a black barge ... not far off, high and dry on the ground, with an iron funnel sticking out of it for a chimney and smoking very cosily.
>
> 'That's not it?' said I. 'That ship looking thing?'

'That's it, Mas'r Davy,' returned Ham. If it had been Aladdin's palace, roc's egg and all, I suppose I could not have been more charmed with the romantic idea of living in it. There was a delightful door cut in the side, and it was roofed in, and there were little windows in it; but the wonderful charm of it was, that it was a real boat which had no doubt been upon the water hundreds of times, and which had never been intended to be lived in on dry land … never having been designed for any such use, it became a perfect abode.

This 'perfect abode' was probably based by Dickens upon the 'Black Hut' of one James Sharman which stood near the Nelson Monument. (There were, apparently, several imitations of Dan'l Peggotty's upside-down boat house in existence after the publication of David Copperfield.)

Later, young David leaves Great Yarmouth, bound for Salem House in London (see also BLACKHEATH and HAMPSTEAD ROAD); his point of departure being the Duke's Head Hotel, where 'the friendly waiter' assists him in the demolition of a huge meal.

Having made friends with the charismatic Steerforth at Salem House, David brings him to Yarmouth. Here Steerforth makes the acquaintance of Emily, with whom he later elopes.

74 Middlegate Street was, in Dickens's day, the premises of an undertaker. Here, David hears the 'Rat-tat-tat. Rat-tat-tat' of the men making his mother's coffin.

GREENWICH, LONDON — In *Our Mutual Friend* Bella Wilfer dines with her father at the Ship Tavern in Greenwich:

> …the little room overlooking the river into which they were shown for dinner was delightful. Everything was delightful. The park was delightful, the punch was delightful, the dishes of fish were delightful, the wine was delightful. Bella was more delightful than any other item in the festival…
>
> And then, as they sat looking at the ships and steamboats making their way to the sea with the tide that was running down, the lovely woman imagined all sorts of voyages for herself and Pa.

It is at The Ship (now gone, site occupied by the dry-dock which later housed the

The Ship Inn, now the site of the Cutty Sark.

famous tea clipper Cutty Sark) that Bella celebrates her marriage to John Rokesmith:

> the marriage dinner was the crowning success, for what had bride and bridegroom plotted to do, but to have and to hold that dinner in the very room of the very hotel where Pa and the lovely woman had once dined together! Bella sat between Pa and John, and divided her attentions pretty equally, but felt it necessary (in the waiter's absence before dinner) to remind Pa that she was his lovely woman no longer.

The wedding ceremony had taken place in Greenwich Church:

> the church porch, having swallowed up Bella Wilfer for ever and ever, had it not in its power to relinquish that young woman, but slid into the happy sunlight, Mrs John Rokesmith instead.

In the essay 'Greenwich Fair' in *Sketches by Boz* Dickens admits: 'In our earlier days we were a frequenter of Greenwich Fair.' In *David Copperfield* a servant of Dora and David, 'a young person of genteel appearance … went to Greenwich Fair in Dora's bonnet'.

Dickens remained an admirer of Greenwich and often dined on whitebait there, either at the Ship Tavern or at the Trafalgar Inn.

GRETA BRIDGE, NORTH YORKSHIRE — During his trip to Yorkshire in the winter of

1838 Dickens stayed – with Hablot Knight Browne – for one night at the George and New Inn, Greta Bridge (see also BARNARD CASTLE, BOWES and GRANTHAM).

GROSVENOR SQUARE, LONDON — In *Little Dorrit* the home of Tite Barnacle, of the Circumlocution Office, is situated at 24 Mews Street, Grosvenor Square:

> It was a hideous little street of dead wall, stables, and dunghills, with lofts over coach-houses inhabited by coachmen's families, who had a passion for drying clothes and decorating their window-sills with miniature turnpike-gates …

The house was:

> a squeezed house, a ramshackle bowed front, little dingy windows, and a little damp area like a damp waistcoat-pocket.
> … To the sense of smell, the house was like a sort of bottle filled with a strong distillation of mews, and when the footman opened the door, he seemed to take the stopper out.

In *Barnaby Rudge* Lord Rockingham's house in Grosvenor Square was among several blockaded by the army against the Gordon Rioters.

GUILDFORD, SURREY — Prior to meeting with Nicholas and Smike in *Nicholas Nickleby*, Vincent Crummles and his travelling theatrical company had fulfilled 'an engagement at Guildford with the greatest applause'.

In *David Copperfield* David and Dora picnic somewhere 'near Guildford', although David has difficulty in recalling the geography of the area:

> it was all Dora to me. The sun shone Dora, and the birds sang Dora. The south wind blew Dora, and the wild flowers in the hedges were all Dora, to a bud.

GUILDHALL, LONDON — On 'the eventful morning of the fourteenth of February' the Pickwickians, and the lawyer Perker, repair to the Guildhall Court (partly rebuilt) in King Street, where the case of Bardell v Pickwick was due to be heard.

Unfortunately for Mr Pickwick, the performance of Mr Winkle, as a witness on his behalf, proves so inept that it effectively seals the case against him: he is charged with costs of £750 which he steadfastly refuses to pay.

'The Trial' in *The Pickwick Papers* became a favourite passage with Dickens's readers and would later provide the author with one of the most popular pieces in his Public Reading repertoire. The carved figures of Gog and Magog – the City Giants – at the west end of the Great Hall, were 'overheard' by Joe Toddyhigh in *Master Humphrey's Clock*.

> He was very much astonished, when he approached the gallery again to see a light in the building ... But how much greater yet was his astonishment at the spectacle which this light revealed.
>
> The statues of the two giants, Gog and Magog, each above fourteen feet in height ... were endowed with life and motion. These guardian genii of the City had quitted their pedestals, and reclined in easy attitudes in the great stained-glass window. Between them was an ancient cask, which seemed to be full of wine; for the younger Giant, clapping his huge hand upon it, and throwing up his mighty leg, burst into an exulting laugh, which reverberated through the hall like thunder.

These famous 18th-century carvings were destroyed during a bombing raid in World War II and were replaced in 1953.

H

HAMMERSMITH, LONDON — In *Oliver Twist*, Sikes and Oliver pass through Hammersmith en route to CHERTSEY. The family home of the Pockets in *Great Expectations* is situated by the river in Hammersmith. In the same novel Estella is 'completing her education at an establishment in Hammersmith'. In *Nicholas Nickleby* we learn that Miss Browdock – Nicholas's father's cousin's sister-in-law – 'was taken into partnership by a lady that kept a school in Hammersmith'.

HAMPSTEAD, LONDON — Following the sudden death of his beloved sister-in-law Mary Hogarth in May 1837, Dickens took his wife and his firstborn son, Charley, to stay in mourning at Wylde's Farm on Hampstead Heath, where they remained for some weeks until he felt able to settle once more to his work.

One of Mr Pickwick's earliest claims to fame was as 'the man who had traced to their source the mighty ponds of Hampstead'. Later in *The Pickwick Papers* and while enjoying an afternoon in the tea-garden of the Spaniard Inn, on the Heath, Mrs Bardell is tracked down by Mr Jackson, 'the young man from Dodson and Fogg's', who proceeds to remind her that she is liable for the unpaid costs in the case of Bardell v Pickwick. Jackson arrests the lady and transports her to the Fleet Prison (see also FARRINGDON STREET].

The Spaniards (pluralized in later years) was well known to Dickens and the building still remains – tea-garden intact – much as it was in his day.

Another Hampstead inn, Jack Straw's Castle (now residential flats), was also a great favourite of the author's. During the writing of *Oliver Twist* he wrote to John Forster with Jack Straw's in mind:

> You don't feel disposed, do you, to muffle yourself up, and start off with me for a

The Spaniards Inn, Hampstead Heath.

good brisk walk over Hampstead Heath? I knows a good 'ouse there where we can have a red-hot chop for dinner, and a glass of good wine.

Throughout their lifelong friendship, the two men would often meet at this inn.

In *Oliver Twist* we see Bill Sikes, having murdered Nancy, skirting Caen Wood (now Ken Wood) and Hampstead Heath on his desperate flight out of London. In *The Old Curiosity Shop*, Dick Swiveller, when married to the Marchioness, occupies: 'A little cottage in Hampstead . . . which had in its garden a smoking-box.' In *Barnaby Rudge*, the Gordon Rioters were bent upon destroying the country seat of Lord Mansfield at Caen Wood:

and lighting a great fire there, which from that height should be seen all over London. But, in this, they were disappointed, for a party of horse having arrived before them they retreated faster than they went, and came straight back to town.

In a fit of depression, *David Copperfield* walks to Hampstead – following a plunge into the Roman Bath in Strand Lane (see also STRAND) – and there takes his breakfast on the Heath.

HAMPSTEAD ROAD, LONDON — When, at last, Charles Dickens's days in Warren's Warehouse (see also STRAND and COVENT GARDEN) were terminated, at his father's insistence, the boy was sent to collect a card-of-terms from the Wellington House Classical and Commercial Academy in Hampstead Road. In the spring of 1825 he became a day pupil at this school.

The establishment was run by one William Jones – known locally as a bullying, sadistic headmaster. But even Jones's presence did little to discourage young Dickens, for whom the metamorphosis from labouring urchin to smart young schoolboy was well suited. His nimble mind quickly grasped the Latin, History and Mathematics offered by the Academy, and he wrote several short stories (now lost) for the school's newspaper.

In the playground and streets, too, he became a normal schoolboy, full of normal schoolboy pranks. He indulged in a secret 'lingo' with his pals, and kept white mice and other pets which the boys 'trained better than the masters trained the boys'. He once led a mass impersonation of 'beggar boys', stopping old ladies in the street and asking for alms (an act which he might have considered to be in unthinkably bad taste just a few months earlier). In short, Charles Dickens was happy at Wellington House and remained there for a little over two years.

The Academy, which stood at the corner of Hampstead Road and Granby Terrace, was eventually demolished in order to make way for the London and North-Western Railway out of Euston Station.

In the essay 'Our School' in *Reprinted Pieces* Dickens describes a visit to the school after the railway had arrived:

The coming of the railways to London is a recurrent theme in Dickens's novels.

A great trunk-line had swallowed the playground, sliced away the schoolroom, and pared off the corner of the house: which, thus curtailed of its proportions, presented itself, in a green stage of stucco, profile-wise towards the road, like a forlorn flat-iron without a handle, standing on end.

The building and Dickens's days there undoubtedly provided some inspiration for the Salem House school in *David Copperfield*, albeit removed to BLACKHEATH.

George Cruickshank, illustrator of *Sketches by Boz* and *Oliver Twist*, lived at

263 Hampstead Road, a fact now commemorated by a plaque.

HAMPTON, MIDDLESEX — In *Little Dorrit* Mrs Gowan lives in 'certain shady and sedate apartments in the Palace at Hampton Court.' Her son Henry, however, considers that she lives 'in the most primitive fashion down in that dreary red brick dungeon at Hampton Court'.

In *Oliver Twist* the small town of Hampton is passed through by Oliver and Bill Sikes en route to 'crack the crib' at CHERTSEY. In *Nicholas Nickleby* the fatal quarrel between Lord Verisopht and Sir Mulberry Hawk begins at Hampton Racecourse (now gone). In *Our Mutual Friend* Mortimer Lightwood and Eugene Wrayburn share a cottage near Hampton.

HARLEY STREET, LONDON — In *Little Dorrit* the ill-fated Mr Merdle lives with his family in what Fanny Dorrit considers 'the handsomest house' in Harley Street. Later, however, we learn the author's true opinion of this house and its neighbours:

Like unexceptional Society, the opposing rows of houses in Harley Street were very grim with one another. Indeed, the mansions and their inhabitants were so much alike in that respect, that the people were often to be found drawn up on opposite sides of dinner-tables, in the shade of their own loftiness, staring at the other side of the way with the dullness of the houses.

HATFIELD, HERTFORDSHIRE — In *Oliver Twist* Bill Sikes, in flight from London following his murder of Nancy, 'shaped his course for Hatfield'. There he:

turned down the hill by the church of the quiet village and, plodding along the little street, crept into a small public house, whose scanty light had guided them there. There was a fire in the taproom, and some country-labourers were drinking before it. They made room for the stranger, but he sat down in the furthest corner and ate alone.

The Eight Bells was Dickens's most likely original for this inn. While in Hatfield, Sikes watches the arrival of the stagecoach from London, whose passengers carry news of the murder 'down Spitalfields way'. He also assists in the fighting of a fire which has broken out at a large house in the district. Dickens was in fact remembering the fire of 1835 at Hatfield House.

The Christmas story 'Mrs Lirriper's Legacy' sees Mrs Lirriper recalling her honeymoon at the Salisbury Arms. Her husband is buried in Hatfield Churchyard.

HATTON GARDEN, LONDON — Having been wrongfully arrested as 'a young fogle-hunter' (a pickpocket specializing in silk handkerchiefs), Oliver Twist was led towards:

a very notorious metropolitan police office. The crowd had only the satisfaction of accompanying Oliver through two or three streets, and down a place called Mutton Hill, when he was led beneath a low archway, and up a dirty court, into this dispensary of summary justice, by the back way.

Once inside, Oliver is brought before the magistrate Fang – 'the reknowned Mr Fang':

The office was a front parlour, with a panelled wall. Mr Fang sat behind a bar, at the upper end; and on one side the door was a sort of wooden pen in which poor little Oliver was already deposited, trembling very much at the awfulness of the scene.

(Dickens based the character of Fang on a real-life magistrate, one A. S. Laing, and the 'dispensary of summary justice' was modelled on the Police Court, at 54 Hatton Garden.)

Thankfully, the book-shop owner has witnessed the pick-pocketing by Dawkins and Bates and is able to vouchsafe Oliver's innocence. The boy is then taken into the care of Mr Brownlow. Later in *Oliver Twist*, Nancy is despatched to Hatton Garden by Fagin in search of Oliver.

In *Bleak House*, the Jellyby family once lived 'in furnished lodgings in Hatton Garden'. Mr Jellyby:

feeling that he was in the way, went out and walked about Hatton Garden in the wet. The poor children scrambled up and tumbled down the house, as they had always been accustomed to do.

HAYMARKET, LONDON — In May 1848 Dickens played as Justice Shallow in eight performances of *The Merry Wives of Windsor* at the Theatre Royal Haymarket in aid of the fund to preserve William Shakespeare's birthplace at STRATFORD-UPON-AVON. One of these charity performances was viewed by Queen Victoria and Prince Albert.

Certain 'dark-complexioned men . . . who congregrate under the opera colonnade, and about the box-office in the season' are mentioned in *Nicholas Nickleby*.

The Theatre Royal Haymarket, where Dickens acted in 1848.

In *Bleak House*, Prince, son of Mr Turveydrop, advises his father to 'dine out comfortably, somewhere', to which Turveydrop senior replies: 'My dear child, I intend to. I shall take my little meal, I think, at the French house, in the Opera Colonnade.'

The Opera Colonnade is now the Royal Opera Arcade.

HENLEY-ON-THAMES, OXFORDSHIRE — Marsh Mill, half a mile above Henley on the river Thames, is the most likely original for Paper Mill where Lizzie Hexam found employment, and near which Betty Higden died, in *Our Mutual Friend*. The attempted murder of Eugene Wrayburn by Bradley Headstone took place on the tow-path between Henley and Marsh Mill. The Anglers' Inn, where Wrayburn was staying and where he is later nursed by Lizzie Hexam was based upon the Red Lion Inn where, in 'a darkened and hushed room', this couple are eventually married.

HIGHGATE, LONDON — In *David Copperfield* Mrs Steerforth lives in 'an old brick house at Highgate on the summit of the hill'. Church House, in South Grove, is the most likely original of her home. Dr and Annie Strong later take a cottage in Highgate. 'But quite on the opposite side of the little town [to Mrs Steerforth's house] ... a pretty old place, on which he seemed to have expended some money.'

Whilst on a visit to Dr Strong's house David spots a cottage to let:

It would do for me and Dora admirably: with a little front garden for Jip to run about in, and bark at the tradespeople through the railings, and a capital room upstairs for my aunt.

Indeed it is here that the newlyweds later set up home. (Aunt Betsey Trotwood takes a small cottage close by.) And it is here that Dora Copperfield suffers her fatal illness.

In *The Pickwick Papers* Mr Pickwick undertakes some 'unwearied researches' in the vicinity of Highgate. In *Oliver Twist* Bill Sikes, in flight after the murder of Nancy 'strode up the hill at Highgate' en route to HATFIELD and ST ALBANS. In *Barnaby Rudge* Joe Willet, 'pondering on his unhappy lot' (his love affair with Dolly Varden has come to an end):

went out by Islington and Highgate, and sat on many stones and gates, but there were no voices in the bells to bid him turn. Since the time of noble Whittington, fair flower of merchants, bells have come to have less sympathy with humankind.

In *Bleak House* Inspector Bucket and Esther Summerson first pick up the trail of Lady Dedlock at Highgate. Bucket says 'I heard of her first at the Archway toll, over at Highgate, but couldn't make quite sure'.

Dickens's parents, John and Elizabeth, are both buried in Highgate Cemetery, as is his ninth child, Dora Annie Dickens (1850–1851) and his elder sister, Fanny (1810–1848).

HOLBORN, LONDON — In *The Pickwick Papers* Job Trotter, on his way to visit the lawyer Mr Perker with some important news from Pickwick:

> ran up Holborn, sometimes in the middle of the road, sometimes on the pavement, and sometimes in the gutter, as the chances of getting along varies with the press of men, women, children and coaches, in each division of the thoroughfare, and, regardless of all obstacles, stopped not for an instant until he reached the gate of Gray's Inn.

In *Oliver Twist* Bill Sikes, glancing up at the clock of St Andrew's church – which shows the time 'hard upon seven', urges the young Oliver to 'step out' as they make their way towards CHERTSEY.

In *Barnaby Rudge* the Holborn distillery owned by Mr Langdale is burned down during the Gordon Riots. In *Little Dorrit* Mr Plornish sorts out Tip Dorrit's problems in 'a stable-yard in High Holborn'.

Sairey Gamp of *Martin Chuzzlewit* fame, arguably Dickens's finest female creation, lived in Kingsgate Street (demolished 1902), off High Holborn:

> This lady lodged above a bird-fancier's, next door but one to the celebrated mutton-pie shop, and directly opposite to the original cat's meat warehouse, the renown of which establishments was duly heralded on their respective fronts. It was a little house, and this was the more convenient, for Mrs Gamp being, in her highest walk of art, a monthly nurse, or, as her signboard boldly had it, 'Midwife', and lodging in the first-floor-front, was easily assailable at night by pebbles, walking-sticks, and fragments of tobacco pipe – all much more efficacious than the street door knocker, which was so constructed as to wake the street with ease, and even spread alarms of fire to Holborn, without making the smallest impression on the premises to which it was addressed.

In *Bleak House* Mr Snagsby tells his apprentices of a time when 'a brook "as clear as crystal" once ran down the middle of Holborn, when Turnstile really was a turnstile, leading slap way into meadows'. Today Great Turnstile is a narrow passageway between Holborn and LINCOLN'S INN.

HOLLOWAY, LONDON — In *Our Mutual Friend* the impoverished Wilfer family live 'in the Holloway region of North London'. Here Mrs Wilfer 'a tall woman and angular' attempted, like Dickens's own mother (see also GOWER STREET), to make a success of running a school. However, like that of Mrs Wilfer's real-life counterpart, the venture failed, and Mrs Wilfer notices something amiss with the front door-plate.

> 'Yes,' said Mrs Wilfer, 'the man came himself with a pair of pincers, and took it off, and took it away. He said that as he had no expectation of ever being paid for

it, and as he had an order for another LADIES' SCHOOL door-plate, it was better (burnished-up) for the interests of all parties.'

HORNSEY, LONDON — In *David Copperfield* the 'late' Mr Trotwood, husband of Aunt Betsey is both born and, eventually, buried in Hornsey.

HORSE GUARDS PARADE, LONDON — In *Martin Chuzzlewit* Mark Tapley apologises for 'remarking that the clock at Horse Guards was striking', during the meeting between his master Martin Chuzzlewit and Mary Graham in nearby ST JAMES'S PARK.

In *Barnaby Rudge* Sam Tappertit, having lost his legs, is 'established in a business as a shoeblack, and opened a shop under the archway near Horse Guards'.

THE HOUSES OF PARLIAMENT, LONDON — By February 1832 John Dickens was working as a reporter for the *Mirror of Parliament*, a newspaper owned by his brother-in-law, John Henry Barrow. Barrow, greatly impressed with Charles's growing reputation at DOCTORS' COMMONS, invited him also to join the *Mirror*'s reporting staff.

And so it was, shortly after his twentieth birthday, that Charles Dickens found himself working in the Gallery of the House of Commons. A few weeks later his income was further improved when a radical new evening paper, the *True Sun*, also invited him to contribute parliamentary reports to its pages.

A reporter's life inside the old Palace of Westminster was far from comfortable, their quarters being invariably cramped and over-crowded. He later wrote of this time:

Horse Guards Parade, featured in *Barnaby Rudge* and *Martin Chuzzlewit*.

I have worn my knees by writing on them in the old Gallery of the Old House of Commons; and I have worn my feet by standing to write in a preposterous pen in the Old House of Lords.

Despite the conditions he soon became, as his fellow scribe Tom Beard later testified, 'a first class reporter'. Indeed, Dickens quickly made his name in the Gallery and was soon well known for his accuracy and his speed of transcription – just as he had been at Doctors' Commons. When the Chief Secretary, Edward Stanley, addressed the House during the reading of the Irish Coercion Bill, he spoke for so long that all eight members of the *Mirror of Parliament*'s reporting staff worked a shift system to record his outpourings, Dickens working the first and the last of these shifts. When that edition of the *Mirror* was published, Stanley read through the entire speech and found only the first and last parts recorded precisely as he had spoken them. He asked to meet the reporter who had so painstakingly recorded his every syllable, and was shocked to see so young a man when Dickens was brought before him.

Dickens was to remain a parliamentary reporter until 1836 by which time he was a successful author (a course in life later shared by David Copperfield).

The Houses of Parliament were burned to the ground in 1834 following a fire which had started in a storeroom. Both the old House of Lords and the old House of Commons were completely destroyed (later

Westminster Hall, part of the original Palace of Westminster which Dickens knew as a parliamentary reporter.

rebuilt). However, Westminster Hall, the oldest part of the original Palace, did survive.

Following the publication of his first fictional piece 'A Dinner at Poplar Walk' in the *Monthly Magazine* for December 1833, the proud Dickens spent half an hour in the peace and quiet of Westminster Hall 'because my eyes were so dimmed with joy and pride that they could not bear the street, and were not fit to be seen there' (see also FLEET STREET and STRAND).

The Houses of Parliament appear in several of the novels: in *Barnaby Rudge*

Lord George Gordon presents his No Popery petition of 1778 there, an event witnessed by Geoffrey Haredale who had entered to find:

> There were many little knots and groups of persons in Westminster Hall: some few looking upward at its noble ceiling and at the rays of evening light, tinted by the setting sun, which streamed aslant through its small windows, and growing dimmer by degrees, were quenched in the gathering gloom below.

In *Martin Chuzzlewit* we learn: 'There was unquestionably a Chuzzlewit in the Gunpowder Plot, if indeed the arch traitor, Fawkes himself, were not a scion of this remarkable stock.' In *Bleak House* the interminable chancery court case of Jarndyce v Jarndyce eventually breaks down in Westminster Hall. In *Our Mutual Friend* Mr Twemlow considers the House of Commons to be 'the best club in London'.

Hurley Lock, Berkshire — Hurley Lock provided Dickens with his original for Plashwater Weir-Mill Lock in *Our Mutual Friend*:

> Plashwater Weir-Mill Lock looked tranquil and pretty on an evening in the summer time. A soft air stirred the leaves of the fresh green trees, and passed like a smooth shadow over the river, and like a smoother shadow over the yielding grass. The voice of the falling water, like the voice of the sea and the wind, was an outer memory to a contemplative listener; but not particularly to Mr Riderhood, who sat on one of the blunt wooden levers of his lock-gates dozing.

Into this scene sails the light boat carrying Eugene Wrayburn to see Lizzie Hexam at HENLEY:

> The creaking lock-gates opened slowly, and the light boat passed in as soon as there was room enough, and the creaking lock-gates closed upon it, and it floated low down in the dock between the two sets of gates, until the water should rise and the second gates should open and let it out.

Wrayburn is in turn followed by Bradley Headstone, a course which eventually leads Headstone into direct confrontation with Rogue Riderhood. Their final part in the story takes place at the edge of the lock:

> Bradley had caught him round the body. He seemed to be girdled with an iron ring. They were on the brink of the Lock, about midway between the two sets of gates.
>
> 'Let go!' said Riderhood, 'or I'll get my knife out and slash you wherever I can cut you. Let go!'
>
> Bradley was drawing to the Lock-edge. Riderhood was drawing away from it. It was a strong grapple and a fierce struggle, arm and leg. Bradley got him round, with his back to the Lock, and still worked him backwards.

'Let go!' said Riderhood. 'Stop! What are you trying at? You can't drown me. Ain't I told you that the man as has come through drowning can never be drowned? I can't be drowned.'

'I can be!' returned Bradley, in a desperate clenched voice. 'I am resolved to be. I'll hold you living, and I'll hold you dead. Come down!'

Riderhood went over into the smooth pit, backward, and Bradley Headstone upon him. When the two were found, lying under the ooze and scum behind one of the rotting gates, Riderhood's hold had relaxed, probably in falling, and his eyes were staring upward. But he was girdled still with Bradley's iron ring, and the rivets of the iron ring held tight.

IPSWICH, SUFFOLK — In *The Pickwick Papers*, Samuel Pickwick and Sam Weller travel to Ipswich, where they put up at The Great White Horse Hotel, which is to be found in Tavern Street:

> on the left-hand side of the way, a short distance after you have passed through the open space fronting the Town Hall.

Dickens had stayed here for three weeks in 1835 and he is less than glowing in his praise of the establishment in *The Pickwick Papers*, in which the hotel is:

The Pickwickians arrive at The Great White Horse Hotel, Ipswich.

rendered the more conspicuous by a stone statue of some rampacious animal with flowing mane and tail, distantly resembling an insane cart-horse, which is elevated above the principal door. The Great White Horse is famous in the neighbourhood, in the same degree as a prize ox, or county-paper-chronicled turnip, or unwieldy pig – for its enormous size. Never were such labyrinths of uncarpeted passages, such huge numbers of small dens for eating or sleeping in, beneath any one roof, as are collected together between the four walls of the Great White Horse at Ipswich.

When Mr Pickwick enquires if Messrs Tupman, Snodgrass and Winkle are at the hotel, a waiter answers bluntly 'No' on all three counts. The meal, 'a bit of fish and a steak', arrived 'after a lapse of an hour', while the port wine was of 'the worst possible standard' and the 'highest possible price'. One wonders just what the Great White Horse did to Dickens's sensibilities to warrant such a catalogue of anti-advertisement. Perhaps, during his stay, he had been involved in an episode similar to that endured by Mr Pickwick who, on his first night at the hotel, finds himself lost whilst in search of his pocket-watch:

The more stairs Mr Pickwick went down, the more stairs there seemed to be to descend, and again and again, when Mr Pickwick got into some narrow passage, and began to congratulate himself on having gained the ground floor, did another flight of stairs appear before his astonished eyes … Passage after passage did he explore; room after room did he peep into; at length, just as he was on the point of giving up the search in despair, he opened the door of the identical room in which he had spent the evening, and beheld his missing property on the table. … If his progress downwards had been attended with difficulties and uncertainty, his journey back was infinitely more perplexing. Rows of doors, garnished with boots of every shape, make, and size, branched off in every possible direction. A dozen times did he softly turn the handle of some bed-room door, which resembled his own, when a gruff cry from within of 'Who the devil's that?' or 'What do you want here?' caused him to steal away, on tiptoe, with a perfectly marvellous celerity. He was reduced to the verge of despair, when an open door attracted his attention. He peeped in – right at last. There were two beds, whose situation he perfectly remembered, and the fire still burning. His candle, not a long one when he first received it, had flickered away in the drafts of air through which he had passed, and sunk into the socket, just as he closed the door after him. 'No matter,' said Mr Pickwick, 'I can undress myself just as well by the light of the fire.'

Unfortunately for Mr Pickwick, he has mistakenly entered the bed-chamber of a middle-aged lady – Miss Witherfield – who is wearing curl papers and preparing herself for a good night's slumber.

> 'Bless my soul,' thought Mr Pickwick, 'What a dreadful thing!' ... 'I never met with anything so awful as this' . . . 'Never. This is fearful'...
>
> ...'A Gentleman!' said the lady with a terrific scream.
>
> 'It's all over,' thought Mr Pickwick.
>
> 'A strange man!' shrieked the lady. Another instant and the house would be alarmed. Her garments rustled as she rushed towards the door.

Thankfully for Pickwick the house is not alarmed, and he ejects himself from the lady's room only to find that he is once again lost in the hotel's dim and labyrinthine corridors. He resigns himself to the fact that he must spend the night 'crouched in a little recess in the wall to wait for morning as philosophically as he might'. Fortunately Sam Weller discovers him and, endowed with a superior sense of direction, is able to lead his master back to his right and proper room.

Next morning, when details of Pickwick's nocturnal adventure come to light, Peter Magnus, suitor for the hand of Miss Witherfield, becomes threatening towards our hero; Pickwick responds by becoming more and more stubborn in his innocence of the matter. Miss Witherfield, meanwhile, imagines that the two gentlemen are about to fight a duel over her. She goes directly with this intelligence to

George Nupkins, the local magistrate:

> 'In Ipswich, ma'am! A duel in Ipswich!'
> ... 'Impossible ma'am; nothing of the kind can be contemplated in this town!'

Nupkins sends a division of special constables to deal with the matter: armed with an old sedan chair in which to arrest Pickwick and his newly arrived 'accomplice', Tracy Tupman. The specials, followed by Winkle and Snodgrass, carry their quarry through the crowded streets of Ipswich until they are halted by Sam Weller. A fracas ensues among the crowd, and Pickwick's head protrudes from the roof of the sedan chair; and 'in this order they reached the magistrate's house; the chairmen trotting, the prisoners following, Mr Pickwick orating and the crowd shouting'.

In fact, Nupkins's house turns out to be a green-gated dwelling in St Clement's Lane, from which Sam Weller had seen his arch-enemy Job Trotter emerging that very morning. During the course of Mr Pickwick's confrontation with Nupkins we learn that Henrietta, the magistrate's socially ambitious daughter, is the latest object of Alfred Jingle's amorous and avaricious designs. Much to Nupkins's embarrassment Pickwick and his friends are able to unmask Jingle's latest piece of villainy. When later confronted by Pickwick, Jingle audaciously brazens it out, safe in the knowledge that the embarrassed Nupkins family will carry the case against him no further. Once again Jingle and Trotter disappear into the night.

Sam Weller, meanwhile, has experienced true love for the first time, for Mary, the Nupkins's housemaid.

Ipswich is also mentioned in *David Copperfield*. On the day of the storm at sea, which kills Ham and Steerforth, David Copperfield is travelling by stagecoach between London and great Yarmouth.

> When the day broke, it blew harder and harder. I had been in Yarmouth when the seamen said it blew great guns, but I had never known the like of this, or anything approaching it. We came to Ipswich – very late, having had to fight every inch of ground since we were ten miles out of London; and found a cluster of people in the market-place, who had risen from their beds in the night, fearful of falling chimneys. Some of these, congregating about the inn-yard while we changed horses, told us of great sheets of lead having been ripped off a high church-tower, and flung into a by-street, which they then blocked up. Others had to tell of country people, coming in from neighbouring villages, who had seen great trees lying torn out of the earth, and whole ricks scattered about the roads and fields. Still, there was no abatement in the storm, but it blew harder.

The inn-yard mentioned in the above passage was in all probability that of the Great White Horse.

Dickens gave three of his famous Public Readings in Ipswich, the first in October 1859 in the Mechanics' Institute Hall. October 1861 saw him at the Public Hall – this was also the venue on his Farewell Tour in March 1869.

ISLE OF WIGHT — In June 1849 Dickens wrote to his wife from Shanklin, Isle of Wight:

> I have taken a most delightful and beautiful house belonging to White [his friend the Rev. James White] at Bonchurch; cool, airy, private bathing, everything delicious. I think it is the prettiest place I ever saw in my life, at home or abroad. Anne may begin to dismantle Devonshire Terrace. I have arranged for carriages, luggage, and everything.
>
> P.S. A waterfall in the grounds, which I have arranged with a carpenter to convert into a perpetual shower-bath.

Dickens's plan was to make this house, Winterbourne at Bonchurch, an alternative holiday spot to BROADSTAIRS, with which he had long been familiar.

As the holiday at Winterbourne progressed, Dickens grew more and more distressed; the island's climate did not agree with him, nor he with it:

> Of all the places I have ever been in, I have never been in one so difficult to exist in, pleasantly. Naples is hot and

Shanklin on the Isle of Wight, where the Lammles honeymooned in *Our Mutual Friend*.

dirty, New York feverish, Washington bilious, Genoa exciting, Paris rainy – but Bonchurch smashing. I am quite convinced that I should die here, in a year. It's not hot, it's not close. I don't know what it is, but the prostration of it is awful … For me, when I leave here at the end of this September, I must go down to some cold place; as Ramsgate for example, for a week or two; or I seriously believe I shall feel the effects of it for a long time.

In October the family were back in the familiar territory of Broadstairs.

Vincent Crummles's theatrical troup spent a week in Ryde in *Nicholas Nickleby*. In the same novel Mr Lillyvick and Miss Petowker spent their brief honeymoon there – accompanied by the 'infant phenomenon', a 'travelling bridesmaid'.

Another Dickensian honeymoon took place on the Isle of Wight – that of the Lammles in *Our Mutual Friend*. They spent two weeks in Shanklin, with unhappy results:

Mr and Mrs Lammle have walked for some time on Shanklin sands, and one may see by their footprints that they have not walked arm in arm, and they have not walked in a straight track, and that they have walked in a moody humour; for, the lady has prodded little spiriting holes in the damp sand before her with a parasol, and the gentleman has trailed his stick after him. As if he were of the Mephistopholes family indeed, and had walked with a drooping tail.

Dickens took the name of Mr Dick in *David Copperfield* from an inhabitant of Bonchurch (he wrote part of that novel here in 1849); and local legend has it that the character of Miss Havisham was also inspired by a local lady, who, jilted at the altar, had kept her wedding breakfast untouched until it crumbled to dust (see also OXFORD STREET).

ISLINGTON, LONDON — Robert Seymour, the first illustrator of *The Pickwick Papers*, lived in Islington. It was here that he committed suicide in April 1836.

The district, being at the end of the Great North Road, is passed through by several of Dickens's travellers. In *Nicholas Nickleby*, the northbound coach stops at the Peacock Inn (now gone) while later a southbound coach carrying Mr and Mrs John Browdie:

> traversed, with cheerful noise, the yet silent streets of Islington, and, giving brisk note of its approach with the lively winding of the guard's horn, clattered onwards to its halting-place hard by the Post-office.

From here Browdie catches his first sight of St Paul's Cathedral. 'There be Paul's church. 'Ecod, he be a soizable 'un, he be.'

In *Bleak House*, Esther Summerson and Inspector Bucket pass through Islington upon their return from ST ALBANS.

In *Martin Chuzzlewit* Tom and Ruth Pinch look for lodgings in Islington:

> 'It used to be called Merry Islington, once upon a time,' said Tom. 'Perhaps it's merry now; if so, it's all the better. Eh?'
> 'If it's not too dear,' said Tom's sister... After roaming up and down for hours looking at some scores of lodgings, they began to find it rather fatiguing, especially as they saw none which were at all adapted to their purpose. At length, however, in a singular old-fashioned house, up a blind street, they found two small bedrooms and a triangular parlour, which promised to suit them well enough.

This house is thought to have been in Terrett's Place, off Upper Street.

View of Upper Street, Islington, in 1830.

J

JACOB'S ISLAND, LONDON — Jacob's Island once lay a mile to the east of London Bridge on the south side of the River Thames. The area has long since been 'improved away' and now forms that part of Bermondsey bounded by Mill Street, Jacob Street and George Row. In the 1830s the island – so named because it was cut off at high tide by a stretch of water known as Folly Ditch - was a maze of narrow, muddy alleyways between grim tenement buildings and was described by Dickens as 'the filthiest, the strangest, the most extraordinary, of the many localities that are hidden in London, wholly unknown, even by name, to the great mass of its inhabitants.' Here, in 'an upper room of … a detached house of fair size, ruinous in other respects, but strongly defended at the door and window' was the home of Toby Crackit, where Bill Sikes decides to hide out whilst on the run following the murder of Nancy. Unfortunately for Sikes his ever-faithful dog, Bullseye, follows him and eventually gives him away. Sikes is accidentally hanged whilst attempting to lower himself on to the bed of Folly Ditch by means of a rope:

> At the very instant when he brought the loop over his head previous to slipping it beneath his arm-pits … the murderer, looking behind him on the roof, threw his arms above his head and uttered a yell of terror.
>
> 'The eyes again!' he cried in an unearthly screech.
>
> Staggering as if struck by lightning, he lost his balance and tumbled over the parapet. The noose was on his neck. It ran up with his weight, tight as a bowstring and swift as the arrow it speeds. He fell for five-and-thirty feet. There was a sudden jerk, a terrific convulsion of the limbs, and there he hung with the open knife clenched in his stiffening hand.

The widespread cholera epidemics of 1849 and 1866 were believed to have started in Jacob's Island.

K

KENILWORTH, WARWICKSHIRE — In *Dombey and Son*, Mr Dombey and Edith Granger visit 'the haunted ruins' of Kenilworth Castle on the day that he decides to propose to her.

Dickens had visited Kenilworth Castle with Hablot Knight Browne in October 1839. He considered making the town a summer resort, although he never did so.

KENNINGTON, LONDON — In *Bleak House*, William Guppy takes a house in Walcot Square, Kennington, a fact which he imparts to Esther Summerson when proposing marriage to her for a second time: 'I beg to lay the 'ouse in Walcot Square, the business and myself, before Miss Summerson.'

KENSINGTON, LONDON — Following his engagement to Catherine Hogarth in May 1835, Dickens decided to rent an apartment that would bring him nearer to his fiancée. He found 11 Selwood Place, Queen's Elm, South Kensington, just a short distance from the Hogarth family home in nearby York Place (now gone).

Despite efforts to find a sub-tenant for his FURNIVAL'S INN chambers, the move left Dickens with two rents to pay for the remainder of 1835. Bearing these expenses in mind – as well as those of his somewhat over-burdening family – Charles and Catherine decided to wait for an improvement in his financial standing before embarking on married life.

This improvement came, of course, with the writing of *The Pickwick Papers*, and the wedding subsequently took place on 2 April 1836 (see also CHELSEA).

In the essay 'Watkins Tottle' in *Sketches by Boz*, Tottle's friend Gabriel Parsons meets secretly with his future wife, Fanny, in Kensington Gardens. Kensington is also mentioned in *The Pickwick Papers* and *Oliver Twist*.

KING'S CROSS, LONDON —

I live over Maiden-lane way – out Holloway direction ... where I live ... is called The Bower. Boffin's Bower is the name Mrs Boffin christened it when we came into it as a property. If you should meet with anybody that don't know it by that name (which hardly anybody does), when you've nigh upon about a odd mile, or say and a quarter if you like, up Maiden-lane, Battle Bridge, ask for Harmony Jail, and you'll be put right.

Such were the directions given to Silas Wegg the ballad-monger, by Nicodemus Boffin, the 'Golden Dustman', in *Our Mutual Friend*. Boffin, in his Bower, presided over a golden dust heap, a heap of rubbish, refuse and junk from which he made his fortune.

Workers in a 19th-century London dustyard.

The King's Cross area now stands on what was once Battle Bridge, and Maiden-lane has become York Road. 'Boffin's Bower' was based by Dickens on a real dust-heap known as Mr Starkey's, which was situated a little to the north of the present King's Cross Station.

KINGSTON, SURREY — 'Which way?' asks Newman Noggs of Nicholas in *Nicholas Nickleby*, as he prepares to accompany him and Smike on the first leg of their journey out of London and away from the clutches of Wackford Squeers. 'To Kingston first,' replies Nicholas.

After a couple of hours on the road Nicholas turns Newman back towards London and then proclaims to Smike: 'We are bound for Portsmouth.'

There is no further mention in the novel of the two friends' trek through Kingston.

KNEBWORTH HOUSE, HERTFORDSHIRE — Dickens's good friend Sir Edward Bulwer-Lytton lived within the magnificent splendour of Knebworth House. Here, in 1850, the two men laid plans for the Guild of Literature and Art, a body devoted to the financial welfare of struggling and impoverished authors, of which Dickens later became Chairman. In fund-raising efforts on behalf of the Guild he acted in several performances of Jonson's *Every Man in his Humour* and Bulwer-Lytton's *Not so Bad as We Seem*. Unfortunately the Guild of Literature and Art was to prove something of a disappointment to its

founders, although both continued to support it for many years.

The author named his tenth child Edward Bulwer-Lytton Dickens in honour of his great friendship with the master of Knebworth House.

LAMBETH, LONDON — In *Nicholas Nickleby* Wackford Squeers pursues Peg Sliderskew after her robbery of the money-lender Arthur Gride. She is tracked down to 'an upper room of a mean house situated in an obscure street, or rather court, near Lambeth'.

LEADENHALL STREET, LONDON — Sol Gills's nautical instruments shop in *Dombey and Son* was based upon Norie and Wilson's establishment at 157 Leadenhall Street (now demolished) whose entrance was adorned by the wooden figure of a little Midshipman:

> Anywhere in the immediate vicinity there might be seen pictures of ships speeding away full sail to all parts of the world; outfitting warehouses ready to pack off anybody anywhere, fully equipped in half an hour; and little timber midshipmen in obsolete naval uniforms, eternally

employed outside the shop-doors of nautical instrument-makers in taking observations of the hackney coaches.

This particular wooden effigy later moved with Norie and Wilson to their new premises at 156 MINORIES, and is preserved in the Dickens House Museum. The offices of 'Dombey and Son' were also situated in the vicinity of Leadenhall Street.

The figure of the 'Little Midshipman', which once decorated a shop in Leadenhall Street.

Leadenhall Market (which has now been rebuilt) features in *Dombey and Son*, as the place where Captain Cuttle makes arrangement with 'a private watchman on duty there, to come and put up and take down the shutters of the Wooden Midshipman every night and morning'. Cuttle later proposes that 'the daughter of the elderly lady who usually sat under the blue umbrella in Leadenhall Market should, for prudential reasons and consideration of privacy, be superseded in the temporary discharge of the household duties [of the Wooden Midshipman] by someone who was not unknown to them, and in whom they could safely confide'.

In *The Pickwick Papers*, Sam Weller writes his 'walentine' to Mary whilst enjoying the hospitality of the Blue Boar Inn, whose origin was the Green Dragon in Bull's Head Passage, Leadenhall Market.

In *Nicholas Nickleby* Tim Linkinwater 'pooh-poohs' the idea of country living:

> ... 'don't tell me country!' (Bow was quite a rustic place to Tim), 'nonsense! What can you get in the country but new-laid eggs and flowers! I can buy new-laid eggs in Leadenhall market any morning before breakfast...'

LEAMINGTON, WARWICKSHIRE — In *Dombey and Son*, Mr Dombey and Major Bagstock travel by train to the spa town of Leamington. Mr Dombey, however, did not approve of this particular mode of travel:

> he carried monotony with him through the rushing landscape ... Away with a shriek, and a roar, and a rattle, from the town, burrowing among the dwellings of

men and making the streets hum ... through the fields, through the woods, through the corn, through the hay, through the chalk, through the clay, through the rock, among objects close at hand, and almost in the grasp, ever flying from the traveller, and a deceitful distance ever moving slowly with him; like as in the track of the remorseless monster, Death.

Having survived the rail-journey, Dombey and Bagstock put up at Copp's Royal Hotel (now demolished). Next day, en route to the pump room, the two gentlemen encounter Mrs Skewton, in her wheeled-chair, and Edith Granger, the woman who will eventually become Dombey's second wife.

Dickens had stayed at Copp's Royal Hotel with Hablot Knight Browne on 29 October 1838, and reported in a letter to his wife 'We found a roaring fire, and elegant dinner, a snug room and capital beds all ready for us at Leamington, after a very agreeable but very cold ride.'

He gave Public Readings in the town, at the Music Hall, in 1858 and in 1862.

LEICESTER SQUARE, LONDON — Following the completion of *The Pickwick Papers*, in October 1837, Dickens held a celebratory dinner at the Prince of Wales Tavern (now gone) in Leicester Place, north of Leicester Square.

A shop (now rebuilt) in Green Street (now Orange Street) laid claim to being Dickens's original for his Old Curiosity Shop.

In *Barnaby Rudge* the home of Sir George Saville stands in Leicester Field (now Leicester Square). In *Bleak House* Mr George's Shooting Gallery is situated in the vicinity of HAYMARKET and Leicester Square.

LIMEHOUSE, LONDON — Several times during the stay in CAMDEN TOWN Dickens's father took Charles to visit his godfather Christopher Huffam in Limehouse. Limehouse was then a thriving naval district where Huffam plied his trade as a ships' rigger; John Forster describes him as living in 'a substantial handsome sort of way' at 12 Church Row (now gone). Here young Charles would often perform something from his repertoire of comic

The Grapes, Limehouse, the original for the Six Jolly Fellowship Porters in *Our Mutual Friend*.

Lizzie Hexam looking for her father in *Our Mutual Friend*.

songs learnt in Chatham, and the delighted Huffam proclaimed him, prophetically enough, a 'prodigy'.

Limehouse most probably appears in *Dombey and Son* as the location of Brig Place where Captain Cuttle lodged at No. 9 (the home of Mrs MacStinger) and of his meeting with Jack Bunsby who is on his way to marry Mrs MacStinger.

In *Our Mutual Friend* the Hexam family live in Limehouse Hole:

> 'Here's my father's sir; where the light is.' The low building had a look of once having been a mill. There was a rotten

wart of wood upon its forehead that seemed to indicate where the sails had been, but the whole was very indistinctly seen in the obscurity of the night.

In the same book Rogue Riderhood 'dwelt deep and dark in Limehouse Hole'; while Dickens modelled the Six Jolly Fellowship Porters Tavern on the Grapes Inn, Narrow Street. This was:

> a tavern of dropsical appearance ... long settled down into a state of hale infirmity. In its whole constitution it had not a straight floor, and hardly a straight line;

but it had outlasted, and clearly would outlast, many a better-trimmed building, many a sprucer public-house.

Dickens was entirely correct in the latter assumption, for the inn survives and still boasts:

> a bar to soften the human breast. The available space in it was not much larger than a Hackney-coach; but no one could have wished the bar bigger.

Abbey Potterson, landlady of the 'Porters', was christened at Limehouse church. In *The Uncommercial Traveller* Dickens describes the leadmills once situated near the church.

LINCOLN'S INN, LONDON — The Chancery court case of Jarndyce v Jarndyce – which forms the central core of *Bleak House* – 'drones on' within the Old Hall of Lincoln's Inn, a building we first discover in the dense, swirling fog at the opening of the novel:

> ...at the very heart of the fog, sits the Lord High Chancellor in his High Court of Chancery.
>
> Never can there come fog too thick, never can there come mud and mire too deep, to assort with the groping and floundering conditions which this High Court of Chancery, most pestilent of hoary sinners, holds, this day, in the sight of heaven and earth.

In the same novel the offices of the solicitors Kenge and Carboy are situated in Old Square, Lincoln's Inn (the same square also provided the office of Sergeant Snubbin in *The Pickwick Papers*). Mr Krook's rag and bottle shop in *Bleak House* is situated in nearby Chichester Rents; Miss Flite lodges at the top of this house 'in a pretty large room from which she had a glimpse of the roof of Lincoln's Inn Hall'. This 'little, mad old woman' often enjoys the garden of Lincoln's Inn 'in contemplation'.

Dickens's good friend and first biographer John Forster lived at 58 Lincoln's Inn Fields; this fine house became the home of Mr Tulkinghorn – legal adviser to Sir Leicester Dedlock and later blackmailer to Lady Dedlock – in *Bleak House*:

> The crow flies straight across Chancery Lane and Lincoln's Inn Garden, into Lincoln's Inn Fields.
>
> Here, in a large house, formerly a house of state, lives Mr Tulkinghorn. It is let off in sets of chambers now, and in these shrunken fragments of its greatness lawyers lie like maggots in nuts.

It was in John Forster's house on 2 December 1844 that Dickens first read his new Christmas story *The Chimes* to distinguished company, including Thomas Carlyle, Daniel Maclise, and Douglas Jerrold. The story was subsequently published to enormous success.

In *David Copperfield*, Aunt Betsey Trotwood stays 'at a kind of private hotel in Lincoln's Inn Fields'. This building was chosen by her because of its stone staircase and its 'convenient door in the roof', both admirable precautions in case of fire.

LITTLE PORTLAND STREET, LONDON

— Having become interested in Unitarian doctrine on his visit to America in 1842 (see also LIVERPOOL and STRAND), Dickens attended a sermon delivered by Dr Channing on 20 November 1842 at the Little Portland Street Chapel (now gone). He later became a seat-holder at this chapel.

LIVERPOOL, MERSEYSIDE — Dickens

first visited Liverpool following his tour of North Wales with Hablot Knight Browne in 1838. They met up with John Forster at the Adelphi Hotel, where they stayed overnight before travelling on to Manchester. Dickens's diary for Tuesday 6 November 1838 records: 'Bill for Adelphi £4. 10s. 9d.'

Following the comparative failure of *Barnaby Rudge* and the subsequent closure of *Master Humphrey's Clock* in November 1841, Dickens paused to consider his career. He had been writing virtually non-stop for the past six years and, until now, had known nothing but success. He decided that a rest from the writing desk might provide the antidote, and that travel might broaden his imaginative horizon. Having made suitable arrangements with Chapman and Hall for the publication of

his next work, Dickens planned to visit America. He had long been 'haunted by visions of the New World', and he looked forward to seeing at first hand many of the enlightened institutions – prisons, asylums, etc. – of the West and reporting his findings back to their grim English counterparts. In a letter from New York the author Washington Irving assured Charles Dickens that his visit 'would be a triumph ... from one end of the States to the other'.

On New Year's Day 1842 Charles and Catherine Dickens climbed aboard a Liverpool-bound train at Euston Station, en route to America. They were accompanied on this, the first leg of their Great Western Adventure, by John Forster, who had helped to make the arrangements for the journey. They stayed for three nights at the Adelphi Hotel and there enjoyed a farewell dinner with Forster before setting sail on 4 January aboard the Cunard paddle-steamer *Britannia*. The promised stateroom on board turned out to be a tiny cabin. Dickens wrote of it to his friend, Thomas Mitton: 'Anything so utterly and monsterously absurd as the size of our cabin 'No gentlemen of England who lives at home at ease' can for a moment imagine. Neither of the portmanteaus would go into it…'.

Upon his return to England Dickens began to commit to paper his collected impressions and observations. When the resulting book was published in London it caused no great stir, but more than 50,000 pirated copies were sold within two days in New York alone.

Dickens delivers an address to the Liverpool Mechanics' Institute, 1844.

Liverpool was again Dickens's embarkation point for his second trip to America in November 1867. This time he occupied the second officer's cabin aboard the *SS Cuba*, yet still complained of its size, which was 'of such vast proportions that it is almost large enough to sneeze in'. He arrived back in England in the spring, on 1 May 1868.

Dickens gave several of his Public Readings in Liverpool, and they were extremely popular; on one memorable occasion, in April 1866, more than 3000 people had to be turned away from the door of St George's Hall. The city appears briefly in *Martin Chuzzlewit* and its dockside haunts are described in the essay 'Poor Mercantile Jack' in *The Uncommercial Traveller*.

LOMBARD STREET, LONDON — In May 1830 the eighteen-year-old Dickens met a young woman named Maria Beadnell. She was the daughter of George Beadnell, manager of Smith, Payne and Smith's Bank at 1 Lombard Street in the City.

Maria was pretty and popular and Charles quickly found himself totally infatuated with her. Although the Beadnell family welcomed him into their home at 2 Lombard Street, they nevertheless could have felt that socially he was beneath them, and perhaps not the proper prospective husband for their daughter.

One day Dickens spotted Maria out in the street with her mother and her sisters. The keen young suitor politely accompanied the ladies to their destination, a dressmaker's shop in ST MARY AXE. In the shop doorway Mrs Beadnell turned to him and said 'And now, Mr Dickin, we'll wish you good morning'. (She never managed to learn his proper surname.)

Despite early encouragement from Maria and the eventual acceptance by her family, the day came when his feelings for her were no longer returned. He wrote her a passionate letter, but her reply was cold towards him and confirmed his worst fears, that their relationship must end. The liaison lasted a little over two years, but he would feel its hurtful reverberations for many years to come, until he was eventually able to exorcise its ghosts with his pen.

Dickens met Maria again – then Mrs Winter – in May 1855. He was disappointed to see what middle-age had done to his youthful ideal of girlhood: he found her dull and silly and she unwittingly became his model for the foolish but good-hearted Flora Finching in *Little Dorrit*.

In *The Pickwick Papers* Tony Weller, father of Sam:

> returned with a cheque on Smith, Payne and Smith, for five hundred and thirty pounds; that being the sum of money to which Mr Weller at the market price of the day, was entitled, in consideration of the balance of the second Mrs Weller's funded savings.

In *Little Dorrit* 'it was a rapturous dream to Mr Dorrit to find himself set aloft in this public car of triumph, making a magnificent progress to that benefiting destination, the golden street of Lombards'. The office of the Barbox brothers in the Christmas story *Mugby Junction* was situated in a 'dim den up a corner of a court off Lombard Street'. And, in *The Poor Relation's Story*, Little Frank and the Poor Relation often walked in Lombard Street.

Castle Court, a narrow passage near to Lombard Street, boasts a famous Dickensian location: 'very good, old-fashioned and comfortable quarters, to wit, the George and Vulture'. This charming old inn became Mr Pickwick's new headquarters following the law suit brought against him by Mrs Bardell (see also GOSWELL ROAD and CORNHILL). Thankfully, the George and Vulture survives and successfully retains a distinctly Dickensian atmosphere. The inn is approached from Lombard Street, via George Yard, and can also be reached from CORNHILL, via St Michael's Alley.

LONDON — Charles Dickens was an honorary cockney if ever there was one. George Lear, a fellow clerk with Dickens in the office of Ellis and Blackmore (see also GRAY'S INN), believed that he personally was very knowledgeable about the city and its environs: 'but after a little talk with Dickens, I found I knew nothing at all,' he later said. 'He knew it all from Brentford to Bow.'

LONDON BRIDGE — In *Oliver Twist*, the fateful nocturnal meeting between Nancy and Rose Maylie takes place on the steps of

London Bridge at the Surrey side:

> The church clock chimed three quarters
> past eleven as two figures emerged on
> London Bridge … It was a very dark
> night. The day had been unfavourable,
> and at that hour and place there were few
> people stirring … A mist hung over the
> river, deepening the red glare of fires that
> burnt upon the small craft moored off the
> different wharfs, and rendering darker
> and more indistinct the murky buildings
> on the banks. The old smoke-stained
> store-houses on either side rose heavy
> and dull from the dense mass of roofs and
> gables, and frowned sternly upon water
> too black to reflect even their lumbering
> shapes. The tower of old Saint Saviour's
> church, and the spire of Saint Magnus, so
> long the giant-warders of the ancient
> bridge, were visible in the gloom, but the
> forest of shipping below bridge, and the
> thickly scattered spires of churches above,
> were nearly all hidden from the sight.

Nancy warns Rose of Fagin's plans for
Oliver. Unfortunately she has been followed
by Noah Claypole, who reports the meeting
to Fagin and Sikes. This information leads
to Sikes's brutal murder of Nancy, one of
the most powerful scenes in all of Dickens.

Dickens knew two London Bridges in
his lifetime. Old London Bridge – which
features briefly in *Barnaby Rudge* and
David Copperfield – was replaced between
1824 and 1831 by the structure which
contained 'Nancy's Steps' on its southern

side. This bridge was shipped stone by
stone to Lake Havasu City, Arizona, in
1973 and was replaced in turn by the
present wider structure.

LONDON WALL, LONDON — In *Martin
Chuzzlewit* Tom Pinch finds himself lost
near London Wall while on a search for the
monument. In *Little Dorrit* Arthur
Clennam and Daniel Doyce 'shared a
portion of a roomy house in one of the grave
old fashioned City streets lying not far from
the Bank of England, by London Wall'.

LONG ACRE, LONDON — In *The Old
Curiosity Shop*, Dick Swiveller, used to
living on credit and false promises, is forced
to take:

> a greasy memorandum book from his
> pocket and made an entry therein.
> 'Is that a reminder, in case you should
> forget to call?' said Trent with a sneer.
> 'Not exactly, Fred,' replied the
> imperturbable Richard, continuing to
> write with a business-like air; 'I enter in
> this little book the names of the streets that
> I cannot go down while shops are open.
> This dinner today closes Long Acre…'

In the essay 'Brokers' and Marine-store
Shops' in *Sketches by Boz*, Dickens
describes Long Acre 'which is composed
almost entirely of brokers' shops'.

In 1858 Dickens gave his first series of
professional Public Readings at St Martin's
Hall (now gone) in Long Acre.

LOWESTOFT, SUFFOLK — It was at a hotel (probably the Royal Hotel) in Lowestoft that young David Copperfield first hears the name 'Brooks of Sheffield', as he listens to the following exchange:

> 'That's Davy,' returned Mr Murdstone.
> 'Davy who?' said the gentleman. 'Jones?'
> 'Copperfield,' said Mr Murdstone.
> 'What! Bewitching Mrs Copperfield's incumberance?' cried the gentleman. 'The pretty little widow?'
> 'Quinion,' said Mr Murdstone, 'take care if you please. Somebody's sharp.'
> 'Who is?' asked the gentleman, laughing.
> I looked up quickly, being curious to know.
> 'Only Brooks of Sheffield,' said Mr Murdstone.
> I was quite relieved to find that it was only Brooks of Sheffield, for at first I really thought it was I.

Mr Murdstone's allusion between the boy and 'Mr Brooks' was, in fact, towards a cutlery manufacturer in Sheffield.

LUDGATE HILL, LONDON — The Belle Sauvage, a coaching inn, once stood near the foot of Ludgate Hill (the inn was demolished in 1837). In *The Pickwick Papers* the twice-widowed Tony Weller declares to his son: 'I have come to the determination o' ... puttin' up vunce more at the Bell Savage vich is my nat'ral-born element, Sammy.'

In *Nicholas Nickleby* Smike dawdles up Ludgate Hill prior to his recapture by Wackford Squeers of Dotheboys Hall (see also BOWES). In *David Copperfield*, David and his Aunt Betsey are spied by Betsey's errant husband as they cross Ludgate Hill.

LUTON, BEDFORDSHIRE — In *Barnaby Rudge*, Barnaby and Mrs Rudge lived for five years in:

> a small English country town, the inhabitants of which supported themselves by the labour of their hands in plaiting and preparing straw for those who made bonnets.

The most likely location for the original of this town is the hatting-centre, Luton.

M

MAIDSTONE, KENT — Maidstone may have provided Dickens with his model for Muggleton in *The Pickwick Papers*, just a short distance from Dingley Dell (see also SANDLING and WEST MALLING).

MANCHESTER, GREATER MANCHESTER — The 'Coketown' of *Hard Times* is an amalgam of the Lancashire towns of PRESTON and Manchester:

It was a town of red brick, or of brick that would have been red if the smoke and ashes had allowed it … It was a town of machinery and tall chimneys, out of which the interminable serpents of smoke trailed themselves for ever and ever, and never got uncoiled. It had a black canal in it, and a river that ran purple with ill-smelling dye, and vast piles of buildings full of windows where there was a rattling and trembling all day long, and where the piston of the steam-engine worked monotonously up and down, like the head of an elephant in a state of melancholy madness. It contained several large streets still more like one another, inhabited by people equally like one another, who all went in and out at the same hours, with the same sound upon the same pavements, to do the same work, and to whom every day was the same as yesterday and tomorrow, and every year the counterpart of the last and next.

'Stone Lodge', home of Thomas Gradgrind, 'situated on a moor within a mile or two of a great town, called Coketown in the present faithful guidebook', has never been satisfactorily identified; neither has the home of Josiah Bounderby, 'A red house with black outside shutters, green inside blinds, a black street door up two white steps with "Bounderby" upon a brazen plate and a round brazen door underneath it, like a brazen full stop.' In truth, these houses were probably

imaginative constructions built by Dickens to suit the needs of the novel.

Dickens first visited Manchester in 1838, following a tour of North Wales with Hablot Knight Browne. During this trip he first met the philanthropic Grant brothers, William and Daniel, of the Stocks, Cheetham Hill, who provided the originals for the kindly Cheeryble brothers, Charles and Edwin, of *Nicholas Nickleby* fame. (The Grants owned a drapery business in Manchester and it is probable that John Dickens had been acquainted with them many years before the young author first met them.)

Dickens's elder sister Frances ('Fanny') married a music teacher, Henry Burnett, in 1837 and they settled in Manchester. Her fragile son seems to have helped inspire Dickens to the characters of Tiny Tim in *A Christmas Carol*, and Paul Dombey in *Dombey and Son*. Frances died of consumption in 1848.

Dickens gave several Public Readings in the city, the last in March 1869, during which his health suffered considerably.

MILE END, LONDON — During a particularly lean period only two customers in ten days call at Sol Gills's establishment in *Dombey and Son*, and one of those turns out to be a woman wanting nothing more than directions towards the Mile-End turnpike.

Sam Weller and Mr Pickwick pass the turnpike en route for IPSWICH in *The Pickwick Papers*. In *Bleak House*, the charitable Mrs Jellyby goes 'to Mile End directly after breakfast, on some Borrioboolan business'.

MILLBANK, LONDON — In *David Copperfield*, Martha Endell contemplates suicide in the Thames at Millbank, not far from Millbank Penitentiary (now gone, site occupied by the Tate Gallery: transporteers were kept at Millbank prior to their departure to the colonies).

In *Barnaby Rudge* Simon Tappertit, apprentice to Gabriel Varden and later Captain of the 'Prentice Knights', marries the 'widow of an eminent bone and rag collector, formerly of Millbank'.

MINCING LANE, LONDON — In *Our Mutual Friend* Reginald Wilfer works as a clerk in the offices of Chicksey, Veneering and Stobbles, druggists, which are situated 'near Mincing Lane', then the centre of the herb trade. Here Bella Wilfer visits her father: 'She directed herself to be driven to the corner of that darksome spot.' The area gives her the impression 'of having just opened a drawer in a chemist's shop'.

MINORIES, LONDON — The wooden figure of the Little Midshipman featured in *Dombey and Son* was obtained by the Dickens House Museum (see also DOUGHTY STREET) from Norie and Wilson's shop at 156 Minories. Previously it had adorned the wall of that company's former premises in LEADENHALL STREET, where Dickens saw it.

MONUMENT, LONDON — The Monument, designed by Christopher Wren and erected 1671–77, commemorates the Great Fire of London of 1666. In *Martin Chuzzlewit* Mrs Todger's boarding house is situated somewhere nearby:

> Surely there never was, in any other borough, city or hamlet in the world, such a singular sort of place as Todger's. And surely London, to judge from that part of it which hemmed Todger's round, and hustled it, and crushed it, and stuck its brick-and-mortar elbows into it, and kept the air from it, and stood perpetually between it and the light, was worthy of Todger's, and qualified to be on terms of close relationship and alliance with hundreds and thousands of the odd family to which Todger's belonged.
>
> You couldn't walk about in Todger's neighbourhood as you could in any other neighbourhood. You groped your way for an hour through lanes and bye-ways, and courtyards and passages, and never once emerged upon anything that might be reasonably called a street ... Instances were known of people who, being asked to dine at Todger's had travelled round and round it for a weary time, with its very chimney pots in view, and finding it, at last, impossible of attainment, had gone home again with a gentle melancholy on their spirits, tranquil and uncomplaining. Nobody had ever found Todger's on a verbal direction, though given within a minute's walk of it...

Monument

The Monument to the Great Fire of London.

As to Todger's itself ... The top of the house was worthy of notice ... Whoever climbed into this observatory was stunned at first from having knocked his head against the little door in coming out, and, after that, was for the moment choked from having looked, perforce, straight down the kitchen chimney; but these two stages over, there were things to gaze at from the top of Todger's, well worth your seeing too. For, first and foremost, if the day were bright, you observed upon the house-tops, stretching far away, a long dark path – the shadow of the Monument, and, turning round, the tall original was close beside you, with every hair erect upon his golden head, as if the doings of the city frightened him.

Later in the novel Tom Pinch 'in his guileless distrust of London' found that 'The Man in the Monument was quite as mysterious a being ... as the Man in the Moon.'

In *Barnaby Rudge* John Willet recommends to his son, Joe, the diversion of 'going to the top of the Monument and sitting there. There's no temptation there, Sir – no drink – no young women – no bad characters of any sort – nothing but imagination. That's the way I enjoyed myself when I was your age, Sir.'

In *Little Dorrit* Mr F's aunt refers to the Monument: 'it was put up after the Great Fire of London and the Great Fire of London was not the fire in which your Uncle George's workshops was burned down.'

N

NEWGATE PRISON, LONDON — The Central Criminal Court – known as the Old Bailey – now covers the site of Newgate Prison. It was here that Fagin spent his last hours before his death on the gallows. He is visited by Oliver and Mr Brownlow:

> They were immediately admitted into the lodge.
>
> 'Is the young gentleman to come too, Sir?' said the man whose duty it was to conduct them. 'It's not a sight for children, Sir.'
>
> 'It is not indeed, my friend,' rejoined Mr Brownlow; 'but my business with this man is intimately connected with him, and as this child has seen him in the full career of his success and villainy – even at the cost of some pain and fear – that he should see him now.'

The two are led through the prison to Fagin's cell:

> The condemned criminal was seated on his bed, rocking himself from side to side, with the countenance more like that of a snared beast than the face of a man. His mind was evidently wandering to his old life, for he continued to mutter, without appearing conscious of their presence otherwise than as a part of his vision…

Day was dawning when they again emerged. A great multitude had already assembled; the windows were filled with people, smoking and playing cards to beguile the time; the crowd were pushing, quarrelling, and joking. Everything told of life and animation, but one dark cluster of objects in the very centre of all – the black stage, the cross beam, the rope, and all the hideous apparatus of death.

Dickens had previously written of Newgate in the essay 'A Visit to Newgate' in *Sketches by Boz*. In *Nicholas Nickleby*, Smike satisfies his curiosity by glancing up at Newgate from the foot of LUDGATE HILL. In *The Old Curiosity Shop* Kit Nubbles finds himself for a short while wrongfully imprisoned in the gaol.

In *Barnaby Rudge* Dickens describes Newgate as:

> then a new building, recently completed at a vast expense and considered to be of enormous strength.

Later in the same novel, however, the prison is attacked and set on fire by the Gordon Rioters. Lord George Gordon, leader of the riots, was imprisoned in Newgate, where:

> Deserted by his friends, and treated in all respects like the worst criminal in the jail, he lingered on, quite cheerful and resigned, until on 1st of November 1793, when he died in his cell, being then only three-and-forty years of age.

In *Great Expectations* Pip is taken within the walls of Newgate by John Wemmick, who is attending the prison on a matter of some business on behalf of his employer Mr Jaggers:

> We were at Newgate in a few minutes, and we passed through the lodge where some fetters were hanging up on the bare walls among the prison walls, into the interior of the jail ... It was visiting time when Wemmick took me in; and a potman was going his rounds with beer; and the prisoners, behind bars in yards, were buying beer, and talking to friends; and a frousy, ugly, disorderly, depressing scene it was.

In the same novel the execution of Abel Magwitch is due to take place at Newgate – but Pip's benefactor dies of his injuries before he can be committed to the gallows.

In *A Tale of Two Cities* Charles Darnay was tried for treason at the Old Bailey:

> ...the Old Bailey was famous as a kind of deadly inn-yard, from which poor travellers set out continually, in carts and coaches, on a violent passage into the other world.

Darnay is acquitted thanks to his exact likeness to Sydney Carton.

NORTHAMPTON, NORTHAMPTONSHIRE

— Having proven himself a great humorist with *The Pickwick Papers*, Charles Dickens next turned his attentions to a wholly more serious topic – albeit an equally entertaining one to his readers. His second novel, *Oliver Twist* (1837–1839), was a satirical/ironical attack on the new Poor Law (the Poor Law Amendment, of 1834) and the workhouse system then prevalent in England.

Like all good bestsellers, *Oliver Twist* quickly grabs the reader's attention. Within the opening pages our hero is born, orphaned and condemned to a life of drudgery as the machinations of the workhouse system are unleashed upon him (even his name is the result of an alphabetical formula). Since he was dealing with the country-wide implications of the new Poor Law, Dickens was necessarily vague as to the location of the 'certain town',

Oliver Twist asks for more gruel in the workhouse.

seventy-five miles north of London, in which stood the dismal workhouse of Oliver's birth. It is likely, however, that he based this town on Northampton – or upon its close neighbour Kettering (both towns lie approximately seventy-five miles from London and both are on a direct route to BARNET, which is the next stop on Oliver's travels). Dickens had reported on the Northamptonshire by-election of December 1835 and had stayed in both towns. (ST ALBANS in Hertfordshire has also been named as the possible original of the 'certain town'.)

NORWICH, NORFOLK — Dickens visited Norwich in December 1848 prior to writing *David Copperfield* (see also BLUNDESTON and GREAT YARMOUTH), but the city is only mentioned once in the novel.

In *The Pickwick Papers* the Pickwickians, en route to Eatanswill (see also SUDBURY) travel there aboard the Norwich coach. In *The Mystery of Edwin Drood* Mr Grewgious informs Rosa Bud that he has the good fortune to receive each Christmas, a present of a turkey 'from the neighbourhood of Norwich'. Dickens gave Public Readings here in 1859, 1861 and 1867.

NORWOOD, LONDON — In *Dombey and Son*, James Carker lives in the London suburb of Norwood:

It is not a mansion; it is of no pretensions as to size; but it is beautifully arranged and tastefully kept. The lawn, the soft, smooth slope, the flower-garden, the clump of trees where graceful forms of ash and willow are not wanting, the conservatory, the rustic verandah with sweet-smelling creeping plants entwined about the pillars, the simple exterior of the house, the well-ordered offices, though all upon the diminutive scale proper to a mere cottage, bespeak an amount of elegant comfort within that might serve a palace.

In the essay 'Watkins Tottle' in *Sketches by Boz*, Dickens mentions Beulah Spa (now gone), then a popular recreation centre, complete with a maze, in Norwood.

OLD ST PANCRAS CHURCH, LONDON — In *A Tale of Two Cities* Jerry Cruncher, followed by his 'grisly urchin', Jerry Cruncher junior, goes 'fishing' with a spade at 'the old church of St Pancras, far off in the fields'. His hoped-for 'catch' is the recently buried body of the Old Bailey spy, Roger Cly.

Having witnessed this nocturnal body-snatching, young Jerry next day confides to his father: 'Oh Father, I should so like to be a Resurrection-Man when I'm quite growed up,' an ambition which fills the 'honest tradesman' Cruncher with a quiet pride.

Old St Pancras Church, where Jerry Cruncher goes body-snatching in *A Tale of Two Cities*.

OLD STREET, LONDON — In *Bleak House* Mr Guppy's mother lives in:

> a little property, which takes the form of a small life annuity; upon which she lives in an independent though unassuming manner, in the Old Street Road.

OSNABURGH TERRACE, LONDON — Dickens rented 9 Osnaburgh Terrace, Regent's Park, between May and July, 1844; his home at 1 Devonshire Terrace having been leased out, prior to the family's holiday in Italy.

OXFORD, OXFORDSHIRE — The famous university city is mentioned in *David Copperfield* when Mrs Steerforth informs David that her son 'had gone away with one of his Oxford friends … I was so fond of him [remembers David], that I felt quite jealous of his Oxford friends.'

Dickens gave Public Readings in Oxford in November 1858.

OXFORD STREET, LONDON — In *Nicholas Nickleby* Nicholas first sees his future wife, Madeleine Bray, in the General Agency Office – 'this temple of promise' – in Oxford Street where they have both gone in search of employment. Later in the same novel Nicholas makes his first acquaintance with Charles Cheeryble (see also BOW and MANCHESTER) at the same venue. And Mrs Nickleby relates the tale of her mother, who, turning a corner into Oxford Street, bumped into her hairdresser who in turn was escaping from a bear.

In *Dombey and Son*, Thomas Towlinson, footman to Mr Dombey, has 'visions of leading an altered and blameless existence as a serious greengrocer' in Oxford Market, which once lay to the north of Oxford Street.

In *Bleak House* Mr Jarndyce and his charges – Esther, Ada and Richard – live for a while at 'a cheerful lodging … over an upholsterer's shop' near Oxford Street. In the same novel Mr Turveydrop's dancing academy is situated at 26 Newman Street, a turning off the north side of Oxford Street:

> I found the academy established in a sufficiently dingy house at the corner of an archway, with busts in all the staircase windows. In the same house there were also established as I gathered from the plates on the door, a drawing-master, a coal-merchant (there was, certainly, no room for his coals), and a lithographic artist.

Following their marriage, Prince Turveydrop and Caddy Jellyby also move into this house.

In his essay 'Where We Stopped Growing' – published in *Household Words* in January 1853 – Dickens writes of a woman of Berners Street, to the north of Oxford Street:

> She is dressed entirely in white, with a ghostly white plaiting round her head and face, inside her white bonnet. She even carries (we hope) a white umbrella. With white boots, we know she picks her way through the winter dirt. She is a conceited old creature, cold and formal in manner, and evidently went simpering mad on personal grounds alone – no doubt because a wealthy Quaker wouldn't marry her. This is her bridal dress. She is always walking up here, on her way to church to marry the false Quaker.

This woman in white would seem to have laid some of the foundations for the character of Miss Havisham in *Great Expectations* (see also ISLE OF WIGHT).

The 'Uncommercial Traveller' lodges in Bond Street (to the south of Oxford Street) in the essay 'Arcadian London'.

P

PALL MALL, LONDON — In *Martin Chuzzlewit* the offices of 'The Anglo-Bengalee Disinterested Loan and Life Assurance Company' are situated 'over a tailors' near Pall Mall. The company's chairman Tigg Montague (he of the reversible name) lives in rooms in Pall Mall:

> …and splendid looking it was. The room in which he received Jonas was a spacious and elegant apartment, furnished with extreme magnificence.

In *Our Mutual Friend* Melvin Twemlow, whilst canvassing for the prospective parliamentary candidate Veneering at his club, 'promptly secures a large window, writing materials, and all the newspapers, and establishes himself, immoveable, to be respectfully contemplated by Pall Mall'.

PARLIAMENT STREET, LONDON — In *David Copperfield* David, while employed by Murdstone and Grinby, enters the Red Lion Inn, in Parliament Street:

> I remember one hot evening I went into the bar of a public house and said to the landlord –
> 'What is your best – your VERY BEST – ale a glass?…'
> 'Twopence-halfpenny,' says the landlord, 'is the price of the Genuine Stunning ale.'
> 'Then,' says I, producing the money, 'just draw me a glass of the Genuine Stunning, if you please, with a good head to it.'
> The landlord looked at me in return over the bar, from head to foot, with a strange smile on his face; and instead of drawing the beer, looked round the

> screen and said something to his wife. She came out from behind it, with her work in her hand, and joined him in surveying me … They asked me a good many questions; as what my name was, how old I was, where I lived, how I was employed, and how I came there. To all of which, that I might commit nobody, I invented, I am afraid, appropriate answers. They served me with the ale, though I suspect it was not the Genuine Stunning; and the landlord's wife, opening the little half-door of the bar, and bending down, gave me my money back, and gave me a kiss that was half admiring, and half compassionate, but all womanly and good, I am sure.

The young Dickens, during his days at Warren's Blacking Warehouse (see also COVENT GARDEN and STRAND), had a similar experience.

PECKHAM, LONDON — In *The Old Curiosity Shop* Dick Swiveller is ordered by Sampson Brass to deliver a letter in Peckham Rye. In *Dombey and Son*, Walter Gay is educated at a weekly boarding school in Peckham. In the same novel B. A. Feeder informs Mr Toots that he is going to board with his two maiden aunts in Peckham in order to study 'the dark mysteries of London'.

PEGWELL BAY, KENT — In *Sketches by Boz* the Tuggs family takes a trip to the shrimping centre Pegwell Bay in the story 'The Tuggses at Ramsgate' (see also RAMSGATE).

PENTONVILLE, LONDON — Oliver Twist's saviour, Mr Brownlow, lives in 'a neat house in a quiet shady street near Pentonville', where he is tended by his housekeeper, Mrs Bedwin. Here Oliver spends a period of recuperation before his recapture by Fagin's crew.

In *David Copperfield*, the Micawbers lodge for a while in Pentonville. In *Little Dorrit*:

> The private residence of Mr Pancks was in Pentonville, where he lodged on the second floor of a professional gentleman in an extremely small way, who had an inner door within the street door, poised on a spring and starting open with a click like a trap.

In *Bleak House* Esther Summerson's suitor William Guppy proclaims to her that he lives in:

> lodgings at Penton Place, Pentonville. It is lowly, but airy, open at the back and considered one of the 'ealthiest outlets.

PETERSFIELD, HAMPSHIRE — In *Nicholas Nickleby* Nicholas and Smike en route to Portsmouth find themselves in the small town of Petersfield. 'Twilight had already closed in, when they turned off the path to the door of a roadside inn, yet twelve miles short of Portsmouth.' The most likely original for this inn is the Bottom Inn (now gone). Here, Nicholas and Smike meet Vincent Crummles. The

following morning sees the two friends, having agreed to join with Crummles's remarkable theatrical troupe, boarding his 'vehicle of unknown design, on which he bestowed the appellation of a four-wheeled phaeton' pulled along by 'a strange four-legged animal ... which he called a pony'.

PETERSHAM, SURREY — Dickens first visited the charming village of Petersham in 1836. From April to August 1839 his family stayed at Elm Cottage (now Elm Lodge) where he wrote part of *Nicholas Nickleby*.

PICCADILLY, LONDON — On 16 May 1851 Dickens acted before Queen Victoria and Prince Albert at Devonshire House, Piccadilly, in a performance of Bulwer-Lytton's *Not So Bad As We Seem*. Eleven days later he acted again at the same venue in his own farce *Mr Nightingale's Diary*. Both performances were given in aid of the Guild of Literature and Art (see also KNEBWORTH HOUSE) and were followed by a fund-raising provincial tour.

Devonshire House (now demolished, site occupied by Mayfair Place and Berkeley Street) was the London residence of the Duke of Devonshire.

In *David Copperfield* the ever-optimistic Mr Micawber, having advertised his services 'in all the papers', sees a rosy future for himself and his family:

> There would probably be an interval, he explained, in which he should content himself with the upper part of a house,

over some respectable place of business – say in Piccadilly – which would be a cheerful situation for Mrs Micawber; and where, by throwing out a bow-window, or carrying up the roof another story, or making some little alteration of that sort, they might live, comfortably and reputably, for a few years.

In *Barnaby Rudge* soldiers were posted, during the Gordon Riots, outside the Lord President's house, in Piccadilly. In *The Pickwick Papers* Mr Pickwick and Sam Weller, en route to Bath, depart from the White Horse Cellar, a well-known coaching inn. The same inn provides a meeting place for Esther Summerson and William Guppy in *Bleak House*.

In *Our Mutual Friend* Alfred and Sophorina Lammle are married at St James's church in Piccadilly, and they take a temporary apartment in nearby Sackville Street. 'Fascination' Fledgeby lives in chambers in Albany, off Piccadilly (elegant residential quarters occupied over the years by many famous bachelor gentlemen). Mr Twemlow, friend of the Veneerings, and 'an

innocent piece of dinner-furniture that went upon easy castors', was 'kept over a livery stable-yard in Duke Street, Saint James', off Piccadilly.

St James's Hall (now demolished, site later occupied by the Piccadilly Hotel) was the venue of many of Dickens's final Public Readings, including his Farewell Readings of 1870.

Bleak House: Mr Skimpole holds forth.

PLYMOUTH, DEVON — In *David Copperfield* the in-laws of Mr Micawber hail from Plymouth. The Micawbers move there, having been turned out of their Windsor Terrace home (see also CITY ROAD). Plymouth is also mentioned in *Bleak House*. Dickens gave Public Readings in the town in 1858 and 1862.

POLYGON, LONDON — In *Bleak House* we learn from Esther Summerson that the unprincipled Harold Skimpole lives:

in a place called Polygon, in Somers Town ... It [his house] was in a state of dilapidation quite equal to our expectation. Two or three of the area railings were gone; the water butt was

The birthplace of Charles Dickens in Portsmouth, now a Dickens museum.

broken; the knocker was loose; the bell-handle had been pulled off a long time, to judge from the rusty state of the wire; and dirty footprints on the steps were the only signs of it being inhabited.

The Polygon, a motley collection of dwellings in Somers Town, was later demolished. The Dickens family lived briefly at No. 17 in 1827.

PORTSMOUTH, HAMPSHIRE — In the summer of 1809 John Dickens was transferred from Somerset House (see also

STRAND) in London, to the Portsmouth Dockyard where he was to work as a Naval Pay Clerk. With him went his young wife, Elizabeth: the couple had only recently married, their wedding having taken place on 13 June at the church of St Mary-le-Strand in London.

They moved into 1 Mile End Terrace in Landport, a middle-class Portsmouth suburb. The house was a pleasant but tiny two-up, two-down dwelling with a basement room, and an attic which served as servants' quarters. There was a small garden at the front and a walled yard at the rear.

The Dickens's first child, Frances Elizabeth – 'Fanny' – was born on 10 November, 1810. Their second child Charles – destined to become one of the most famous Englishmen of all time – was born in the early hours of 7 February 1812 in the upstairs front bedroom of 1 Mile End Terrace.

The boy was christened Charles John Huffam Dickens on 4 March 1812 at St Mary's Church, Kingston, Portsmouth. The Huffam – misspelled as Huffham in the Parish Register – was for his godfather, Christopher Huffam, an old friend of the family (see also LIMEHOUSE).

John Dickens was a naturally generous man, frequently given to entertaining his friends on a somewhat lavish scale. (His parents had been butler and housekeeper to Lord Crewe at Crewe Hall (see also CREWE) in Cheshire and perhaps this tentative connection with the nobility had contributed more than any other factor towards his perpetually unfulfilled pretensions to gentility – a characteristic of many new recruits to the middle classes of the time.) In general he enjoyed the appearance of a man living the good life. In reality, he was living far beyond his means and was constantly plagued by financial worries. He once described himself an 'avowed optimist' who was like a cork – when pushed underwater in one place it would always 'bob up cheerfully in another'. In 1849 Dickens would affectionately model the memorable character of Wilkins Micawber on that of

his own father. Indeed both men appear to have shared a common financial philosophy:

'Annual income twenty pounds, annual expenditure nineteen, nineteen six, result happiness. Annual income twenty pounds, annual expenditure twenty pounds ought and six, result misery'

as Mr Micawber says in *David Copperfield*. Unfortunately neither man was able profitably to apply the equation to his own life; both were simply content to wait in the hope that 'something will turn up'.

The yearly rental of 1 Mile End Terrace was £35, which represented a sizeable portion of John Dickens's annual salary; too sizeable as it turned out, for his increasingly precarious financial position quickly forced him to seek a cheaper, more manageable home for his family and servants.

On 24 June 1812, less than five months after the birth of his first son, he moved the family to 16 Hawk (later Hawke) Street, Portsea. This was a smaller, more cramped house, albeit in an equally prestigious neighbourhood. There was no front garden, and the bay window of the tiny sitting-room literally overhung the cobbled pavement. The Dickens family were to remain here until the end of 1813. (Hawke Street suffered badly during German bombing raids in World War II and Number 16 was destroyed.) Throughout 1814 they lived at 39 Wish Street (now King's Road), Southsea, and in January

1815 John Dickens was transferred back to London.

Charles Dickens left the city of Portsmouth when he was two years old and he seldom returned there. One visit, however, took place in 1838, during the writing of Nicholas Nickleby: Dickens wanted to brush up on his knowledge of the locality in which he was to set the adventures and performances of Vincent Crummles's theatrical troupe: Crummles stayed 'in the house of one Bulph, a pilot, in St Thomas's Street'; Nicholas and the unfortunate Smike lodged above a tobacconist's shop on the Common Hard in 'two small rooms up three pairs of stairs, or rather two pairs and a ladder'; and the company performed on the stage of the old Portsmouth Theatre in the High Street (all three of these locations have since been demolished).

Another visit to Portsmouth by Dickens occurred in 1866 – this time in the company of his manager George Dolby – during an exhausting Public Reading tour. Turning a corner the world-famous author stopped suddenly in his tracks and declared 'By Jove! here is the place where I was born.' But even Charles Dickens's phenomenal powers of recall were unable to ascertain in precisely which of the houses he had spent the first months of his infancy. (There is some doubt whether the street was Mile End Terrace, for Dolby reported it as Landport Terrace which ran into Wish Street, a locality which Dickens might more easily recall.)

In 1903, the City of Portsmouth, rightly proud of its most famous son, purchased the house of his birth and opened it to the public as a Dickensian Museum. In the late 1960s the building was reconstructed as an early 19th century middle-class dwelling, although the only original fixture is a built-in dresser in what was the kitchen.

Modern city planning has long since changed the address of the house: today it is 393 Old Commercial Road.

PORTSMOUTH STREET, LONDON — Several claims have been made as to the actual location of Dickens's original for *The Old Curiosity Shop*. Most prominent among these is that made by an establishment at 13–14 Portsmouth Street which today bears the legend 'Immortalized by Charles Dickens'. However, beyond the fact that Dickens certainly knew of the existence of this building (his good friend John Forster lived just around the corner, at 58 Lincoln's Inn) there is little further evidence to authenticate the claim.

Other claims have been made for similar small shops in Fetter Lane (see also FLEET STREET), Green Street and Irving Street. Finally, at the end of the novel Kit Nubbles is seen sometimes to take his daughters:

> to the street where she [Nell] had lived, but new improvements had altered it so much it was not like the same. The old house had been long ago pulled down, and a fine broad road was in its place. At first he would draw with his stick a

The 'Old Curiosity Shop', Portsmouth Street.

However, he wrote to John Forster:

> I am afraid I shall not be able to get much here. Except the crowds at the street-corners reading the placards pro and con; and the cold absence of smoke from the mill-chimneys; there is very little in the streets to make the town remarkable. I am told that the people 'sit at home and mope'...

Dickens's next visit to Preston took place in December 1861 when he stayed at the Victoria Hotel and gave a Public Reading at the Corn Exchange. Another Reading was given in Preston early in 1867, after which Dickens and his manager George Dolby reputedly walked the twelve miles to his next reading venue in Blackburn.

During this trek Dickens and Dolby visited Houghton Towers, a location later used by Dickens in the story *George Silverman's Explanation*. In the same story Silverman is born in Preston.

On 22 April 1869 Dickens was due to give a Reading at the Guildhall in Preston; he was midway through a Provincial Tour. However, the author was ordered by his doctor to curtail the tour there and then, for fear of a further deterioration in his health.

square upon the ground to show where it used to stand. But he soon became uncertain of the spot, and would only say it was thereabouts.

The most likely original for 'The Magpie and Stump' of *The Pickwick Papers* was the George IV Inn (now rebuilt) on the corner of Portugal Street and Portsmouth Street.

PRESTON, LANCASHIRE — *Hard Times*, Dickens's tenth and shortest novel, is set chiefly in the northern industrial town of 'Coketown', an amalgam of Preston and MANCHESTER. Whilst working on the novel in 1854, he visited Preston during a mill-workers strike hoping to gather much background information for his story.

PUTNEY, LONDON — In *David Copperfield* Dora Spenlow goes to live with her aunts (Miss Lavinia and Miss Clarissa) in Putney following the death of her father, Francis Spenlow. She and David 'strolled about the common' and are later married in a church of which the most probable original is St Mary's, Putney.

In *Little Dorrit* Arthur Clennam passes through Putney 'for the pleasure of strolling over the Heath' en route to Mr Meagle's 'cottage-residence' at Twickenham.

'QUILP'S WHARF', LONDON — Dickens's original for 'Quilp's Wharf' no longer exists, but once lay among many such wharves 'on the Surrey side of the river', opposite Tower Hill where Quilp lives with his long-suffering wife. Here, the villain of *The Old Curiosity Shop* carried out his business, which was of no 'particular trade or calling, though his pursuits were diversified and his occupations numerous'. Dickens set it in:

> a small rat-infested dreary yard ... in which were a little wooden counting-house burrowing all awry in the dust as if it had fallen from the clouds and ploughed into the ground, a few fragments of rusty anchors, several large iron rings, some piles of rotten wood, and two or three heaps of old sheet copper, crumpled, cracked and battered. On Quilp's Wharf, Daniel Quilp was a ship-breaker, yet to judge from these appearances he must have been a ship-breaker on a very small scale, or have broken his ships up very small indeed.

Quilp eventually meets his end in the murky waters of the Thames while attempting to escape justice.

RAMSGATE, KENT — Dickens knew this seaside resort during his times at nearby BROADSTAIRS. He had previously set the story 'The Tuggses at Ramsgate' there in *Sketches by Boz*: this family considered Ramsgate 'just the place of all others'.

READING, BERKSHIRE — In May 1841 Dickens was offered a Liberal Party candidacy for the constituency of Reading. However, after careful consideration, he declined the offer as he could not afford the necessary expenses involved in such a venture. A second approach by the Liberals was also turned down as Dickens valued his independence as an author more than the chance for glory in Parliament.

In December 1851 Dickens acted in Reading at the Town Hall in Lord Lytton's play *Not So Bad As We Seem*. In November 1858 he gave a Public Reading at the New Hall. The town features in *Bleak House*, when Esther Summerson's narrative informs us that she spent 'six happy quiet years' at Greenleaf, a school run by the Donny twins.

REGENT STREET, LONDON — In *Nicholas Nickleby*, Lord Frederick Verisopht lives in 'a handsome suite of private apartments in Regent Street'. The curve, known as the Quadrant (later rebuilt), at the southern end of Regent Street is mentioned in the essay 'Misplaced Attachment' in *Sketches by Boz*.

RICHMOND, SURREY — In *The Pickwick Papers* Tracy Tupman 'took lodgings' in the elegant district of Richmond 'where he has since resided'. In *Great Expectations* Estella goes to stay with Mrs Brandley in 'a staid old house' in Richmond, believed to be based on a house in Maids of Honour Row.

Dickens often visited the Star and Garter Hotel on Richmond Hill: the first numbers of the early novels were celebrated there, as were family birthdays. And in April 1850 Dickens held an elaborate party at the hotel, in celebration of the resounding success of *David Copperfield*. The site of this hotel is now occupied by a home for disabled ex-servicemen. Richmond also features briefly in *Sketches by Boz* and *Our Mutual Friend*.

ROCHESTER, KENT — Rochester was Charles Dickens's favourite city. As a 'queer small boy' living in neighbouring Chatham ('If anybody … knows to a nicety where

Rochester ends and Chatham begins, it is more than I do,' says Richard Doubledick in 'The Seven Poor Travellers') Charles had enjoyed numerous visits there with his father, during which he had inquisitively 'peeped about the old corners of the city'.

The young Dickens was often taken to the Theatre Royal in Star Hill, usually by James Lamert (the fiancée of his Aunt Fanny). Here the boy had been introduced to the wonders of Shakespeare. He had also witnessed several of the wildly rambling melodramas of the day and had once seen Joe Grimaldi, 'The Prince of Clowns', whose memoirs he would later edit. These all too infrequent visits instilled within him a love of the theatre which would remain throughout his lifetime.

In the essay 'Dullborough Town' in *The Uncommercial Traveller* Dickens writes of a return visit to the Theatre Royal:

> But I found very little, for it was in a bad and declining way … It was TO LET, and hopelessly for its old purposes; and there had been no entertainment within its walls for a long time, except a Panorama; and even that had been announced as 'pleasingly instructive', and I know too well the fatal meaning and the leaden import of those terrible expressions. No, there was no comfort in the Theatre. It was mysteriously gone, like my own youth.

The Royal Function Rooms now occupy the site of the old Theatre Royal. In the same piece 'The Uncommercial Traveller'

Rochester Castle: a 'magnificent ruin' according to Augustus Snodgrass in *The Pickwick Papers*.

walks along the High Street, past the Corn Exchange (now the Prince's Hall):

> There was a public clock in it, which I had supposed to be the finest clock in the world; whereas it now turned out to be as inexpressive, moon-faced, and weak a clock as ever I saw.

Dickens steered the opening episodes of *The Pickwick Papers* towards the familiar territory of his happiest childhood days in Chatham and Rochester. As the 'Commodore' stagecoach crosses Rochester Bridge the friends – Pickwick, Snodgrass, Winkle and Tupman, together with the itinerant actor Alfred Jingle – are confronted with the Norman edifice of Rochester Castle.

> 'Magnificent ruin,' exclaims Snodgrass. 'What a study for an antiquarian,' agrees Pickwick. 'Ah! Fine place!' echoes Jingle.

The Pickwickians begin their travels from the Bull Hotel at Rochester.

'Glorious pile – frowning walls – tottering arches – dark nooks – crumbling staircases.'

After crossing Rochester Bridge, the 'Commodore' pulls up in the yard of The Bull Hotel where, on Jingle's advice – 'Good house – nice beds' – the four Pickwickians decide to stay for a while.

The hotel's grand staircase still remains intact: on it the Pickwickians observed the preparations for the evening's ball – 'devil of a mess on the staircase … forms going up – carpenters coming down – lamps, glasses, harps.'

Later, while Pickwick, Snodgrass and Winkle sleep off the effects of the journey and of the 'ardent spirits' provided by the good house, Tracy Tupman attends the ball. He is accompanied by Jingle who is wearing a coat 'borrowed' from Mr Winkle. Jingle's unseemly behaviour towards a widow at the ball, and some confusion as to the ownership of the coat, leads to the innocent Mr Winkle being challenged to a duel by the irate Dr Slammer.

The hotel also appears in the guise of the 'Blue Boar' in *Great Expectations* and serves as the 'Winglebury Arms' in 'The Great Winglebury Duel' in *Sketches by Boz*.

Before departing for the Wardles's home at Dingley Dell we meet Mr Pickwick as he leans over old Rochester Bridge, contemplating the morning as he awaits breakfast-time:

On either side, the banks of the Medway, covered with cornfields and pastures, with here and there a windmill or a distant church, stretched away as far as the eye could see, presenting a rich and varied landscape, rendered more beautiful by the changing shadows which passed swiftly across it, as the thin and half-formed clouds skimmed away in the light of the morning sun. The river, reflecting the clear blue of the sky, glistened and sparkled as it flowed noiselessly on; and the oars of the fishermen dipped into the water with a clear and liquid sound, as the heavy but picturesque boats glided slowly down the stream.

Old Rochester Bridge was built by the Romans, but was replaced in Dickens's day by the present iron structure. The balustrade (not Roman) over which Mr Pickwick 'contemplated nature' is preserved, however, and now forms part of the balustrade of the Esplanade, overlooking the Medway, below the castle.

For the 1854 Christmas number of his magazine *Household Words*, Dickens wrote 'The Seven Poor Travellers', a story inspired by Watts's Charity in Rochester High Street. Richard Watts (d. 1579) was a local philanthropist who founded a charity which swore to provide 'for six poor Travellers, who not being Rogues or Proctors, May receive gratis for one Night, Lodging, entertainment, and Fourpence each' as is inscribed above the entrance.

Dickens wrote:

It was in the ancient little City of Rochester of all the good days in the year upon Christmas-eve, that I stood reading the inscription over the quaint door in question … 'Now,' I said to myself, as I looked at the knocker, 'I know I am not a Proctor, I wonder whether I am a rogue.'

In the story Dickens makes himself – as narrator – the seventh poor traveller.

Richard Watts is also commemorated by a memorial inside Rochester Cathedral. He lived at a house in Boley Hill, in which he once entertained Queen Elizabeth I. Watts apologized to the monarch for the apparent meagreness of his house – but she replied that it was perfectly 'satis'. Therefore Watts called his home 'Satis House', the name borrowed in turn by Dickens for the home of Miss Havisham where young Pip is sent to play in *Great Expectations*. Estella explains:

'Its other name was Satis; which is Greek or Latin, or Hebrew, or all three – or all one to me – for enough.'

'Enough House!' said I. 'That's a curious name, Miss.'

'Yes,' she replied; 'but it meant more than it said. It meant when it was given, that whoever had this house, could want nothing else…'

The house itself, 'of old brick and dismal', is based upon Restoration House in Crow Lane, so named in commemoration of a brief stay there by King Charles II in May

Restoration House, Crow Lane, Rochester, the original for Miss Havisham's house in *Great Expectations*.

1660 following his return from a visit to France. (Samuel Pepys wrote of this house in his famous diary – in the cherry garden he met a shopkeeper with a pretty wife 'and did kiss her'.)

John Forster records that Dickens was fascinated by Restoration House:

> He would turn out of Rochester High Street, through the Vines where some of the old buildings, (from one of which

called Restoration House he took Satis House for Great Expectations), had a curious attraction for him.

According to Pip in *Great Expectations*, Uncle Pumblechook's establishment in the High Street was:

> of a peppercorny and farinacious character, as the premises of a corn chandler and seedsman should be. It

appeared to me that he must be a very happy man indeed, to have so many little drawers in his shop; and I wondered when I peeped into one or two on the lower tiers, and saw the tied-up brown paper packets inside, whether the flower-seeds and bulbs ever wanted of a fine day to break out of those jails, and bloom ... On the previous night, I had been sent straight to bed in an attic with a sloping roof, which was so low in the corner where the bedstead was, that I calculated the tiles as being within a foot of my eyebrows.

In Dickens's day this shop – built in the late 1600s – was indeed occupied by a seedsman who advertised the premises as 'convenient and commodious'. The building also served Dickens as the home of Mr Sapsea, auctioneer, in *The Mystery of Edwin Drood*.

Indeed, Rochester itself became the 'Cloisterham' of *The Mystery of Edwin Drood*, the 'ancient cathedral town' in which the mystery unfolds:

It was once possibly known to the Druids by another name, and certainly to the Romans by another, and to the Saxons by another, and to the Normans by another ... A monotonous silent city, deriving an earthy flavour throughout from its Cathedral crypt, and so abounding in vestiges of monastic graves, that the Cloisterham children grow small salad in the dust of abbots and abbesses, and make dirt pies of nuns and friars.

The 'earthy flavour' that once emanated from the 13th century crypt has, since Dickens's day, been eliminated by careful restoration work. There is, however, a sense of 'looking down the throat of old time' about Rochester cathedral, as Mr Grewgious exclaimed when gazing in through the west door. (The grave of one John Dorrett and his family, sited at the western end of the cathedral graveyard, may well have inspired Dickens to name the 'Dorrit' family in *Little Dorrit*.)

Dickens's original for The Nun's House, the seminary for young ladies run by Miss Twinkleton in *Edwin Drood*, was Eastgate House in Rochester High Street, an Elizabethan building erected in 1590-91 for Sir Peter Bucke, a naval paymaster. (This house is also the most probable original of Westgate House in *The Pickwick Papers* – see also BURY ST EDMUNDS.) The house was purchased by the Rochester City Council in 1897 and eventually became a Dickensian museum containing many relics of the author's life and times. The museum closed in 2004, although the house continues life as an exhibition centre and a venue for weddings and civil ceremonies.

In the garden of Eastgate House stands the Swiss Chalet presented to Dickens by the actor Charles Fechter in 1864; it had originally been sited in the small shrubbery opposite GAD'S HILL PLACE. Following Dickens's death in 1870 the chalet was exhibited at Crystal Palace, and was later presented to Lord Darnley who placed it in Cobham Park (see also COBHAM). In 1961 the Dickens Fellowship rescued the chalet from deterioration and, in conjunction with the Rochester City Council, restored it to former glory and placed it in the care of Eastgate House. Since then the fragile structure has twice undergone restoration. However, in recent years it fell once again into disrepair, thus prompting the Rochester and Chatham Dickens Fellowship to launch an appeal for restoration funds in 2010, with the aim of reopening the chalet as a cultural centrepiece in time for the 200th anniversary celebrations in 2012.

Edwin Drood paces The Vines, an open stretch of parkland, once a monastery vineyard, criss-crossed with pathways:

> He has walked to and fro, full half an hour by the Cathedral chimes, and it has closed in dark, before he becomes aware of a woman, crouching on the ground near the wicket gate in the corner. The gate commands a little cross-path little used in the gloaming.

Eastgate House, which appears in *Edwin Drood*.

One of the crosspaths of The Vines leads to another Dickensian location, Minor Cannon Row (Dickens called it 'Minor Canon Corner'), 'a row of staid old brick houses' where, in *The Mystery of Edwin Drood*, lives the Rev Canon Crisparkle and his 'Ma', the 'china shepherdess'. 'A quiet place in the shadow of the Cathedral which the cawing of rooks, the echoing footsteps of rare passers, the sound of the Cathedral bell, or the roll of the Cathedral organ, seemed to render more quiet than absolute silence.' Minor Cannon Row remains much as it was in Dickens's day.

'Jasper's Gatehouse', the lodging place of John Jasper, the Cathedral choirmaster in *Edwin Drood*, is modelled on College (or Chertsey's) Gatehouse in Rochester High Street. Beside it stands the house occupied in the same novel by Mr Topes. This was the 'official dwelling ... of modest proportions' of the Cathedral's chief verger, and the lodging place of Mr Datchery. Today the building is a restaurant. On 7 June 1870 Dickens was observed wandering the streets of Rochester. He was seen to lean against the fence of The Vines and to gaze at Restoration House. Sadly, the world of literature never knew what future plans he might have had in mind for this favourite location, for two days later the great author died.

A brass tablet in the South transept of Rochester Cathedral commemorates Dickens's association with the area. It reads:

Charles Dickens
Born at Portsmouth 7th February, 1812.
Died at Gad's Hill Place, by Rochester,
9th June, 1870. Buried in Westminster
Abbey. To connect his memory with the
scene, in which his earliest and latest
years were passed, and with the
association of Rochester Cathedral and
its neighbourhood, which extended over
all his life, this tablet, with the sanction of
the Dean and Chapter, is placed here by
his Executors.

It is entirely fitting that among the last words Charles Dickens ever wrote was this description of his favourite city:

A brilliant morning shines on the old city. Its antiquities and ruins are surpassingly beautiful, with the lusty ivy gleaming in the sun, and the rich trees waving in the balmy air. Changes of glorious light from moving boughs, songs of birds, scent from gardens, woods and fields – or rather, from the one great garden of the whole cultivated island in its yielding time – penetrate into the Cathedral, subdue its earthy odour, and preach the Resurrection and the Life. The cold stone tombs of centuries ago grow warm, and the flocks of brightness dart into the sternest marble corners of the building, fluttering there like wings.

ROCKINGHAM, NORTHAMPTONSHIRE

— Whilst holidaying at Lausanne, Switzerland in 1846, Dickens met with the Hon. and Mrs Richard Watson. Both men found that they shared similar liberal temperaments and quickly became firm friends; Dickens later dedicated David Copperfield to the Watsons.

The Watsons invited the author to their home, Rockingham Castle in Northamptonshire, and his first visit there, with Catherine, was made in November 1849. Dickens wrote of the splendid building to John Forster:

Picture to yourself, my dear F., a large old castle, approached by an ancient keep, portcullis, &c., &c., filled with company, waited on by six-and-twenty servants … Of all the country-houses and estates I have yet seen in England, I think this is by far the best.

Among the guests was one Mary Boyle, a well-known amateur actress, with whom Dickens acted in some impromptu scenes

Rockingham Castle, Northamptonshire: the model for Lady Dedlock's home in *Bleak House*.

from *The School for Scandal* and *Nicholas Nickleby*. The friendship between these two theatrical enthusiasts was cemented at Rockingham Castle and would last throughout Dickens's lifetime.

In 1850 Dickens supervised the building of a small theatre inside the castle where several productions of his own plays *Used Up, The Day after the Wedding* and *Animal Magnetism* were subsequently staged.

Richard Watson died in 1852, but Dickens continued his connection with the family throughout his own lifetime and was a frequent visitor to Rockingham.

Although in *Bleak House* Dickens placed Lady Dedlock's home 'in Lincolnshire', he in fact partly based 'Chesney Wold' on Rockingham Castle. He confirmed as much to Mrs Watson in a letter of 27 August 1853: 'In some of the descriptions of Chesney Wold, I have taken many bits, chiefly about trees and shadows, from observations made at Rockingham,' he wrote.

We are first introduced to the castle and village of Chesney Wold in Chapter 2 of *Bleak House*, during a wintry rainstorm:

The weather, for many a day and night, has been so wet that the trees seem wet through, and the soft lappings and prunings of the woodman's axe can make no crash or crackle as they fall.

The deer, looking soaked, leave quagmires where they pass. The shot of a rifle loses its sharpness in the moist air, and its smoke moves in a tardy little cloud towards the green rise, coppice-topped, that makes a background for the falling rain … The vases on the stone terrace in the foreground catch the rain all day; and the heavy drops fall, drip, drip, drip, upon the broad flagged pavement, called, from old time, the Ghost's Walk, all night.

The torrent continues in Chapter 7:

The rain is ever falling, drip, drip, drip, by day and night, upon the broad flagged terrace-pavement, The Ghost's Walk. The weather is so very bad ... that the liveliest imagination can scarcely apprehend its ever being fine again ... There may be some motions of fancy among the lower animals at Chesney Wold. The horses in the stables – the long stables in a barren, redbrick courtyard, where there is a great bell in a turret, and a clock with a large face, which the pigeons who live near it, and who love to perch upon its shoulders, seem to be always consulting – they may contemplate some mental pictures of fine weather, on occasions, and may be better artists at them than the grooms.

The Ghost's Walk is modelled upon the Yew Walk at Rockingham Castle. The red-

The Long Gallery at Rockingham Castle. Displayed here are several letters from Charles Dickens to his friend the Hon. Richard Watson.

bricked courtyard is based on 'The Street', formerly the domestic quarters of the castle staff. And the River Welland, flowing through the valley below the castle, was often prone to overflowing during heavy rainfalls, thereby presenting Dickens with the watery landscape described above.

Later in the book Esther Summerson, visiting Chesney Wold with John Jarndyce, describes the grounds more fully:

It was a picturesque old house, in a fine park richly wooded … The house with gable and chimney, and tower, and turret, and dark doorway, and broad terrace-walk, twining among the balustrades of which, and lying heaped upon the vases, there was one great flush of roses, seemed scarcely real, in its light solidity, and in the serene and peaceful hush that rested on all around it…

The Great Hall, Rockingham Castle. Dickens often acted here.

I passed before the terrace garden with its fragrant odours, and its broad walks, and its well-kept beds, and smooth turf; and I saw how beautiful and grave it was, and how the old stone balustrades and parapets, and wide flights of shallow steps, were seamed by time and weather; and how the trained moss and ivy grew about them, and around the old stone pedestal of the sundial; and I heard the fountain falling. Then the way went by long lines of dark windows, diversified by turreted towers, and porches, of eccentric shapes, where old stone lions and grotesque monsters bristled outside dens of shadow, and snarled at the evening gloom over the escutcheons they held in their grip. Thence the path wound underneath a gateway, and through a court-yard where the principal entrance was (I hurried quickly on), and by the stables where none but deep voices seemed to be, whether in the murmuring of the wind through the strong mass of ivy holding to the high red wall, or in the low complaining of the weathercock, or in the barking of the dogs, or in the slow striking of a clock. So, encountering presently a sweet smell of limes, whose rustling I could hear, I turned with the turning of the path, to the south front; and there above me, were the balustrades of the Ghost's Walk, and one lighted window that might be my mother's.

Other parts of the Rockingham estate were utilized by Dickens in *Bleak House*. The keepers' lodge, 'that lodge, within sight of the house', becomes the home of Mr George. The church also features in the story, its pathway being the cause of the feud between Sir Leicester Dedlock and Mr Boythorn (they dispute the right of way).

The village of Rockingham becomes the village of Chesney Wold, with the Sondes Arms Inn providing the model for the Dedlock Arms. Lawrence Boythorn lives in 'A real old house, with settles in the chimney of the brick-floored kitchen, and great beams across the ceilings. On one side of it was the terrible piece of ground in dispute.'

ROYAL TUNBRIDGE WELLS, KENT — In *Little Dorrit* we are informed that Mr Finching proposed several times to Flora (see also LOMBARD STREET):

> once in a hackney coach, once in a boat, once in a pew, once on a donkey at Tunbridge Wells and the rest on his knees.

Tunbridge Wells – with its Sussex neighbour Groombridge – provided Dickens with his original for Groombridge Wells in the Christmas Story 'No Thoroughfare'.

RUGBY, WARWICKSHIRE — Rugby provided Dickens with his original for Mugby Junction, 'the maddest place in England' in the Christmas Story 'Mugby Junction'.

S

SAFFRON HILL, LONDON — Simultaneously with its attack on the new Poor Law, *Oliver Twist* also contains a famous and informed portrayal of the criminal society of the 1830s, the 'dregs of life' who invariably inhabited the notorious 'rookeries' of London. Dickens deliberately chose to write of these essentially immoral people in order to contrast them with young Oliver and his 'principle of Good surviving through every adverse circumstance and triumphing at last'. He felt that presenting a truthful picture of 'a knot of such associates in crime as really did exist; to paint them in all their deformity, in all their wretchedness, in all the squalid misery of their lives; to show them as they really are … would be to attempt something which was needed, and which would be a service to society.'

The district in which he decided to centre these underworld goings-on was that around Saffron Hill, which runs parallel with Farringdon Road.

With promises of food, shelter and comfort, Jack Dawkins leads Oliver Twist into the labyrinthine streets of 'the great large place' which is London. Their subsequent trek towards Saffron Hill was as follows:

> It was nearly eleven o'clock when they reached the turnpike at Islington. They crossed the Angel into St John's Road; struck down the small street which terminates at Sadler's Wells Theatre; through Exmouth Street and Coppice Row; down the little court by the side of the workhouse; across the classic ground which once bore the name of Hockley-in-the-Hole; thence into Little Saffron-hill; and so into Saffron Hill the Great.

In these narrow night-time streets Oliver Twist catches his first glimpses of 'the dregs of life' – frightening, dark figures, lurking in the doorways and the shadows. Eventually the 'Artful Dodger' steers him through a doorway near Field Lane (now gone), and into the den of the ' 'spectable old gentleman', the thief-master Fagin. In making welcome the innocent newcomer, Fagin unwittingly weaves the web of intrigue and eventual disaster

Oliver Twist discovers Fagin's den.

more tightly about himself and those most closely associated with him. However, the consequences of Fagin's action lead us along an exciting narrative path through the criminal underworld, the police courts, and the countryside surrounding London.

The Three Cripples Inn, 'or rather the Cripples', stood in Little Saffron Hill (now Herbal Hill). Here we are introduced to Bill Sikes, the house-breaker prone to violence, and Nancy the kind-hearted prostitute:

> …in an obscure parlour of a low public-house, in the filthiest part of Little Saffron Hill – a dark and gloomy den, where a flaring gas-light burnt all day in the winter time, and where no ray of sun ever shone in the summer.

In *Little Dorrit* the Plornish family live in Bleeding Heart Yard, a turning off Greville Street, Saffron Hill:

> As if the aspiring city had become puffed up in the very ground on which it stood, the ground has so risen about Bleeding Heart Yard that you got into it down a flight of steps which formed no part of the original approach, and got out of it by a low gateway into a maze of shabby streets, which went about and about, tortuously ascending to the level again. At the end of the yard and over the gateway was the factory of Daniel Doyce, often heavily beating like a bleeding heart of iron, with the clink of metal upon metal.

Arthur Clennam later becomes a partner to Doyce in his business. The landlord of Bleeding Heart Yard is the hypocritical Christopher Casby whose unscrupulous methods are eventually exposed by Mr Pancks (see also GRAY'S INN). A legend among taxi drivers claims that Bleeding Heart Yard is so-named because it's so 'bleedin' hard' to find. The Saffron Hill area was much altered by the building of Holborn Viaduct in 1867–69.

ST ALBANS, HERTFORDSHIRE — 'Bleak House', home of Mr Jarndyce in *Bleak House*, stands 'near to St Albans'. Esther Summerson's narrative tells us:

> There was a light sparkling on the top of a hill before us, and the driver, pointing to it with his whip and crying, 'That's Bleak House!' put his horses into a canter, and took us forward at such a rate, uphill though it was, that the wheels sent the road drift flying about our head like spray from a watermill. Presently we lost the light, presently saw it, presently lost it, presently saw it, and turned into an avenue of trees, and cantered up towards where it was beaming brightly. It was in a window of what seemed to be an old-fashioned house, with three peaks in the roof in front, and a circular sweep leading to the porch.

No house in the vicinity of St Albans answered precisely to this description, although several have laid claim to being

Dickens's original. The most likely, however, is a house in Catherine Street, which in 1890 altered its name to 'Bleak House'. It is known that Dickens visited St Albans during the writing of *Bleak House*. (See also BROADSTAIRS.)

Following the murder of Nancy in *Oliver Twist*, Bill Sikes, in flight from London, takes 'the road that leads from Hatfield to St Albans'. (It has also been suggested that St Albans was Dickens's original for the 'certain town' of Oliver Twist's birth; see also NORTHAMPTON.) In *David Copperfield*, a friend of Steerforth's lives 'near St Albans'.

St James's Park, London — In *Martin Chuzzlewit*, young Martin meets Mary Graham in St James's Park following an arrangement made by Mark Tapley. Other meetings took place there, between Ralph Nickleby and his former Clerk, Brooker, during a rainstorm in *Nicholas Nickleby*, and between Arthur Clennam, Daniel Doyce and Mr Meagles in Little Dorrit.

St Martin's-le-Grand, London — On the morning of 13 May 1827 Mr Pickwick set off from his chambers in GOSWELL STREET – 'with his portmanteau in his hand, his telescope in his greatcoat pocket and his notebook in his waistcoat pocket' – for the coach stand in St Martin's-le-Grand, near St Paul's Cathedral. From here he orders a cab to take him, as the sullen cab-man notes, 'only a bob's vorth' to Golden Cross (see also TRAFALGAR SQUARE).

St Mary Axe, London — In 1830 St Mary Axe was the scene of the young Dickens's embarrassment when he accompanied his sweetheart Maria Beadnell, her mother and her sisters to a dressmaker's shop there. Mrs Beadnell effectively put him in his place at the shop doorway (see also LOMBARD STREET).

In *Our Mutual Friend* the offices of Pubsey and Co., owned by 'Fascination' Fledgeby and managed by Mr Riah, are situated in 'a yellow overhanging plaster-fronted house' in St Mary Axe. Lizzie Hexam, befriended by Riah, and Jenny Wren often sit in the roof-garden there.

St Marylebone Church, London — St Marylebone Church stands close to the site of 1 DEVONSHIRE TERRACE, Dickens's home from 1839 to 1851. Here, in *Dombey and Son*, little Paul Dombey is christened:

'Please to bring the child in quick out of the air there,' whispered the beadle, holding open the inner door of the church.

Little Paul might have asked with Hamlet 'into my grave?' so chill and earthy was the place. The tall shrouded pulpit and reading desk; the dreary perspective of empty pews stretching away under the galleries, and empty benches mounting to the roof and lost in the shadow of the great grim organ; the dusty matting and cold stone slabs; the grisly free seats in the aisles; and the damp corner by the bell-rope, where the black trestles used for funerals were stowed

The magnificent interior of St Marylebone Church, scene of Paul Dombey's christening.

away, along with some shovels and baskets, and a coil or two of deadly-looking rope; the strange, unusual, uncomfortable smell, and the cadaverous light, were all in unison. It was a cold and dismal scene.

Later in *Dombey and Son* Mr Dombey's doomed second marriage to Edith Granger also takes place in the church. And, following the tragic death of little Paul, the child is buried there. Before their wedding at 'a mouldy old church, in a yard, hemmed in by a labyrinth of back streets and courts', Walter Gay and Florence Dombey pause to look at the monument to Paul.

ST OLAVE'S CHURCH, HART STREET, LONDON — In his essay 'City of the Absent' in *The Uncommercial Traveller*, Dickens declares the church of St Olave's, in Hart Street, to be one of his favourites in all of London – he 're-christened' it 'St Ghastly Grim':

It lies at the heart of the city … a small churchyard, with a ferocious strong spiked iron gate, like a jail. This gate is ornamented with skulls and cross-bones, larger than life, wrought in stone; but it likewise came into the mind of Saint Ghastly Grim that to stick iron spikes a-

Gateway to St Olave's Churchyard, Hart Street: 'St Ghastly Grim', according to Dickens.

top of the stone skulls, as though they were impaled, would be a pleasant device.

St Olave's is the burial place of the diarist Samuel Pepys (d. 1703) and his wife Elizabeth (d. 1669), both of whom were regular worshippers there.

SALISBURY, WILTSHIRE — In *Martin Chuzzlewit* Tom Pinch, assistant to Seth Pecksniff, thinks Salisbury must be 'a very desperate sort of place; an exceedingly wild and dissipated city' as he sets forth on market-day 'on a stroll about the streets with a vague and not unpleasant idea that they teemed with all kinds of mystery and bedevilment'. And, in the same novel, it is

Salisbury Cathedral's 'old grey spire, surmounted by a cross' that the confidence trickster Montague Tigg last sees from the darkening woodland before meeting his death at the hands of Jonas Chuzzlewit.

Salisbury Cathedral provides Pecksniffs' architectural students with a model from which to make 'elevations … from every possible point of sight'. Pecksniff later extols the virtues of the cathedral to Jonas Chuzzlewit:

'Salisbury Cathedral, my dear Jonas, is an edifice replete with venerable associations, and strikingly suggestive of the loftiest emotions. It is here we contemplate the work of bygone ages. It

Salisbury Cathedral, which appears in *Martin Chuzzlewit*.

is here we listen to the swelling organ, as we stroll through the reverberating aisles. We have drawings of this celebrated structure from the North, from the South, from the East, from the West, from the South-East, from the Nor-West.'

SANDLING, KENT — Sandling was probably Dickens's original for the village of Dingley Dell in *The Pickwick Papers*,

and nearby Cob Tree Hall was his model for Manor Farm, the home of the Wardle family, at which the four friends are made most welcome. 'There ain't a better spot o' ground in all Kent,' so they are reliably informed, by the man with the complexion of a ribstone-pippin apple; a feeling echoed next morning by Mr Pickwick as he throws open his bedroom window: 'Pleasant, pleasant country . . .

who could live to gaze from day to day on bricks and slate, who had once felt the influence of a scene like this?'

The plot of *The Pickwick Papers* thickens considerably at Dingley Dell, and the Pickwickians return later to Manor Farm to enjoy Christmas festivities with the Wardle family. During this episode Mr Pickwick has his famous but unfortunate experience on the frozen pond:

> The sport was at its height, the sliding was at the quickest, the laughter was at the loudest, when a sharp smart crack was heard. There was a quick rush towards the bank, a wild scream from the ladies, and a shout from Mr Tupman. A large mass of ice disappeared, the water bubbled over it, and Mr Pickwick's hat, gloves, and handkerchief were floating on the surface; and this was all of Mr Pickwick that anybody could see.

Thankfully our hero is rescued before the icy depths of the pond can claim him.

Sandling, Kent, scene of 'Christmas Eve at Mr Wardle's' from *The Pickwick Papers…*

SEVEN DIALS, LONDON — Towards the conclusion of *Nicholas Nickleby*, Nicholas and Kate find themselves lost in 'that labyrinth of streets which lie between Seven Dials and Soho'. Here, in 'a small boarded cellar' they discover the fate of the philandering Mr Mantalini. They find him:

> There, amidst clothes-baskets and clothes, stripped to his shirt sleeves, but wearing still an old patched pair of pantaloons of superlative make, a once brilliant waistcoat, and moustache and whiskers of yore, but lacking their lustrous dye … and grinding meanwhile as if for very life at the mangle.

Seven Dials – so-named because seven streets meet there – was an area well known to Dickens since his days as a child labourer at Warren's Blacking Warehouse (see also STRAND). Often at night he had wandered, innocent and alone, about this notorious 'rookery' known for its criminal element. Perhaps his very innocence protected him from meeting with anything untoward there. 'I understood little or nothing of what was bad then, and it had no depraving influence on me' was his own explanation.

The essays 'Seven Dials' and 'Meditations in Monmouth Street' in *Sketches by Boz* describe various incidents and characters seen there by Dickens.

SHADWELL, LONDON — In *The Mystery of Edwin Drood* Princess Puffer's opium den was based by Dickens upon one he had visited in the Shadwell district in the autumn of 1869 in the company of his American friend J. T. Fields.

In *The Life of Charles Dickens* John Forster relates Fields's experience:

… and of Mr Pickwick's ice-sliding accident.

'In a miserable court at night,' says Mr Fields, 'we found a haggard old woman blowing at a kind of pipe made of an old ink-bottle; and the words that Dickens puts into the mouth of this wretched creature in Edwin Drood, we heard her croon as we leaned over the tattered bed in which she was lying.'

Shadwell church features in the essay 'Bound for the Great Salt Lake' in *The Uncommercial Traveller.*

SHEERNESS, KENT — In January 1817 John Dickens was transferred to the small town of Sheerness, in Kent. Although little is known of the Dickens's brief stay here (they moved on to CHATHAM probably in March of the same year), it appears that they lived next door to the Sheerness Theatre (now gone). John Dickens reputedly told a tale of joining in with the choruses of several songs overheard from the theatre which adjoined the family sitting-room.

SHEFFIELD, SOUTH YORKSHIRE — Dickens's allusion between young David and 'Brooks of Sheffield' in *David Copperfield* is the only time the city is mentioned in his novels. In December 1855 he gave a reading of *A Christmas Carol* in the Lecture Hall; afterwards he was presented with several examples of cutlery.

SHORNE, KENT — Shorne was one of Dickens's favourite villages. He loved the Saxon church there, and features it briefly in *The Pickwick Papers.* He calls it:

One of the most peaceful and secluded churchyards in Kent, where wild flowers mingle with the grass, and the soft landscape around forms the fairest spot in the garden of England.

This churchyard was one of the places in which Dickens expressed a wish to be buried, the others being COBHAM and ROCHESTER. (See also GAD'S HILL PLACE and WESTMINSTER ABBEY),

SHREWSBURY, SHROPSHIRE — In *A Tale of Two Cities* we learn that Sydney Carton and the lawyer Mr Styver both received their education at Shrewsbury School.

It is possible that in *The Old Curiosity Shop* Dickens based 'the large town', in whose 'streets were a number of old houses built of a kind of earth or plaster', upon that of Shrewsbury.

Dickens had first visited the town, with Hablot Knight Browne, on 31 October 1838; they stayed at the Lion Hotel.

SLOUGH, BERKSHIRE — In July 1851 Dickens took his son Charley, together with three of his schoolfriends, on a picnic to Slough 'accompanied by two immense hampers from Fortnums and Mason, on (I believe) the wettest morning ever seen out of the tropics'. Dickens's friend, the actress Ellen Ternan, lived in Slough for a while during the 1860s.

SMITHFIELD, LONDON — In *Little Dorrit*, following his accident with a mail-coach outside the Cross Keys Inn (see also CHEAPSIDE), John Baptist Cavalletto is taken to St Bartholomew's Hospital, near Smithfield Market. 'St Bart's', London's oldest hospital (founded in 1123) also features in *The Pickwick Papers*, where Jack Hopkins is a student to Slasher the Surgeon. In *Martin Chuzzlewit* the nurse Betsey Prig is:

> of Bartlemy's: or as some said Barkleby's, or as some said Bardlemy's; for by all these endearing and familiar appellations, had the hospital of St Bartholomew become a household word.

In *Oliver Twist* Sikes and Oliver, en route to 'crack the crib' at Chertsey, pass through Smithfield Market at early morning (see also CHERTSEY.).

In *Great Expectations* the lawyer Mr Jaggers – employed by Miss Havisham and by Abel Magwitch – has offices in Little Britain 'just out of Smithfield, and close by the coach office'. Here, Pip learns the true history of Estella when Jaggers puts 'the imaginary case'.

Dickens's *Household Words* essay 'A Monument to French Folly' (1851), which appears in *Reprinted Pieces*, was his contribution to the campaign to get Smithfield modernized and reorganized.

SMITH SQUARE, LONDON — In *Our Mutual Friend* Jenny Wren lives with her alcoholic father, her 'bad boy', in:

> a certain little street called Church Street, and a certain little blind square called

Smith Square, in the centre of which last retreat is a very hideous church with four towers at the four corners, generally resembling some petrified monster, frightful and gigantic, on its back with its legs in the air.

Church Street is now called Dean Stanley Street, and the church in question is St John's, Westminster (now a concert hall).

SNOW HILL, LONDON —

'Mr Squeers is in town, and attends daily, from one till four, at the Saracen's Head, Snow Hill. N.B. An able assistant wanted. Annual salary £5. A master of Arts would be preferred.'

So ran the newspaper advertisement answered by Nicholas Nickleby which led to his being taken on as a master at Dotheboys Hall (see also BOWES).

Prior to the construction of Holborn Viaduct (in 1868) Snow Hill was a steep gradient 'where omnibus horses going eastward seriously think of falling down on purpose, and where horses in hackney cabriolets going westward not infrequently fall by accident'. The Saracen's Head Inn was the chief coaching station for travellers going north and was often the London base for visiting Yorkshire schoolmasters. The building was demolished in 1868; its site is now occupied by a police station.

A doorway (now bricked-in) in the south wall of St Sepulchre's church led, via a passageway, to the condemned cells within nearby NEWGATE PRISON. A handbell, kept in the church, would herald an execution. In *Barnaby Rudge*, during a morning's wait for the execution of two rioters:

The concourse, which had been rapidly augmenting for some hours, and still received additions every minute, waited with an impatience which increased with every chime of St Sepulchre's clock, for twelve at noon.

SOHO, LONDON — While living in CAMDEN TOWN Dickens was often taken to visit his Uncle, Thomas Barrow – his mother's elder brother – who lived in a room above a bookseller's shop in Gerrard Street, Soho. This shop was run by a Mrs Manson, the former proprietor's widow, who would often lend young Charles books to read at his leisure.

During one visit to Gerrard Street, Dickens discovered his Uncle Thomas laid up with a broken leg, and being shaved by a 'very old barber out of Dean Street' who 'never tired of detecting Napoleon's mistakes, and rearranging his whole life for him'.

Soho was to make many such distinct impressions on young Dickens's mind and he would return there in three of his novels: in *Barnaby Rudge*, Emma Haredale 'was with her uncle at the masquerade at Carlisle House' (in Carlisle Street). In *Bleak House*, Esther Summerson meets with Caddy Jellyby in:

a quiet place in the neighbourhood of Newman Street. Caddy was in the garden in the centre, and hurried out as soon as I appeared.

The garden referred to is Soho Square. In *A Tale of Two Cities*:

The quiet lodgings of Doctor Manette were in a quiet street-corner not far from Soho Square ... A quainter corner than the corner where the Doctor lived was not to be found in London. There was no way through it, and the front windows of the Doctor's lodgings commanded a pleasant little vista of the street that had a congenial air of retirement on it ... The summer light struck into the corner brilliantly in the earlier part of the day; but, when the street grew hot, the corner was in shadow so remote but that you could see beyond it into a glare of brightness. It was a cool spot, staid but cheerful, a wonderful place for echoes, and a very harbour from the raging streets ... The Doctor occupied two floors of a large still house. ... In a building at the back, attainable by a courtyard where a plane tree rustled its green leaves, church-organs claimed to be made, and likewise gold to be beaten by some mysterious giant who had a golden arm starting out of the wall of the front hall – as if he had beaten himself precious, and menaced a similar conversion of all visitors.

Houses in Carlisle Street, Greek Street and Manette Street have made claims to being

Sketches of Charles Dickens playing Captain Bobadill in Ben Jonson's play *Every Man In His Humour*.

the original of Doctor Manette's house. The gold-beater's sign was rescued from Manette Street by the Dickens Fellowship and can be seen at the Dickens House Museum, DOUGHTY STREET.

In 1845 Dickens acted at Fanny Kelly's theatre (now gone) in Dean Street: this theatre being attached to the school of dramatic art owned and run by Miss Kelly, a retired actress.

SOUTHWARK, LONDON — Within a few weeks of starting work at Warren's Warehouse in January or February 1824 (see also COVENT GARDEN and STRAND), young Dickens's pride took a further blow when his father was arrested for debt. For three days – while John Dickens languished inside a 'sponging house' – Elizabeth, Charles and other family members frantically attempted to find a solution. But there was no way out of their dilemma and John Dickens was duly imprisoned inside the King's Bench Debtors' prison situated off Borough High Street, Southwark. Shortly afterwards he was removed to the nearby New Marshalsea Debtors' prison.

For a while, at least, Elizabeth was able to retain the house in GOWER STREET North, but it soon proved more economical for her and the younger children to share John's cramped room inside the New Marshalsea.

Charles, being in employment, and his elder sister Fanny – a boarder at the Royal Academy of Music (see also TENTERDEN STREET) – were both excluded from the move. Charles was, however, summoned to appear before an 'appraiser' near St George's Circus, whose task it was to evaluate the worth of the clothes on the boy's back – these were not allowed to exceed a value of £20. Needless to say he passed this test with ease. (The Obelisk, St George's Circus – now in the grounds of the Imperial War Museum, Lambeth Road – was also the place where David Copperfield had his box and half a guinea stolen by 'the long-legged young man'.) Charles was sent to lodge with a Mrs Roylance in Little College Street, CAMDEN TOWN. Here he met several children in circumstances similar to his own – a fact which made his sudden loneliness all the more acute.

On Sundays he and Fanny would visit the family inside the New Marshalsea. On one such occasion John Dickens recognized the desperately unhappy state of his son, and within a few days had arranged a new lodging for him in the back attic of a house in Lant Street, just a few minutes' walk from the prison. The move meant that Charles was able to share breakfast-times with his family before walking northwards to work across Blackfriars Bridge.

One day he was taken ill at work – a result no doubt of undernourishment and worry. Bob Fagin made up a bed of straw for him and tended to him throughout the day – and, when the time came, insisted on accompanying his sick friend home. Inwardly, Dickens was horrified by the prospect as he had told no one at Warren's of his family's current circumstances. And yet he could hardly refuse so kind an offer.

Needing time to think, he led the other boy across Southwark Bridge (instead of taking his usual, quicker route over Blackfriars Bridge). Once across the river, he thanked Fagin profusely, shook him by the hand and then darted up the steps of the nearest large house. As his friend lingered down in the street, Dickens knocked on the door and waved him goodbye. At last Fagin turned back towards London. When the lady of the house eventually answered the door Dickens mumbled an apology to her. Then, checking that his companion was well out of sight, he proceeded alone to Lant Street.

His landlord and landlady here were a friendly old couple, who – with their lame son – unwittingly became models for the Garland family in *The Old Curiosity Shop*. Another fictional resident of Lant Street was Bob Sawyer, the medical student who lodges with Mrs Raddle in *The Pickwick Papers* (see also BRISTOL). Today, Lant Street is almost entirely rebuilt and the Charles Dickens Primary School commemorates the author's brief stay in the area. Several other streets in the vicinity are named after some of his famous fictional characters, such as Copperfield Street.

Life inside the Marshalsea wasn't all bad for John Dickens (chronic debtors were at least protected there from their creditors). He was well-liked by inmates and warders alike. His natural ebullience and optimistic nature quickly won him the chairmanship of the Committee to Regulate the Internal Workings of the Marshalsea – a job into which he typically threw all his energies. His crowning achievement in this office was the successful commissioning of a petition calling for a 'royal bounty', a sum of money with which the inmates would drink a toast to King George IV on the occasion of the monarch's forthcoming birthday. Charles Dickens, who was present at the petitioning, later recalled the incident as an example of 'my early interest in observing people … I made my own little character and story for every man who put his name to that sheet of paper.'

At the end of April 1824, John Dickens's mother died, leaving him the sum of £450 in her will. Although it did not save him from insolvency, this money probably helped in securing his release from the New Marshalsea in May. He returned to his naval post, ostensibly on a full-time basis. However, since he had taken advantage of the Insolvent Debtors' Act, the Navy Board decided that his career could no longer continue; but, taking into consideration his twenty years of loyal service, the fact of his large family and medical evidence of 'a chronic affection of the urinary organs', the Navy Board retired him on a superannuation of £145.

Although it lasted but three short months, the Marshalsea experience left an indelible mark upon Charles Dickens, a mark which found its way into his work. William Dorrit, 'the father of the Marshalsea', is imprisoned within its walls for twenty-five years in *Little Dorrit*. His daughter Amy is born in the prison and often sits gazing out of his cell window, situated – as was John Dickens's cell – 'on the top storey but one.'

Nearby stands the church of St George the Martyr where Little Dorrit (Amy) was christened and is later married to Arthur Clennam. The vestry still remains in which she sleeps for one night, having failed to gain admission to the prison. In commemoration of the church's association with *Little Dorrit* the bottom-left corner of a fine stained-glass window (above the altar) depicts Amy Dorrit kneeling at prayer.

The 'Little Dorrit church', Borough High Street.

Also in the vicinity stood the King's Bench Prison (now demolished), scene of Mr Micawber's incarceration for debt – his expected fortune having failed to 'turn up'. Another Southwark prison, 'The Clink' in Tooley Street, was burned down during the Gordon Riots of 1780 and is mentioned in *Barnaby Rudge*.

It was at the Horsemonger Lane Gaol (site now occupied by Harper Road) in 1849 that Dickens witnessed the public execution of Mr and Mrs Manning (they had murdered their lodger). He was horrified at the reactions of the blood-thirsty crowd and subsequently wrote a celebrated letter to *The Times* criticizing such behaviour. It is in the courtyard of the White Hart Inn, in Borough High Street, that Samuel Pickwick first encounters Sam Weller in *The Pickwick Papers*, as the latter shines the boots of the inn's clientele. The White Hart was one of a number of galleried coaching inns sited in Borough High Street – it is mentioned by Shakespeare in *Henry VI*. Sadly, this important Dickensian landmark has long since been demolished and is now commemorated by a plaque. Fortunately visitors can still enjoy a drink just a short distance along the street at The George Inn, a genuine 17th-century building and the last remaining galleried tavern left in London. Here, in *Little Dorrit*, Edward 'Tip' Dorrit composes a begging letter to Arthur Clennam.

The fateful meeting of Nancy with Rose Maylie and Mr Brownlow – in *Oliver Twist* – takes place on the steps of London Bridge 'on the same side … as St Saviour's Church' (see also LONDON BRIDGE). St Saviour's is also mentioned in *The Uncommercial Traveller*. This church became Southwark Cathedral in 1905 and is the smallest of London's cathedrals. Southwark Bridge provides the venue for Little Dorrit's first meeting with Arthur Clennam; and *Our Mutual Friend* has its magnificently atmospheric opening passage on the Thames, 'between Southwark Bridge which is of iron and London Bridge which is of stone.'

A contemporary illustration of the train crash at Staplehurst of which Dickens was a survivor.

STAPLEHURST, KENT — On 9 June 1865 Dickens (accompanied by his friend the actress Ellen Ternan) returned by steamer to Folkestone, following a brief visit to Paris. He boarded the 'tidal' train, bound for London; his destination was ROCHESTER, from where he would complete the journey to GAD'S HILL PLACE. Shortly after 3 p.m., the train was speeding towards Staplehurst.

Unfortunately, and unbeknownst to the driver, essential maintenance work was being carried out along that stretch of track, which involved the temporary removal of a 40-foot (12m) length of rail. Due to a misunderstanding of the timetable by the foreman of the gang, and to an inadequate warning system, the 'tidal' train was derailed on a bridge across a stream, at a speed of some 40 m.p.h. Several passengers were killed in the accident. Dickens survived, and was actively involved in the rescue operation of the survivors. He was, moreover, travelling with the manuscript of *Our Mutual Friend*, and had to return to his carriage to retrieve it.

On 10 June he wrote to John Forster:

I was in the terrific Staplehurst accident yesterday, and worked for hours among the dying and dead. I was in the carriage that did not go over, but went off the line, and hung over the bridge in an inexplicable manner. No words can describe the scene.

The horrendous experience shook Dickens considerably. He suffered from nerves for the rest of his days, and never again enjoyed travelling by rail. Always afterwards he took a flask of brandy on a train journey.

STAPLE INN, LONDON — In *Bleak House* the law stationer Snagsby enjoys walking 'in Staple Inn in the summertime and to observe how countrified the sparrows and the leaves are'.

The same Inn of Chancery, which lies behind the row of well-known Tudor shops in Holborn, also appears in *The Mystery of Edwin Drood*:

> Behind the most ancient part of Holborn, London, where certain gabled houses some centuries of age still stand looking on the public way, as if disconsolately looking

Staple Inn, London, where the smoky London sparrows 'play at country'.

for the Old Bourne that has long run dry, is a little nook composed of two irregular quadrangles, called Staple Inn. It is one of those nooks, the turning into which out of the clashing street, imparts to the relieved pedestrian the sensation of having put cotton in his ears, and velvet soles on his boots. It is one of these nooks where a few smoky sparrows twitter in smoky trees, as though they called to one another, 'Let us play at country,' and where a few feet of garden mould and a few yards of gravel enable them to do that refreshing violence to their tiny understanding.

Within Staple Inn lives Hiram Grewgious, guardian to Rosa Bud, in a set of chambers whose doorway bears 'the mysterious inscription':

JPT
1747

which may still be seen.

Despite the attentions of a flying bomb in World War II, the Inn still survives, having been restored to former glory in 1954.

STRAND, LONDON — In January or February 1824 a well-intentioned scheme to add to the dwindling Dickens family coffers was suggested to John and Elizabeth by their brother-in-law, James Lamert, who was then working as the manager of Warren's Boot Blacking Warehouse. He proposed that Charles be set to work in the warehouse, from 8 a.m. to 8 p.m. for six days a week. Much to the boy's horror, the weekly wage of 6s was enough to persuade his parents to agree to the suggestion.

Warren's Blacking Warehouse was a ramshackle wooden building abutting the river Thames at Hungerford Stairs, Hungerford Market (site now occupied by Charing Cross Station). It was decrepit and damp, rotting away in places and running alive with rats.

At first Charles's refined manners did not go down too well in the warehouse, and he was mockingly referred to as the 'Young Gentleman'. But gradually the common drudgery of the work brought him acceptance among his workmates, while his enormous sense of pride enabled him to keep secret his reasons for being there at all.

Among Charles's new companions, who worked in the dim light at covering and labelling the pots of blacking, was a boy named 'Poll' Green, the son of a fireman at Drury Lane Theatre, and another called Bob Fagin (their respective christian and surnames would later find fame in different guises). When Jonathan Warren moved his blacking business to larger premises in Chandos Street (now Chandos Place), COVENT GARDEN, Charles Dickens moved with them.

In *Nicholas Nickleby*, Miss La Creevy, the painter of miniatures, lives and works in the Strand. Her apartment/studio lies within 'a private door about half-way down that crowded thoroughfare'.

In *Oliver Twist* the interview between Mr Brownlow and Rose Maylie which leads towards the recovery of Oliver takes place in an unspecified house in Craven Street, off the Strand.

A rather grotesque door knocker in Craven Street gave Dickens the inspiration to have Scrooge's door knocker change into the face of Jacob Marley in *A Christmas Carol*.

In *Martin Chuzzlewit*, young Martin – upon his return from America – secures lodgings for himself and his servant Mark Tapley 'in a court in the Strand, not far from Temple Bar'.

David Copperfield found lodgings at Mrs Crupp's house in Buckingham Street, off the Strand. Dickens himself lodged at 15 Buckingham Street between May 1832 and November 1834. His room was at the top of the house and his window overlooked the river Thames. His stay here, within easy reach of his reporting work at the HOUSES OF PARLIAMENT, alternated with frequent visits to the family home at 18 BENTINCK STREET. Previously he had lodged at a house in Cecil Street (now gone), Strand. These lodgings proved uncomfortable; the landlord and landlady 'put too much water in their hash' and 'attended on me most miserably'.

On the day of Copperfield's house-warming party, he walked along the Strand:

and observing a hard mottled substance in the window of a ham and beef shop, which resembled marble, but was labelled 'Mock Turtle', I went in and bought a slab of it, which I have since

seen reason to believe would have sufficed fifteen people. This preparation, Mrs Crupp, after some difficulty, consented to warm up; and it shrank so much in a liquid state, that we found it what Steerforth called 'rather a tight fit' for four.

David Copperfield also tells of an 'old Roman bath':

at the bottom of one of the streets out of the Strand – it may still be there – in which I have taken many a cold plunge. Dressing myself as quietly as I could, and leaving Peggotty to look after my aunt, I tumbled head foremost into it, and then went for a walk to Hampstead. I had a hope that this brisk treatment might freshen my wits a little.

Indeed, the 'Roman Bath' is there still in Strand Lane (no longer 'out of the Strand', but now approached by a passageway off Surrey Street) and may be viewed through a window, or entered by appointment. The bath may not be, in fact, of Roman origin, but possibly dates from another period, perhaps the 16th century. The building is currently administered by Westminster County Council.

In *Great Expectations* Pip arranged for 'Mr Provis', alias Magwitch, 'a respectable lodging house in Essex Street'. Essex Street is a turning to the south of the Strand where, in 1842, Dickens attended the Unitarian Chapel (later Essex Hall) having become interested in Unitarian thought on his recent visit to America (see also little PORTLAND STREET and LIVERPOOL).

Adelphi Terrace (now demolished), a fine residential quarter between the Strand and the Thames, was often explored by Dickens during his days as a child labourer at Warren's Blacking Warehouse.

In November 1834, during his father's second term of imprisonment for debt, Dickens arranged cheap accommodation for his mother and her younger children at 21 George Street, Adelphi. He later featured the area in several stories: Mr Pickwick celebrates his release from the Fleet Prison at 'Osbornes Hotel' – based on the Adelphi Hotel (now gone). Later in *The Pickwick Papers* Mr Wardle and his daughter Emily also stay here. In *Little Dorrit* Miss Wade meets Blandois (alias Rigaud) and Tattycoram in the Adelphi, a meeting witnessed by Arthur Clennam. In 'Mrs Lirriper's Lodgings' (*Christmas Stories*) Mrs Edson contemplates suicide from the Terrace.

The Strand also features briefly in *The Old Curiosity Shop*, *Barnaby Rudge*, *A Tale of Two Cities* and *Our Mutual Friend*.

The offices of the *Morning Chronicle* (and later the *Evening Chronicle*), for whom Dickens worked as a Parliamentary Reporter between August 1834 and 1836, stood at 332 Strand. The offices and bookshop of Messrs Chapman and Hall, Dickens's first publishers, were at 186 Strand (now gone). This firm published *The Pickwick Papers*, *Nicholas Nickleby*, *Master Humphrey's Clock*, *The Old*

Curiosity Shop, *Barnaby Rudge*, *American Notes*, *Martin Chuzzlewit*, *A Christmas Carol* and *The Chimes*. Dickens broke with Chapman and Hall in June 1844 (making a new arrangement with Bradbury and Evans) but rejoined them in 1859 for the publication of his weekly journal *All the Year Round*. The firm subsequently published *A Tale of Two Cities*, *The Uncommercial Traveller*, *Great Expectations*, *Our Mutual Friend* and the uncompleted *The Mystery of Edwin Drood*.

Somerset House, between the Strand and Victoria Embankment, also has Dickensian connections. John Dickens was employed there as an Assistant Naval Clerk between 1801 and 1809. There he met Elizabeth Barrow, sister of Thomas Barrow, a fellow clerk. The couple were married at the church of St Mary-le-Strand on 13 June 1809. Shortly after the wedding they moved to Portsmouth where John took up a new post as a Navy Pay Clerk.

Charles Barrow – father of Thomas and Elizabeth – was also employed by the Navy as Chief Conductor of Monies in Town. This was a highly respectable position, involving the conveyance of large sums of money, and carrying with it a suite of rooms inside Somerset House.

Outwardly a pillar of respectability, Charles Barrow had in fact been systematically cheating his employers for a number of years. Between 1803 and 1810 more than £5000 of Naval funds had found its way into his pocket. When confronted with the misdemeanour, Barrow confessed all. But, rather than go to prison, he absconded into Europe and never returned. He spent his last years in the Isle of Man, where he died in 1826.

A secret sense of shame over this skeleton in the family cupboard – and over his own father's ultimately catastrophic financial condition – was felt by Charles Dickens for many years to come.

Rules Restaurant in Maiden Lane, to the north of the Strand, was one of Dickens's favourite eating places, and still boasts a 'Dickens corner'.

STRATFORD-UPON-AVON, WARWICKSHIRE — Dickens first visited Stratford-upon-Avon on 30 October 1838, during a tour of the Midlands and North Wales with Hablot Knight Browne. His diary for that day relates:

> we sat down in the room where Shakespeare was born, and left our autographs and read those of other people, and so forth.

The diary also discloses that the two friends stayed at an inn – not specified – where the bill came to £2. 10s. 0d.

In 1848 Dickens became actively involved with the committee formed to preserve the birthplace of the Immortal Bard. In May of that year he played in eight fund-raising performances as Justice Shallow in *The Merry Wives of Windsor*, at the Theatre Royal HAYMARKET, London, in aid of that cause.

In *Nicholas Nickleby*, Mrs Nickleby tells of a visit to the town made shortly after her wedding:

> '…after we had seen Shakespeare's tomb and birthplace, we went back to the inn there, where we slept that night, and I recollect that all night long I dreamt of nothing but a black gentleman, at full length, in plaster of Paris, with a lay down collar tied with two tassels, leaning against a post and thinking, and when I woke in the morning and described him to Mr Nickleby, he said, it was Shakespeare just as he had been when he was alive, which was very curious indeed.'

STROOD, KENT — Strood is the north-western neighbour to ROCHESTER and CHATHAM. During his days at GAD'S HILL PLACE Dickens would often walk into Strood and there enjoy a drink or two at the Crispin and Crispianus Inn on the London Road (closed in 2010 and badly damaged by fire in 2011).

SUDBURY, SUFFOLK — For their second journey in *The Pickwick Papers* the Pickwickians undertake to travel to the town of 'Eatanswill' to witness the forthcoming Parliamentary election there, between the 'Blues' and the 'Buffs'.

Excepting that it lay somewhere in East Anglia – as the Pickwickians were 'booked by the Norwich coach' – Dickens (or rather 'Boz', editor of the 'papers') claims to have 'in vain searched for proof of the actual existence of Eatanswill'. Considering, however, that the next leg of this journey takes the story to BURY ST EDMUNDS, then the claims for Sudbury as being the original 'Eatanswill' seem the most likely (other claims have been made for IPSWICH but Sudbury is in a more direct line linking London to Bury St Edmunds.) And indeed Dickens had reported on a by-election there for the *Morning Chronicle*, in July 1834.

The Pickwickians arrive with Sam Weller in Eatanswill, only to discover that the inns and hotels are packed to the rafters and the place is awash with election fever. At the Town Arms Mr Pickwick locates his contact – the lawyer Perker, who is acting as political agent to Samuel Slumkey, the Blues candidate. Perker's opposite number – the agent to the Buffs candidate, Horatio Fizkin – has 'three-and-thirty voters in the lockup coach house at the White Hart', and is only likely to release them at voting time. The slightly more sophisticated Perker has matched this move with a more subtle gambit, consisting of the free distribution of forty-five green parasols to certain well-chosen ladies of the town. Perker explains: 'All women love finery – extraordinary the effect of these parasols. Secured half their husbands, and half their brothers – beats stockings, and flannel, and all that sort of thing hollow.'

Perker introduces the Pickwickians to Mr Pott, editor of the pro-Blues Eatanswill Gazette, and deadly rival to Mr Slurk,

editor of the Buffs-biased Eatanswill Independent. In turn, Pott arranges accommodation for the Pickwickians. After a meal at the Town Arms, Tupman, Snodgrass and Weller all repair to the Peacock Inn, while Pickwick and Winkle enter the domestic circle of the Pott household.

Having seen Samuel Slumkey successfully returned in the election, the Pickwickians are invited to attend a fancy-dress breakfast, a 'fête champêtre', at 'The Den, Eatanswill', home of Mrs Leo Hunter, authoress of the mildly celebrated 'Ode to an Expiring Frog'. Here they spot a certain Charles Fitz-Marshall whose appearance causes Mr Pickwick to drop his knife and fork in astonishment, for the stranger is none other than Alfred Jingle, the cause of so much upset within the Pickwickian camp. Under the suddenly frightening gaze of the 'indignant orbs of Mr Pickwick', Jingle makes his excuses and disappears rather sharply.

The pro-Buff Peacock Inn, where the Pickwickians hear 'The Bagman's Tale', is based upon the Swan Inn. The original of the Town Arms, Headquarters of the 'Blues' – where the barmaid is said to 'hocus the brandy and water of fourteen unpolled electors who were staying at the house' – is thought to have been the Rose and Crown, which was unfortunately destroyed by fire in 1922. The locations of the Potts' family home and of 'The Den' are not known.

T

TAVISTOCK HOUSE, LONDON — In November 1851, following the expiry of the lease of 1 DEVONSHIRE TERRACE, the growing Dickens family moved to Tavistock House, Tavistock Square, Bloomsbury: Dickens had paid the owner, artist Frank Stone, £1,450 for the leasehold. This was a much larger house than Devonshire Terrace, of some eighteen rooms, set within private grounds, and was the neighbour to Russell House and Bedford House.

Before settling in and setting to work on his ninth novel, *Bleak House*, Dickens required several alterations to be made. Stone's first-floor studio was to be converted into a drawing room, a movable partition was to be made between this and Dickens's study, and Stone's old drawing room was to become a schoolroom for the Dickens children. A team of workmen were contracted to carry out this work, but the author was soon complaining:

> Curtains and carpets, on a scale of awful splendour and magnitude, are already in preparation and still – still – NO WORKMEN ON THE PREMISES …
> Then Stone presents himself, with a most exasperatingly mysterious visage, and says that a Rat has appeared in the kitchen, and it's his opinion (Stone's, not the Rat's) that the drains want 'composing';

for the use of which explicit language I could fell him without remorse.

Eventually these frustrations were appeased and the necessary work done to Dickens's satisfaction. In later years his daughter Mamie recalled his study at Tavistock House as 'a fine large room, opening into the drawing-room by means of sliding doors … When the rooms were thrown together they gave my father a promenade of considerable length for the constant indoor walking which formed a favourite recreation for him after a hard day's writing.' Dickens later made the schoolroom into a theatre, where he often indulged his passion for amateur dramatics.

Whilst living in Tavistock House Dickens wrote *Bleak House*, *Hard Times*, and *Little Dorrit*, as well as parts of *A Tale of Two Cities*. The house, along with its elegant neighbours, was demolished in 1901. The headquarters of the British Medical Association now occupies the site and a commemorative plaque celebrates Dickens's former occupancy.

THE TEMPLE, LONDON — The Temple, lying between FLEET STREET and the Victoria Embankment, was originally the headquarters of the Knights Templar, founded in 1119 in Jerusalem. The order was dissolved in 1312, and in 1324 the Temple became a legal centre. The four Inns of Court – Middle Temple, Inner Temple, Gray's Inn and Lincoln's Inn – were founded in the mid-1400s. Inner and

Middle Temple Hall in the nineteenth century.

Middle Temple are divided by Middle Temple Lane, with Inner Temple to its east and Middle Temple to its west. The Temple was well known to Dickens; he calls it 'the cloisterly Temple' in *Bleak House* and uses the area in several other novels. In *Martin Chuzzlewit*, Tom Pinch lives and works in chambers in Pump Court and he meets Mr Fips at Middle Temple Gate. The romance between Ruth Pinch and John Westlock begins in Fountain Court, while:

Merrily the fountain plashed and plashed, until the dimples, merging into one another, swelled into a general smile, that covered the whole surface of the basin.

Later in the same relationship:

…the Temple Fountain sparkled in the sun, and laughingly its liquid music played, and merrily the idle drops of water danced and danced, and, peeping out in sport among the trees, plunged lightly down to hide themselves, as little Ruth and her companion came towards it.

And why they came towards the Fountain at all is a mystery, for they had no business there. It was not in their way. It was quite out of their way. They had no more to do with the Fountain, bless you, than they had with – with Love, or any out-of-the-way thing of that sort ... Oh wicked little Ruth!

In *Barnaby Rudge* we learn that:

> There are still worse places than the Temple on a sultry day, for basking in the sun or resting idly in the shade. There is yet a drowsiness in its Courts and a dreamy dullness in its trees and gardens; those who pace its lanes and squares may yet hear the echoes of their footsteps on the sounding stones, and read upon its gates 'Who enters here leaves noise behind.'

When, in the same novel, Maypole Hugh 'plied the knocker of Middle Temple Gate' he received the reply 'We don't sell beer here'. The object of his visit was the chambers of Sir John Chester in Paper Buildings.

In *A Tale of Two Cities* the lawyer, Mr Styver, has chambers within the Temple. His clerk, Sydney Carton:

> turned into the Temple, and, having revived himself by twice pacing the pavements of King's Bench Walk and Paper Buildings, turned into the Styver chambers.

In *Great Expectations* Pip and Herbert Pocket, after a year in BARNARD'S INN, share rooms in Garden Court:

> Alterations have been made in that part of the Temple since that time, and it has not now so lonely a character as it had then, nor is it so exposed to the river. We lived at the top of the last house, and the wind rushing up the river shook the house that night, like discharging of cannon, or breakings of a sea.

'That night' was the night on which Pip discovers the truth behind his good fortunes when Abel Magwitch appears at Garden Court. It is at the Whitefriars' Gate entrance to the Temple that Pip receives Wemmick's note with its warning 'Don't go home'.

Later in the same novel, when Magwitch has died in the ill-fated attempt to flee the country, Pip falls sick in his chambers. Upon regaining consciousness he finds himself in the care of Joe Gargery, the gentle blacksmith. The boat used by Pip and Herbert in Magwitch's escape attempt is kept at Temple Stairs (now gone) at the foot of King's Bench Walk. This location serves the same purpose for Mr Tairter's boat in *The Mystery of Edwin Drood*.

In *Our Mutual Friend* the young solicitors, Mortimer Lightwood and Eugene Wrayburn, live in chambers on a site now occupied by Goldsmith's Buildings. Here we see Mr Boffin 'in consultation' with Lightwood with regard to his surprise inheritance following the death of Mr Harmon. Here the two men attempt to discover the address of Lizzie Hexam from Mr Dolls by plying him with several 'threepenn'orths Rum'. And Bradley Headstone waits near the Temple Gate for Eugene Wrayburn to appear.

TENTERDEN STREET, LONDON — In 1823 Dickens's elder sister, Frances (known as Fanny), won a scholarship to attend the Royal Academy of Music, then situated in Tenterden Street, off Hanover Square, where she stayed as a boarder. Although he loved her dearly, Charles nevertheless felt a deep resentment at the time that his own education had been simultaneously cut short (he had not attended school since leaving Chatham and would soon know even worse circumstances when sent to work in Warren's Blacking Warehouse – see also COVENT GARDEN and STRAND). Fanny Dickens later taught at the Academy.

TEWKESBURY, GLOUCESTERSHIRE — En route to Birmingham the Pickwickians stop to dine at the Hop Pole Inn (now the Royal Hop Pole Hotel), in Tewkesbury:

> upon which occasion there was more bottled ale, with some more Madeira, and some port besides; and here the case-bottle was replenished for the fourth time. Under the influence of these combined stimulants, Mr Pickwick and Mr Ben Allen fell fast asleep for thirty miles, while Bob and Mr Weller sang duets in the dickey.

THAMES STREET, LONDON — In *Nicholas Nickleby* Ralph Nickleby acquires a rather depressing lodging for his sister-in-law and his niece in 'a large old dingy house in Thames Street, the doors and windows of which were so bespattered by mud that it would have appeared to have been uninhabited for years'.

In *Barnaby Rudge*, Joe Willet settles his annual account with 'a certain vintner and distiller in the City of London' whose place of business was to be found 'down in some deep cellars hard by Thames Street'. In the same novel Simon Tappertit is on his way to deliver a lock 'to be fitted on a ware'us door in Thames Street', when he pauses to speak to Sir John Chester.

Thames Street, now divided into Upper and Lower Thames Street, runs from Blackfriars Bridge to Tower Hill.

THAVIES INN, LONDON — In *Bleak House* Mrs Jellyby lived in Thavies Inn, 'a narrow street of high houses, like an oblong cistern to hold the fog'. Esther Summerson, Ada Clare and Richard Carstone all lodge here.

THREADNEEDLE STREET, LONDON — In Dickens's first published piece of fiction, 'A Dinner at Poplar Walk' (later published in *Sketches by Boz* as 'Mr Minns and His Cousin'), Mr Minns begins his journey to Poplar Walk from the coaching-stand near the Flower Pot Inn (now demolished) which stood at the corner of Threadneedle Street. This street's most famous building, the Bank of England (built 1788), features in *The Pickwick Papers*, *Nicholas Nickleby*, *Barnaby Rudge*, *Dombey and Son* and *Little Dorrit*.

TONG, SHROPSHIRE — Having met once more with the kindly schoolmaster Mr Marton in *The Old Curiosity Shop*, Little Nell and her grandfather accompany him on the remainder of his journey to take up a new post at 'a village a long way from here'. On arrival in the village the trio halt their journey in order to 'contemplate its beauties':

'See – here's the church!' cried the delighted schoolmaster, in a low voice; 'and that old building close beside it is the schoolhouse, I'll be sworn. Five-and-thirty pounds a year in this beautiful place!'

Little Nell and her grandfather arrive at the church in *The Old Curiosity Shop*.

They admired everything – the old gray porch, the mullioned windows, the venerable gravestones dotting the green churchyard, the ancient tower, the very weathercock; the brown thatched roofs of cottage, barn and homestead, peeping from among the trees; the stream that rippled by the distant windmill; the blue Welsh mountains far away. It was for such a spot the child had wearied in the dense, dark, miserable haunts of labour.

The village in question is Tong in Shropshire, a fact confirmed by Dickens himself in conversation with the Venerable T. B. Lloyd (Archdeacon of Salop from 1824 to 1896). Indeed, the church of St Bartholomew was undoubtedly George Cattermole's original for the engraving which illustrates the first and several subsequent editions of the novel.

Little Nell and her grandfather move into a small cottage close to the church and next door to Mr Marton, who watches over the couple. Nell is entrusted with the tasks of keeping the keys to the church, opening it up for services, and conducting visitors around its ancient portals.

Dickens gives a detailed description of the church's interior:

…the very light, coming through sunken windows, seemed old and gray, and the air redolent of earth and mould, seemed laden with decay, purified by time of all its grosser particles, and sighing through arch and aisle and clustered pillars like the breath of ages gone! Here was the broken pavement, worn so long ago by pious feet, that Time, stealing on the pilgrims' steps, had trodden out their track and left but crumbling stones. Here were the rotten beam, the sinking arch, the sapped and mouldering wall, the lowly trench of earth, the stately tomb on which no epitaph remained – all – marble, stone, iron, wood and dust – one common monument of ruin. The best work and the worst, the plainest and the richest, the stateliest and the least imposing – both of Heaven's work and Man's – all found one common level here, and told one common tale.

Some part of the edifice had been a baronial chapel, and here were effigies of warriors stretched upon their beds of stone with folded hands – crossed-legged, those who had fought in the Holy Wars – girded with their swords, and cased in armour as they had lived. Some of these knights had their own weapons, helmets, coats of mail, hanging upon the walls hard by, and dangling from rusty hooks. Broken and dilapidated as they were, they yet retained their ancient form, and something of their ancient aspect. Thus violent deeds live after men upon the earth, and traces of war and bloodshed will survive in mournful shapes, long after those who worked the desolation are but atoms of earth themselves.

Although Little Nell finds happiness in the village, her health gradually declines and she eventually dies in peace. She is buried

St Bartholomew's, Tong, Little Nell's final resting place.

inside the church. Her heartbroken grandfather dies soon afterwards.

The first issue of *Master Humphrey's Clock* was published by Chapman and Hall on 4 April 1840 and some 60,000 copies were quickly sold. However, Dickens's readership, anticipating another good long yarn in the instalment tradition of *Oliver Twist* and *Nicholas Nickleby* were sorely disappointed to find that no such plan had been laid. Subsequent sales of the second and third numbers had dropped dramatically. Dickens realized, of course, that he must do something about the situation, and quickly.

His solution was to expand one of the stories into a full-length work. The result – *The Old Curiosity Shop* – began in the fourth number. The story immediately caught the public imagination and sales of *Master Humphrey's Clock* rose once more, often hovering between 70,000 and 100,000 copies per week. Such was the power of the story that it was said to move grown men to tears. The Irish M.P. Daniel O'Connell was aboard a train whilst reading the instalment containing the death of Little Nell, and was so incensed by the episode that he threw the magazine from his carriage window. Quayside crowds in New York were said to ask incoming

Interior of St Bartholomew's, Tong. The building was restored in 1892.

English sailors for news of Little Nell. John Forster considered that the story ranked 'with the most attractive pieces of English fiction' and that it 'added to his [Dickens's] popularity more than any other of his works,' and made 'the bond between himself and his readers one of personal attachment'.

The legend of Little Nell lived on in Tong and indeed still does. In the early 1900s a particularly enterprising verger at St Bartholomew's would show visitors two cottages near the church, reputed to be those once occupied by Nell, her grandfather and Mr Marton. He would also point out the very spot in the churchyard where Little Nell was 'buried' (he was obviously unconcerned by the fact that Dickens had buried his heroine inside the church). It seems that the weather also played a part in this man's enterprise; on a fine day he would solemnly lead his pilgrims to an unmarked grave in a far corner of the churchyard. If, however, it happened to be raining, then the verger showed an alternative plot close to the church porch. This 'grave' still remains and bears a plaque proclaiming it as 'The Reputed Grave of Little Nell'. Its contents, if any, are unknown.

A search of the parish records for 1841 by Robert Jeffery, Archdeacon of Salop, revealed the name of one 'Nelly Gwynne'. The entry appears boldly scratched in Post Office ink in the normally vacant space at the foot of a column of names which are written in a now faded brown ink.

TOTTENHAM COURT ROAD, LONDON — Dickens first knew Tottenham Court Road as a child labourer at Warren's Blacking Warehouse (see also COVENT GARDEN and STRAND). He wrote of those days, 'I could not resist the stale pastry put out at half-price on those trays at the confectioners' doors in Tottenham Court Road; and I often spent in that, the money I should have kept for my dinner…'

Tottenham Court Road features in the essays 'Horatio Sparkins' and 'Hackney Coach-Stands' in *Sketches by Boz*. In *Nicholas Nickleby* Mortimer Knag lives 'in a bye-street off Tottenham Court Road', from where he sells ornamental stationery and lends out 'the newest old novels' from his circulating library. In *David Copperfield* the missing items of furniture belonging to Sophy Crewler and Tommy Traddles are tracked down to a brokers' shop in Tottenham Court Road.

TOWCESTER, NORTHAMPTONSHIRE — On their return journey from Birmingham to London, via Coventry, Dunchurch and Daventry, the Pickwickians' stagecoach pulls up in a rain-storm at the door of the Saracen's Head, in Towcester.

'I think it's quite impossible to go on tonight,' interposed Ben.

'Out of the question, sir,' remarked Sam Weller, coming to assist the conference: 'it's a cruelty to animals, sir, to ask 'em to do it. There's beds here, sir,' said Sam addressing his master,

The Saracen's Head, Towcester, where Mr Pickwick and his friends enjoy a good meal.

'everything clean and comfortable. Wery good little dinner, sir, they can get ready in half an hour – pair of fowls, sir, and a weal cutlet; French beans, 'taturs, tart, and tidiness. You'd better stop vere you are, sir, if I might recommend. Take advice, sir, as the doctor said.'

Take 'advice' Pickwick did, and:

The candles were brought, the fire was stirred up, and a fresh log of wood thrown on. In ten minutes' time, a waiter was laying the cloth for dinner, the curtains were drawn, the fire was blazing brightly, and everything looked (as everything always does, in all decent English inns) as if the travellers had been expected, and their comforts prepared, for days beforehand.

In the Saracen's Head the Pickwickians meet again with the rival newspaper editors Pott and Slurk (of the Eatanswill Gazette and the Eatanswill Independent respectively – see also SUDBURY), between whom a battle-royal ensues, involving a carpet-bag 'well stuffed with moveables', a fire-shovel, and a meal bag. Sam Weller saves the day by intervening in the fracas and the rival editors retire to their beds only to continue the fight at a later date – albeit in print – in Eatanswill.

The Saracen's Head survives today, proud of its Pickwickian association and ever-ready to serve up the modern equivalent of 'taturs, tart, and tidiness'.

THE TOWER OF LONDON — Daniel Quilp, the moneylender and the bane of Little Nell's life in *The Old Curiosity Shop*:

> resided on Tower Hill; and in her bower on Tower Hill Mrs Quilp was left to pine the absence of her lord, when he quitted her on the business which he has already been seen to transact.

Dickens's original for this dwelling, which 'comprised, besides the needful accommodation for himself and Mrs Quilp, a small sleeping-closet for that lady's mother, who resided with the couple and waged perpetual war with Daniel, was most probably 2 Tower Hill (now gone).

In *Barnaby Rudge* Joe Willet takes the King's Shilling at the Crooked Billet, which stood in Tower Street: 'In the course of five minutes after his arrival at that house of entertainment, he was enrolled among the gallant defenders of his native land.' In the same novel Lord George Gordon, the prime mover in the 'No Popery' riots, is imprisoned inside the Tower:

> in a dreary room whose thick stone walls shut out the hum of life and made a stillness which the records left by former prisoners with those silent witnesses seemed to deepen and intensify.

The Tower of London is also mentioned in *David Copperfield* and *Our Mutual Friend*.

TRAFALGAR SQUARE, LONDON — Part of South Africa House in Trafalgar Square now occupies the site of Golden Cross, once London's central coaching station, where in *The Pickwick Papers* Mr Pickwick meets up with his three travelling companions – Snodgrass, Winkle and Tupman – as well as the eccentric strolling player Alfred Jingle, who eventually proves the bane of his life. Here the party climb aboard 'The Commodore', a ROCHESTER-bound stagecoach.

In *David Copperfield* David meets Mr Peggotty and Martha Endell on the steps of the church of St Martin-in-the-Fields, during his search for Little Em'ly.

TURNHAM GREEN, LONDON — In *A Tale of Two Cities* Dickens reports that the 'magnificent potentate, the Lord Mayor of London,' was robbed at Turnham Green 'by one highwayman, who despoiled the illustrious creature in sight of all his retinue'.

TWICKENHAM, MIDDLESEX — In *Nicholas Nickleby*, the duel between Lord Verisopht and Sir Mulberry Hawk takes place in 'one of the meadows opposite Twickenham, by the riverside'. The result sees the end of the young Lord's life.

Later in the same novel Morleena Kenwigs receives an invitation to enjoy a picnic on Eel Pie Island, which sits in mid-

Thames at Twickenham. She arrives 'per steamer from Westminster Bridge' and makes merry 'upon a cold collation, bottled beer, shrub, and shrimps'.

In *Little Dorrit* Mr Meagles 'had a cottage-residence of his own' in Twickenham. 'It was a charming place (none the worse for being a little eccentric), on the road by the river.' Dickens was very familiar with Twickenham, having stayed in the town for a few months in 1838, during the writing of *Nicholas Nickleby*, at 2 Ailsa Park Villas.

W

WALWORTH, LONDON — 'Wemmick's Castle', in *Great Expectations*, lay in Walworth, then a quite rural district of London where John Wemmick lived with his 'Aged Parent'. Pip thinks Walworth 'a collection of back lanes, ditches, and little gardens' while Wemmick's house:

> was a little wooden cottage in the midst of plots of garden, and the top of it was cut out and painted like a battery mounted with guns.
>
> 'My own doing,' said Wemmick. 'Looks pretty; don't it?'
>
> …I think it was the smallest house I ever saw, with the queerest gothic windows (by far the greater part of them

sham), and a gothic door, almost too small to get in at.

'That's a real flagstaff, you see,' said Wemmick, 'and on Sundays I run up a real flag. Then, look here. After I have crossed this bridge, I hoist it up – so – and cut off the communication.'

The bridge was a plank, and it crossed a chasm about four feet wide and two deep. But it was very pleasant to see the pride with which he hoisted it up and made it fast; smiling as he did so, with a relish and not merely mechanically.

'At nine o'clock every night, Greenwich time,' said Wemmick, 'the gun fires. There he is, you see! And when you hear him go, I think you'll say he's a Stinger!'

The piece of ordnance referred to, was mounted in a separate fortress, constructed of lattice-work. It was protected from the weather by an ingenious little tarpaulin contrivance in the nature of an umbrella.

'…At the back there's a pig, and there are fowls and rabbits; then, I knock together my own little frame, you see, and grow cucumbers; and you'll judge what sort of a salad I can raise. So, sir,' said Wemmick, smiling again, but seriously too, as he shook his head, 'if you can suppose the little place besieged, it would hold out a devil of a time in point of provisions.

This marvellous little edifice has, alas, never been positively identified, and was in all probability a product of Dickens's vivid imagination.

Walworth also features in 'The Black Veil' in *Sketches by Boz*, and the essay 'Refreshment for Travellers' in *The Uncommercial Traveller*.

WARWICK, WARWICKSHIRE — Dickens was uncharacteristically vague in naming many of the locations of his fourth novel *The Old Curiosity Shop*. Whether intentional or not, this omission adds greatly to the book's haunting, rather enigmatic quality.

This unsignposted route has provided food for thought for many notable Dickensian topographers, resulting in several contradictory itineraries. It is certain, however, that the eventual destination of Little Nell and her aged grandfather in their desperate flight from the evil, dwarfish Daniel Quilp was the delightful village of TONG in Shropshire.

It follows, therefore, that – en route to Tong – the most likely meeting place with Mrs Jarley's caravan, 'a smart little house upon wheels', was just south of Warwick. Mrs Jarley gives the odd couple a lift and offers Nell employment ('dust the figures and take the checks, and so forth') in her celebrated waxworks, 'the only stupendous collection of real waxworks in the world … the genuine and only Jarley'.

At midnight the caravan draws up just inside an old town gate, most probably Warwick. A little later, in the same gateway,

Nell catches a glimpse of none other than Quilp himself: 'The street beyond was so narrow, and the shadow of the houses on one side of the way so deep, that he seemed to have risen out of the, earth.' Thankfully, Quilp disappears mysteriously into the shadows and, for a while at least, Nell is again able to breathe easily.

But soon the knowledge of Quilp's likely presence in the district, and of her grandfather's weakness at the card-table of the Valiant Soldier Inn (location not known), a weakness which even forces him to steal from her purse, persuades Nell that it is time to move on once more.

A visit to Warwick Castle is greatly appreciated by Mrs Skewton in *Dombey and Son*:

> 'The Castle is charming,' said Mrs Skewton, 'associations of the Middle Ages – and all that – which is so truly exquisite.'

A viewing of the pictures inside the castle finds Mrs Skewton in:

> such ecstasies with the works of art, after the first quarter of an hour, that she could do nothing but yawn (they were such perfect inspirations, she observed as a reason for that mark of rapture).

Dickens had visited Warwick and its castle on a tour of the Midlands with Hablot Knight Browne ('Phiz') in November 1838.

WELBECK STREET, LONDON — Lord George Gordon, leader of the 'No Popery' riots of 1780, lived at 64 Welbeck Street (since rebuilt), off Wigmore Street; a fact used by Dickens in his historical novel *Barnaby Rudge*.

WEST MALLING, KENT — Whilst staying with the Wardle family at Manor Farm (see also SANDLING), the Pickwickians are invited to witness a cricket match between the men of Dingley Dell and the men of Muggleton.

Muggleton, 'a corporate town, with a mayor, a burgess and a foreman', situated two miles from Dingley Dell and reached by 'shady lanes and sequestered footpaths' was probably based on the small town of West Malling.

After the match both teams – the All Muggletons and the Dingley Dellers – together with the Pickwickians and Alfred Jingle, retire for refreshment at the Blue Lion Inn, probably based on the real-life Swan Inn, which is indeed within walking distance of a cricket pitch.

Another candidate for Dickens's Muggleton model is nearby MAIDSTONE.

WESTMINSTER ABBEY, LONDON — 'I never knew an author's death to cause such general mourning. It is no exaggeration to say that this whole country is stricken with grief.' So wrote Longfellow in America on the effects of the news of Charles Dickens's death on 9 June 1870. The same feelings were echoed all around the world wherever the news was heard.

In England, Queen Victoria telegraphed her condolences to the family at GAD'S HILL PLACE, relaying her 'deepest regret at the sad news of Charles Dickens's death'. John Forster wrote: 'In his own land it was as if a personal bereavement had befallen everyone.'

Dickens had expressed a wish to be buried without any fuss. Indeed his Last Will and Testament states:

> I emphatically direct that I be buried in an inexpensive, unostentatious, and strictly private manner; that no public announcement be made of the time or place of my burial; that at the utmost not more than three plain mourning coaches be employed; and that those who attend my funeral wear no scarf, cloak, black bow, long hat band, or other such revolting absurdity. I direct that my name be inscribed in plain English letters on my tomb, without the addition of 'Mr' or 'Esquire'. I conjure my friends on no account to make me the subject of any monument, memorial or testimonial whatever. I rest my claims to the remembrance of my country upon my published works, and to the remembrance of my friends upon their experience of me in addition thereto.

Despite this wish and his own preferred choice of final resting places as ROCHESTER, COBHAM, or SHORNE, much pressure was brought to bear on his immediate family – chiefly by the *Times* newspaper – to the

195
Westminster Abbey

Visitors cluster around the grave of Charles Dickens in Westminster Abbey shortly after his death in 1870.

effect that his rightful place was alongside the finest of English writers in Poets' Corner, Westminster Abbey.

So it was that early on the morning of Tuesday 14 June 1870, Charles Dickens made his final journey. His coffin was transported by train from Rochester to Charing Cross Station.

His wish to be 'buried in an inexpensive, unostentatious, and strictly private manner' was duly honoured. The service took place in the south transept of Westminster Abbey shortly after nine-thirty. Forster wrote: 'Nothing so grand or so touching could have accompanied it, as the stillness and the silence of the vast Cathedral.'

Afterwards the grave of England's best-loved author remained open for two days as a seemingly endless procession of his devoted readers filed past to pay their last respects to the 'Old Inimitable'.

WESTMINSTER BRIDGE, LONDON — The first Dickensian characters to cross old Westminster Bridge (replaced by the present structure in 1862) were the four Pickwickians and Alfred Jingle, aboard the 'Commodore' coach bound for ROCHESTER in *The Pickwick Papers*. The bridge is also crossed in *Nicholas Nickleby*, *David Copperfield* and *Our Mutual Friend*.

Astley's Royal Equestrian Amphitheatre, which once stood in

Westminster Bridge Road, on the southern side of the river, is described in the essays 'Astley's' and 'Horatio Sparkins' in *Sketches by Boz*, and visited by Kit Nubbles and friends in *The Old Curiosity Shop*; and by Trooper George in *Bleak House*.

Manchester Buildings once stood on the site now occupied by Westminster Underground station and provided lodging quarters for junior members of parliament. It is here in *Nicholas Nickleby* that Nicholas applies for work as secretary to 'Mr Gregsbury, the great member of parliament'.

> I don't know what the number is,' said Tom; 'but Manchester Buildings isn't a large place, and if the worst comes to the worst, it won't take you very long to knock at all the doors on both sides of the way till you find him out…

Nicholas eventually arrives at his destination which is found:

> …in one street of gloomy lodging-houses, from whose windows in vacation time there frown long melancholy rows of bills, which say, as plainly as did the countenances of their occupiers, ranged on ministerial and opposition benches in the session which slumbers with its fathers, 'To Let', 'To Let' … In damp weather the place is rendered close by the steams of moist Acts of Parliament and frowsy petitions … This is Manchester Buildings; and here, at all hours of the night, may be heard the rattling of

latchkeys in their respective keyholes, with now and then – when a gust of wind, sweeping across the water which washes the Building's feet, impels its sound towards its entrance – the weak, shrill voice of some young member practising tomorrow's speech…

Following the interview with the pompous M.P., Nicholas refuses to work for him.

WHITECHAPEL, LONDON — In *The Pickwick Papers*, Mr Pickwick, in the company of Peter Magnus, boards a coach at the Bull Inn (now demolished), Whitechapel; they are bound for IPSWICH.

A typical London fishmonger's of the time.

In the same novel Sam Weller observes that poverty and oysters seem to go together: he also notes that there are a great many oyster stalls in Whitechapel.

Upon his recapture by Bill Sikes's crew, Oliver is taken to a house in Whitechapel in *Oliver Twist*. In *Barnaby Rudge* Joe Willet enjoys many meals at the Black Lion Inn (now gone), Whitechapel Road. In *David Copperfield* David's first arrival in London is at the Blue Boar Inn (now gone).

WHITEHALL, LONDON — In *The Pickwick Papers* as 'The Commodore' stagecoach transports the Pickwickians southwards along Whitehall, Alfred Jingle points out the window of the Banqueting House, outside of which King Charles I was beheaded in 1649: '– fine place – little window – somebody else's head off there, eh, sir! – He didn't keep a sharp look-out enough,' notes Jingle, alluding to his previous anecdote about a lady who lost her head aboard a stagecoach as it passed out beneath the archway of the Golden Cross Hotel (see also TRAFALGAR SQUARE).

In *Little Dorrit* the Circumlocution Office stands in Whitehall. Dickens used this office to explain satirically 'the whole science of Government':

> The Circumlocution Office was (as everybody knows without being told) the most important Department under government. No public business of any kind could possibly be done at any time without the acquiescence of the Circumlocution Office. Its finger was in the largest public pie and in the smallest public tart. It was equally impossible to do the plainest right and undo the plainest wrong without the express authority of the Circumlocution Office. If another Gunpowder Plot had been discovered half-an-hour before the lighting of the match, nobody would have been justified in saving the Parliament until there had been half-a-score of boards, half-a-bushel of minutes, several sacks of official memoranda, and a family-vaultful of ungrammatical correspondence on the part of the Circumlocution Office.
>
> This glorious establishment had been early in the field, when the one sublime principal involving the difficult art of governing a country was first distinctly revealed to statesmen. It had been foremost to study that bright revelation, and to carry its shining influence through the whole of the official proceedings. Whatever was required to be done, the Circumlocution Office was beforehand with all the public departments in the art of perceiving – HOW NOT TO DO IT.

WINDSOR, BERKSHIRE — In November 1841 Dickens stayed at the White Hart Hotel (now the Harte and Garter Hotel) in Windsor, while recovering from an operation for a fistula. Here he completed *Barnaby Rudge*.

Y

The Black Swan Inn, York. Dickens and Hablot Knight Browne stayed here in February 1838.

In *Bleak House* we learn from Esther Summerson's narrative that she 'had passed (as far as I know) my whole life', in Windsor.

YORK, NORTH YORKSHIRE — While returning to London from BARNARD CASTLE in February 1838, Dickens and Hablot Knight Browne stayed at the Black Swan Inn, in Corey Street. They attended a service in York Minster and there first heard the 15th-century legend of the Five Sisters of York, which is commemorated by a fine stained-glass window in the north transept of the cathedral. Dickens's own version of the legend subsequently found its way into the pages of *Nicholas Nickleby*. According to Dickens the Five Sisters:

> dwelt in an old wooden house – old even in those days – with overhanging gables and balconies of rudely-carved oak, which stood within a pleasant orchard, and was surrounded by a rough stone wall, whence a stout archer might have winged an arrow to St Mary's abbey. The old abbey flourished then, and the five sisters living on its far domains paid yearly dues to the black monks of St Benedict, to which fraternity it belonged.

The ruins of the Benedictine Abbey of St Mary are to be found in the Museum Gardens.

CHECKLIST OF LOCATIONS

SKETCHES BY BOZ
Clare Market; Covent Garden; Doctors' Commons; Farringdon Street; Furnival's Inn; Gravesend; Greenwich; Hampstead Road; Kensington; Long Acre; Newgate Prison; Pegwell Bay; Ramsgate; Richmond; Rochester; Seven Dials; Threadneedle Street; Tottenham Court Road; Walworth; Westminster Bridge.

THE PICKWICK PAPERS
Aldgate; Bath; Beckhampton; Birmingham; Bristol; Brixton; Bury St Edmunds; Chatham; Chelmsford; Chelsea; Cobham; Cornhill; Covent Garden; Doctors' Commons; Dorking; Dover; Dulwich; Farringdon Street; Furnival's Inn; Goswell Road; Gray's Inn; Guildhall; Hampstead; Highgate; Holborn; Ipswich; Islington; Kensington; Leadenhall Street; Leicester Square; Lombard Street; Ludgate Hill; Maidstone; Mile End; Norwich; Piccadilly; Portsmouth Street; Richmond; Rochester; St Martin's-le-Grand; Sandling; Shorne; Smithfield; Southwark; Strand; Sudbury; Threadneedle Street; Tewkesbury; Towcester; Trafalgar Square; West Mailing; Westminster Bridge; Whitechapel; Whitehall.

OLIVER TWIST
Barbican; Barnet; Bow Street; Brentford; Chertsey; Clerkenwell; Covent Garden; Hammersmith; Hampstead; Hampstead Road; Hampton; Hatfield; Hatton Garden; Highgate; Holborn; Jacob's Island; Kensington; Northampton; Pentonville; Saffron Hill; St Albans; Smithfield; Strand; Whitechapel.

NICHOLAS NICKLEBY
Aldgate; Barnard Castle; Beak Street; Birmingham; Bow; Bowes; Bow Street; Cadogan Place; Cavendish Square; Cheapside; Chelsea; Dawlish; Devil's Punch Bowl; Drury Lane; Eaton Socon; Exeter; Godalming; Golden Square; Grantham; Guildford; Hammersmith; Hampton; Haymarket; Isle of Wight; Kingston; Lambeth; Leadenhall Street; Ludgate Hill;

Manchester; Newgate Prison; Oxford Street; Petersfield; Petersham; Portsmouth; Regent Street; St James's Park; Seven Dials; Snow Hill; Strand; Stratford-upon-Avon; Threadneedle Street; Thames Street; Tottenham Court Road; Twickenham; Westminster Bridge; York.

THE OLD CURIOSITY SHOP

Bath; Chelsea; Covent Garden; Finchley; Fleet Street; Hampstead; Leicester Square; Long Acre; Newgate Prison; Peckham; Portsmouth Street; 'Quilp's Wharf'; Shrewsbury; Southwark; Strand; Tong; Tower of London; Warwick; Westminster Bridge.

BARNABY RUDGE

Barbican; Birmingham; Bristol; Chelsea; Chigwell; Clerkenwell; Cornhill; Drury Lane; Finchley; Fleet Street; Gravesend; Grosvenor Square; Hampstead; Highgate; Horse Guards Parade; Houses of Parliament; Leicester Square; London Bridge; Luton; Millbank; Monument; Newgate Prison; Piccadilly; Snow Hill; Soho; Temple; Threadneedle Street; Thames Street; Tower of London; Welbeck Street; Whitechapel; Windsor.

MARTIN CHUZZLEWIT

Aldersgate Street; Amesbury; Austin Friars; Barbican; Brixton; Cheapside; Cornhill; Covent Garden; Finchley; Fleet Street; Furnival's Inn; Holborn; Horse Guards Parade; Houses of Parliament; Islington; London Wall; Liverpool; Monument; Pall Mall; St James's Park; Salisbury; Smithfield; Strand; Temple.

DOMBEY AND SON

Aldgate; Ball's Pond Road; Birmingham; Bishopsgate; Brighton; Brook Street; Camden Town; Cheapside; City Road; Finchley; Fulham; Kenilworth; Leadenhall Street; Leamington; Limehouse; Mile End; Minories; Norwood; Oxford Street; Peckham; St Marylebone Church; Threadneedle Street; Warwick.

DAVID COPPERFIELD

Blackheath; Blundeston; Broadstairs; Camden Town; Canterbury; City Road; Covent Garden; Doctors' Commons; Dover; Ely Place; Fleet Street; Golden Square; Gravesend; Great Yarmouth; Greenwich; Hampstead Road; Highgate; Hornsey; Ipswich; Isle of Wight; Lincoln's Inn; London Bridge; Lowestoft; Ludgate Hill; Millbank; Norwich; Oxford; Parliament Street; Pentonville; Piccadilly; Plymouth; Putney; Richmond; Rockingham; St Albans; Sheffield; Strand; Tottenham Court Road; Tower of London; Whitechapel.

BLEAK HOUSE
Barnet; Bath; Broadstairs; Chancery Lane; Clare Market; Deal; Dover; Drury Lane; Elephant and Castle; Fleet Street; Gravesend; Hatton Garden; Haymarket; Highgate; Holborn; Houses of Parliament; Islington; Kennington; Leicester Square; Lincoln's Inn; Mile End; Old Street; Oxford Street; Pentonville; Piccadilly; Plymouth; Polygon; Reading; Rockingham; St Albans; Soho; Thavies Inn; Westminster Bridge; Windsor.

HARD TIMES
Manchester; Preston.

LITTLE DORRIT
Barbican; Billingsgate; Brook Street; Canterbury; Cheapside; Coram's Fields; Cornhill; Dover; Fleet Street; Folkestone; Gray's Inn; Grosvenor Square; Hampton; Harley Street; Holborn; Lombard Street; London Wall; Oxford Street; Pentonville; Putney; Royal Tunbridge Wells; Saffron Hill; St James's Park; Southwark; Strand; Threadneedle Street; Twickenham; Whitehall.

A TALE OF TWO CITIES
Blackheath; Cambridge; Clerkenwell; Dover; Fleet Street; Newgate Prison; Old St Pancras Church; Shrewsbury; Soho; Strand; Temple; Turnham Green.

THE UNCOMMERCIAL TRAVELLER
Billingsgate; Brixton; Canterbury; Chatham; Cornhill; Covent Garden; Dover; Gad's Hill Place; Gray's Inn; Limehouse; Liverpool; Rochester; St Olave's Church; Shadwell; Southwark; Walworth.

GREAT EXPECTATIONS
Barnard's Inn; Billingsgate; Brentford; Cambridge; Chalk; Cheapside; Cooling; Gravesend; Hammersmith; Newgate Prison; Oxford Street; Richmond; Rochester; Smithfield; Strand; Temple; Walworth.

OUR MUTUAL FRIEND
Blackheath; Brentford; Cavendish Square; Chancery Lane; Clerkenwell; Cornhill; Covent Garden; Doctors' Commons; Fleet Street; Greenwich; Hampton; Henley-on-Thames; Holloway; Houses of Parliament; Hurley Lock; Isle of Wight; King's Cross; Limehouse; Mincing Lane; Pall Mall; Piccadilly; Richmond; St Mary Axe; Smith Square; Strand; Temple; Tower of London.

THE MYSTERY OF EDWIN DROOD

Aldersgate Street; Chatham; Furnival's Inn; Norwich; Rochester; Shadwell; Staple Inn; Temple.

Places mentioned in the shorter works

A CHRISTMAS CAROL
Camden Town; Cornhill.

THE CHIMES
Covent Garden; Fleet Street; Lincoln's Inn.

GEORGE SILVERMAN'S EXPLANATION
Cambridge; Preston.

A MESSAGE FROM THE SEA
Barnstaple; Bideford; Clovelly.

REPRINTED PIECES
Broadstairs; Deal; Hampstead Road.

MRS LIRRIPER'S LODGING
Cambridge: Strand.

MRS LIRRIPER'S LEGACY
Hatfield.

THE MUDFOG PAPERS, ETC.
Chatham.

MUGBY JUNCTION
Lombard Street; Rugby.

THE POOR RELATION'S STORY
Lombard Street.

NO THOROUGHFARE
Royal Tunbridge Wells.

MASTER HUMPHREY'S CLOCK
Barnard Castle; Birmingham; Guildhall.

Travellers' Information

BROADSTAIRS

The Dickens House Museum

2 Victoria Parade

Broadstairs

Kent CT10 1QS

Tel: 01843 861232 (or 01843 863453 when museum is closed)

Web: www.dickensfellowship.org/branches/broadstairs

CHATHAM

Dickens World

Leviathan Way

Chatham Maritime

Kent ME4 4LL

Tel: 01634 890421

Web: www.dickensworld.co.uk

LONDON

The Charles Dickens Museum

48 Doughty Street

London

WC1N 2LN

Tel: 020 7405 2127

Web: www.dickensmuseum.com

PORTSMOUTH

The Charles Dickens Birthplace Museum

393 Old Commercial Road

Portsmouth

PO1 4QL

Tel: 02392 827261

Web: www.charlesdickensbirthplace.co.uk

ROCHESTER

Restoration House

17–19 Crow Lane

Rochester

Kent ME1 1RF

Tel: 01634 848520

Web: www.restorationhouse.co.uk

ROCKINGHAM

Rockingham Castle

Rockingham

Market Harborough

Leicestershire LE16 8TH

Tel: 01536 770240

Web: www.rockinghamcastle.com

SELECT
BIBLIOGRAPHY

Listing works consulted during the compilation of *Dickens's England*.

Charles Dickens: The Public Readings ed. Philip Collins (Oxford University Press, 1975)

The England of Dickens by Walter Dexter (Cecil Palmer, 1925)

The Letters of Charles Dickens ed. Mamie Dickens and Georgina Hogarth (Chapman and Hall, 1880)

The Life of Charles Dickens by John Forster (Chapman and Hall, 1872)

Charles Dickens – A Critical Study by George Gissing (The Gresham Publishing Co., 1902)

The Dickens Companion ed. J. A. Hammerton (The Educational Book Co., 1910)

Dickens' England by Michael and Mollie Hardwick (J. M. Dent, 1970)

The Charles Dickens Encyclopedia compiled by Michael and Mollie Hardwick (Osprey, 1973)

The Dickens Encyclopedia by Arthur L. Hayward (Routledge, 1924)

The Making of Charles Dickens by Christopher Hibbert (Longman Green and Co., 1967)

Charles Dickens: His Tragedy and Triumph by Edgar Johnson (revised edition Allen Lane, 1977)

Dickens' Rochester by John Oliver (John Hallewell, 1978)

Charles Dickens by Una Pope-Hennessy (Chatto and Windus, 1945)

Charles Dickens and his World by J. B. Priestley (Thames and Hudson, 1961)

Charles Dickens 1812–1870: A Centenary Volume ed. E. W. F. Tomlin (Weidenfeld and Nicolson, 1969)

The Real Dickens Land by H. Snowden Ward and Catherine Weed Barnes Ward (Chapman and Hall, 1904)

The World of Charles Dickens by Angus Wilson (Seeker and Warburg, 1970)

The London of Charles Dickens (London Transport and Midas Books, 1979)

PICTURE CREDITS